T0302164

"The team coaching profession needs a book like this! It places this emerging profession on a rigorous foundation that draws on diverse relational philosophies, theories and practical psychology, using relevant historical sources. With an integrative approach of theory and practice, the authors take us on an exciting learning journey to explore what relational team coaching is all about. In an exceptional manner, the authors emphasise the value of taking a more dynamic, relational-systemic view on team coaching, walking us through many real-life case examples from their own experience. Instead of prescribing certain tools and techniques as 'best practice', the authors invite us to grow our relational courage by gently exploring the complex dynamics of human interaction in the moment, helping teams to progress. By practising what they preach, the authors taught me to be more comfortable with 'not knowing'. As a team coach myself, they helped me reflect and appreciate more who I am and to be curious in the emerging moment. Ultimately, this handbook significantly helps to further continue my self-discovery in helping teams deal with complex challenges and anxieties."

Daniel Aalbersberg, *Senior Manager, Leadership &
Team Development, Accenture*

"What I really enjoyed and connected with in this book was the encouragement to bring one's whole self into group coaching practice – embracing the resulting uncertainty and unpredictability and engaging with the deeper and more relational outcomes that can emerge. In Chapter 3 I enjoyed the offering of a 'hunch' as a coaching tool (or hypothesis in Chapter 4). In Chapter 4 I appreciated the encouragement to actively engage and utilise your own experience in a group as well as their response to your presence and interventions. In Chapter 5 I connected strongly with the long-term impact of founders on organisational culture – and the importance of taking account of the context in which an organisation works. In Chapters 3 and 4 I found the grids offering 'types' of questions/what to look out for and consider extremely useful – providing guides to shaping responses rather than offering a linear process. Overall the content resonated with and shone a mirror on practices of eco-psychology, non-hierarchical governance and consensual decision making which I have experienced in my working and voluntary fields."

Hilary Jennings, *Independent Consultant and Director, Happy Museum*

"It is a very important topic and a timely piece of work – and one that in our Executive Development practice we are seeking to deepen our experience and expertise. Which is to say, I come at this from a practitioner but in no way an expert perspective. I fully support the premise of relational team coaching and I think your introduction and Chapter 1 describe your rationale very clearly. I am particularly struck by the nature of power dynamics in any process and relationship where one party may be perceived to be more 'expert' than another, and am drawn to how the nature of relational coaching can bring a different tenor to this work. In some ways, as you articulate later in the book (e.g. in Chapter 4, pg 64, such as the notion that 'The coach will … encounter resistance to the work'), this power dynamic is inevitable and mirrors what goes on between team members. It is an interesting paradox for a coach to hold, i.e. to bring a presence and skillset that is by definition missing from the team (an expertise), whilst also sitting alongside the team as an 'equal' or peer. A theme that felt very figural, to deploy a Gestalt term, through my reading was the challenge you are posing to us as team coaches to raise our game and develop an elevated presence, mindset and awareness to do this work well."

Senior leader, *Head of Executive Development (anonymous)*

"I really like this book! The book feels really useful and comprehensive and well thought through. I imagine it will quickly become one of the top recommendations for anyone working with team coaching."

Naja Felter, *Deputy Director, Organisation, Development & Design Practice, Cabinet Office, UK Civil Service*

"In terms of readability, I found the book pretty easy to read and the content easy to digest. It's not a book that can be skim-read though and, for me, required a degree of focus and concentration to ensure that I understood the key hypotheses and messages. Perhaps understandably, I found the tone of the book to be on the academic side, but this was nicely balanced by the inclusion of case examples and vignettes and the very practical nature of the book. It did strike me that the book would appeal largely to more experienced and academically/professionally qualified coaches and I assume that this is the target audience you had in mind during the drafting of the book. From a structural perspective, the book lends itself well to dipping in and out of depending on the topic of interest/immediate challenge and I could imagine that professional coaches would find this particularly valuable. The Brief Abstracts and the detailed introductions to Parts A, B and C were a helpful orientation and a simple way of directing the reader towards the most relevant section of the book. Part C was for me the most valuable section of the book and the easiest section to digest and relate to. For those with a practical bias, the importance of landing the hypotheses and constructs in practical ways with examples to illustrate the points and with the inclusion of some insightful questions and prompts for the reader, cannot be emphasised enough. I felt that these chapters covered the content with sufficient depth and would be easy to draw from and adopt in real-life situations. I was particularly attracted to the Talik team coaching model for reasons of simplicity and practicality."

Jo Easton, *Senior role in HR in De La Rue PLC*

"I love the super comprehensive collection of material and perspectives that you have captured in this book. This is a topic I am quite passionate about and I felt totally spoilt for choice. I also adore that people can read the chapter(s) that they are most interested in at that time. Brilliantly done!!"

Talia Nikpalj, *Head of Executive Development, Associated British Foods plc*

"I have to say I have really enjoyed reading your book. I haven't read it all yet, but all the chapters I have read or dipped into have been a great, and very accessible summary of their theme. And I have really liked how they have been bought together and illuminated by case studies. And when it comes out in hard copy, I will definitely be wanting to add it to my library, and for my co-coaches and collaborators to read it and discuss themes with me. I've picked up lots of insights, reminders, and new ideas from it so far to build into my work."

Liz Hill-Smith, *Associate Director of Organisation Development, Arup UKIMEA*

"Working relationally is complex and demanding in its unpredictability; this collection offers a rich and varied framework for coaching professionals to turn to when orthodox methods fall short."

Kate Trench, *Head of Clinical Training, WPF Therapy*

Relational Team Coaching

Relational Team Coaching is a state-of-the-art reference book detailing what makes team coaching effective, with a focus on being able to work at a relational level within the here and now, about what is going on in the present in the team and between the team and the coach.

The scope of the book is comprehensive, exploring challenging and topical issues. Part A presents an introduction to team coaching and to a relational, integrative approach to team coaching, providing access to all relevant background, research and case studies of team coaching in action. Part B deepens how this relational philosophy looks in practice and what it means for choices and working methodology of the team coach. Part C, finally, explores how the team coach can step up to face or address the more challenging or professional aspects of practice (e.g., of contracting, diversity and inclusion, and the shadow side of boards).

This book is an essential guide to relational-based effectiveness in team coaching. It will be a key text for all coaching practitioners, including those in training.

Erik de Haan is the director of the Ashridge Centre for Coaching, Hult International Business School, and professor of organisation development and coaching at VU University Amsterdam. He has an MSc in theoretical physics, an MA in psychodynamic psychotherapy, and a PhD in psychophysics, and specialises in team coaching and one-to-one coaching for executives.

Dorothee Stoffels is an experienced team and executive coach and Organisation Development (OD) practitioner. Originally trained in systemic psychotherapy, she takes a keen interest in how organisations function as systems. Her interventions focus on the relational aspects of interactions and change. She is a founding member and director of the Ashridge Team Coaching Programme.

Relational Team Coaching

Edited by Erik de Haan and
Dorothee Stoffels

Routledge
Taylor & Francis Group

LONDON AND NEW YORK

Designed cover image: Borchee © Getty Images

First published 2024
by Routledge
4 Park Square, Milton Park, Abingdon, Oxon OX14 4RN

and by Routledge
605 Third Avenue, New York, NY 10158

Routledge is an imprint of the Taylor & Francis Group, an informa business

© 2024 selection and editorial matter, Erik de Haan and Dorothee Stoffels; individual chapters, the contributors

The right of Erik de Haan and Dorothee Stoffels to be identified as the authors of the editorial material, and of the authors for their individual chapters, has been asserted in accordance with sections 77 and 78 of the Copyright, Designs and Patents Act 1988.

All rights reserved. No part of this book may be reprinted or reproduced or utilised in any form or by any electronic, mechanical, or other means, now known or hereafter invented, including photocopying and recording, or in any information storage or retrieval system, without permission in writing from the publishers.

Trademark notice: Product or corporate names may be trademarks or registered trademarks, and are used only for identification and explanation without intent to infringe.

British Library Cataloguing-in-Publication Data
A catalogue record for this book is available from the British Library

ISBN: 978-1-032-35196-4 (hbk)
ISBN: 978-1-032-35195-7 (pbk)
ISBN: 978-1-003-32578-9 (ebk)

DOI: 10.4324/9781003325789

Typeset in Times New Roman
by Newgen Publishing UK

Contents

About the contributors

Erik de Haan, MSc, MA, PhD, is Director of Ashridge's Centre for Coaching and Professor of Organisation Development at the VU University Amsterdam. He joined Ashridge Business School in 2002. His consulting approach is informed by his psychodynamic psychotherapy and team-dynamics training. He specialises in working with the organisational unconscious and in surfacing hidden levels of the company or group culture. He has (co)written 16 books and well over 200 professional and research articles.

Dorothee Stoffels, DipSW, MSc, MA, is an experienced team and executive coach, OD practitioner and an associate at Ashridge. Originally trained as a systemic psychotherapist, she has always taken a keen interest in how organisations function as systems and her interventions focus on the relational aspects of human interaction and change. She is one of the founding members of faculty for the Ashridge Team Coaching Programme and is the programme director.

Judith Bell, Dip Clin Psych, DPsych, AFBPsS, is an experienced chartered psychologist, organisational consultant, and executive coach. Drawing from her background in psychodynamic and systems thinking she is skilled at creating containing spaces with individuals and groups to facilitate a deep understanding of personal and organisational complexity. Previously she established and led an MA programme in working with groups and teams.

David Birch, PGCE, MSc, PG Cert Supervision. His practice is founded on the understanding that change occurs within and through relationships. He has over 30 years' international business experience, helping individuals, groups, and organisations make a difference to the world. He is qualified as a team and executive coach, supervisor, mediator, and psychotherapist.

Simon Cavicchia, MA, MSc, MSc (Org. Devt.), Dip Supervision, APECS Accredited Executive Coach, is an internationally experienced OD consultant, executive coach, coach supervisor, team coach, process consultant, facilitator, and lecturer. Simon draws on his experience in consulting, deep human systems understanding, and psychology to enable organisations to successfully navigate the complexities of transformational change processes, develop leadership cultures, and individuals.

Andrew Day, MSc, C.Psychol., D. Psych., D.C. Psych., is an OD consultant and executive coach who helps individuals, groups, and organisations to navigate complex transitions and to undertake systemic change. His expertise lies in helping his clients to explore and understand the influence of group and cultural dynamics in organisations. He is a partner in Metalogue Consulting.

Rachael Hanley-Browne, MA, AoEC & EMCC Accredited Coach, TIHR Accredited Supervisor, offers a developmental space for her clients to experiment, seek clarity, formulate choices, and subsequently make informed changes. She coaches executives, c-suite teams, and boards with a view to co-creating transformation at an enterprise level. Her niche is in working with organisations led by subject-matter experts, e.g. technologists. She has a background in international commercial leadership including holding P&L accountability, establishing start-ups, and creating new revenue streams. Rachael is President of the European Mentoring and Coaching Council UK and owns a business dedicated to team coaching, The Team Lab. She offers supervision for executive and team coaches.

Ann Knights, MSc (Exec Coaching), MSc (Org Consulting), PG Cert Supervision, PG Cert Relational Organisational Gestalt, is organisation development consultant, coach and team coach with 25 years experience working with people in organisations to develop their capacity to lead and support sustainable, meaningful change. Ann's real passion and expertise is in creating environments for challenge, experimentation, reflection, and learning and translating this into daily organisational life. Ann believes deeply in the power of connected groups in organisations and society and is a skilled group process facilitator: this might mean working with learning and inquiry groups; groups working live on organisational and societal challenges or intact teams. She is Associate Director of Talik and Company.

Charlotte Sills, MA, MSc, TSTA (ITAA), PGCE, works locally and internationally as a coach, supervisor, and team facilitator and is Professor of Coaching at Ashridge Business School. She brings to this role more than 30 years' experience as a practitioner of psychological therapy and as a teacher and supervisor of counsellors, therapists, and coaches.

Alexandra Stubbings, MSc, CMI, DProf. With over 20 years' international experience in organisation development, Alexandra specialises in coaching executive teams to make sense of the challenges of low-carbon transformation and develop meaningful strategies to address them. She joined Ashridge Business School in 2005 as a consultant and faculty member, and since 2013 has led Talik to focus wholly on purpose-led business transformation. Her Professional Doctorate (Middlesex, 2013), in organisational engagement with sustainability produced the eponymous 'Talik systemic change model' which has now been applied in the field for ten years in complex change environments.

Tammy Tawadros, MSc, MBPsS, PG Cert Supervision, is a coach, supervisor, OD consultant, and work psychologist with many years' experience of designing, delivering, and supporting a broad range of leadership, organisational development, and change endeavours. She was a mental health social worker and a learning and development manager before becoming an OD consultant and executive coach. Tammy works with individuals, teams, and whole organisations to develop and thrive, in the face of change, disruption, and uncertainty. She is especially interested in how we conceive and experience our world, as well as in how wider external environment shapes our actions and understanding.

Introduction to *Relational Team Coaching*

Erik de Haan and Dorothee Stoffels

In leadership teams at all levels there is a growing awareness that in present-day organisations leadership team members need to look after themselves and each other in order to be ready for an ever-accelerating pace of change, volatility and complexity. They also need to sustain their fitness and internal relationships to keep making good decisions and offer leadership to the teams and individuals that they are together responsible for. Finally, they are learning that good decisions in complex and ambiguous environments need a pooling of the expertise from both within and outside the team, which means they require a relatively open and safe way of collecting information and working together. In such modern teams which face considerable and relentless challenges, there is an increasing understanding that they cannot always do the 'looking after', 'staying fit', motivating, inspiring, deciding and managing all by themselves. More and more leadership teams make use of regular team coaching to sustain their fitness, joy, awareness, and effectiveness. Not to mention the many teams and leaders who feel they need to rely on team coaching for a period in order to overcome conflict or paralysis, or to help the team work together more productively.

At Ashridge we have worked as team coaches for leadership teams for decades, and we have seen team coaching gaining ever more acceptability and prominence. The 11 authors of this book have all met and collaborated at Ashridge and the Hult Ashridge Centre for Coaching. We have taken on countless assignments as team coaches in many different sectors around the world. We have agreed on the finding that team coaching is so helpful because it can bring a deepening of *reflection* to teams – with increasing research (De Haan, 2017) demonstrating that reflection is key to the ability of teams to innovate and stay productive under stress. Although our backgrounds are very different, we all offer forms of team coaching that can help to increase reflection and reflexivity in leadership teams.

Another principle that all authors of this book agree on is expressed by the word 'relational' in the title. We find that in order to enhance reflection within the teams that we work with as their outside 'reflection support', we need to be able to be fully and consciously present with them and invite them to look at that present moment together with us. Amongst an infinity of reflections and reflective interventions, we privilege the ones that are anchored in the here-and-now

DOI: 10.4324/9781003325789-1

relationships that we experience together with the team. This is called *relational* team coaching and that is what this book is about. The phenomena in a team in the here-and-now provide essential information and therefore rich resources for reflection. In the ongoing, evolving and emerging relationships the contract with the team can be formed, made explicit, and strengthened. In these same relationships evidence can be found for the presences of challenges, and for ways of resolving the challenges. And, last but not least, in the present moment the emergence and impact of reflection can be checked, e.g., if there is understandable resistance to new insights or solutions, this can only be discovered and overcome in the present moment.

We faced questions at the beginning of this project whether we would make team coaching more complex and less practical by bringing in the 'relational'. But we believe this book *needs* to be written precisely for very practical and simple reasons. Team coaches need to develop their courage to use their own fleeting hunches, doubts, fear and shame, especially in the midst of a world that does not initially welcome such emoting and doubting, and appears to seek clarity, certainty and predictability. In other words, both for our readers and the team coaches that work with or without this book, there may be an initial yearning for clarity, tips, tricks and guidelines on the part of the coach, client or commissioner. Nevertheless, we trust that that is not the real question but that the real question is more subtle and relevant... something like "teach me how to work with this solution?", "how can I be brave enough to do what I know is right?", or, "how can we implement this solution when currently few people trust us?" This book also addresses further, deeper questions, such as "what does our team challenge tell us about us?" or "why do we keep resisting what we know is the best way forward?"

In our own process of writing this book, we have experienced the challenges that many teams experience that come together temporarily to achieve a task. In order to overcome these challenges, we have adhered to many of the principles and ideas we have laid out in this book. We came together as a group of individuals, connected through only a string of key meetings with the sole purpose of bringing together our ideas on relational team coaching and jointly deciding on the work. During those meetings, the process and timeframe was loosely held and facilitated by us, the two co-editors. We brought the Author Team together in regular intervals and let the process of co-authoring and co-editing emerge as we met. This included an agreement that after the first round of edits done by the editors, authors reviewed each other's work and gave each other feedback. In this way most of the chapters have been shaped by large parts of the team: first by one or two authors, then two co-editors, and then up to two other members from the Author Team. This required a lot of openness, risk-taking and trust amongst the Author Team which probably would not have been possible if we had not already worked together in smaller groups on many client-facing assignments. Difference and diversity in thought and writing styles was a challenge not just for co-authored chapters, but also for the book as a whole. How could we honour everyone's individual contribution and style, whilst still producing a coherent 'whole' for the reader? This tightrope walk required an ebb and flow of challenge and support whilst staying firmly grounded in our working relationships. As the book grew, so did the overall ownership of the process and the product amongst the Author Team.

In this book we introduce relational team coaching and take you through over fifty real-life examples from our own practice (or occasionally borrowed with permission from our wider network), so that you can see relational team coaching in action. We hope this provides you with relevant learning as team coaches, learning that you can apply and test in your own practice. It will also help you to see that relational coaching is not straightforward and requires a degree of courage, where we take a risk in, e.g., naming something fresh and challenging when the situation is already pregnant with anxieties and fears. We think relational risks, trying to name and understand something that has not been named before, are more than worthwhile. Such relational courage directly addresses the elephant in the room or the emperor's lack of clothes. This may initially feel impertinent or daring, and occasionally provocative or abrasive (or even plain wrong) in the eyes of many leaders present, but ultimately by gently exploring and maintaining curiosity (admitting that we do not know and are only guessing), this relational coaching will help every team to progress and develop (e.g. towards more effectiveness and more innovation, in terms of seeing a way forward, agreeing amongst themselves, making a decision, or towards less tangible objectives such as feeling more supported or coping with a loss), provided the difficulties of the session itself are tolerated and faced by both team coach and client team.

The book has been written in three parts which are increasingly more practical. Part A displays our philosophical grounding and team coaching principles, drawn from three long-standing traditions of practical psychology. Part B shows how we work in more detail, showing how team coaching can draw from the past and existing, recurring patterns in teams, how team coaches can work relationally in the present, and how we can help teams preparing for and securing their futures. In this part the reader can find specific interventions linking with past, present and future. Part C is slightly longer and is perhaps the most practical part of the book, showing how specific models of areas that are important to team coaches and their clients, can help guide our interventions. In this part of the book there are models of team effectiveness and diversity; ideas about how to work with top teams and with endings; and underpinning models of contracting and team coaching skills and interventions. If you are interested in any of these themes, then please feel free to jump to one of those chapters. All chapters can be read by themselves, and you can therefore start this book at any point.

At the end of the book there is an Epilogue about the future of team coaching: what do we believe the trends are, what is preoccupying us as we look forward, and what would we predict to emerge in this fast-changing, young profession. At that point we thought it would be best if you would hear from all of the Author Team individually, so we have done no co-reading or feedback-giving on that chapter, in contrast to all the earlier chapters. We have made the book as accessible as we could. For this reason we have made all personal pronouns female and as such straightforward. We have also disguised all cases very carefully so that client teams would struggle to recognise themselves and be reassured that their peers and counterparts in the organisation will not recognise them from our description.

London, June 2023

Erik de Haan & Dorothee Stoffels

Part A

Ways of framing relational team coaching

Introduction to Part A

In this part of the book, we will lay down our convictions and describe the grounding of our practice, including our arguments for drawing from the diverse relational philosophies in this book. We describe the history and main principles of each of the three schools of psychological practice that have informed our own grounding as relational team coaches.

After an introductory chapter that covers relationality and the relational turn in psychotherapy and puts forward the timeliness and other main reasons for wanting to work relationally, Chapters 2, 3 and 4 are dedicated to the three relational schools that we feel indebted to: Chapter 2 introduces the school of Gestalt psychology and elucidates how Gestalt can be relevant for team coaches. Chapter 3 introduces the systemic school of family therapy and how this tradition of working with small (family) groups can be applied in team coaching. Finally, Chapter 4 introduces the school of systems psychodynamics and demonstrates how psychoanalytical concepts from this school can be used by relational team coaches.

DOI: 10.4324/9781003325789-2

Chapter 1

Why relational?

Simon Cavicchia and Dorothee Stoffels

As you start to walk on the way, the way appears.

(Rumi, 13th Century)

1.1 Introduction: two types of team coaching?

"When will you finally teach us tools and techniques?" – this request comes on the last workshop of a Team Coaching Programme for Consultants during an open session where participants can raise questions and notice what is happening for them and in the group. We immediately find ourselves curious about this question. Where has it come from? What is the perceived lack or gap the students are experiencing in regards to their practice? Particularly as this is not an unusual comment or request that we, the authors of this chapter, hear at any point of the Programme.

Equally, when we work with teams, the call for clear tools, processes and methods is strong, whether it be a psychometric measure of the team or a request for a watertight process that leads the team to define and agree on their vision and strategy. We even notice at times our own desire to fill our time with a team with structured activity, some useful 'input' and a clear and pre-determined road map to particular outcomes. So, what is going on in the field of team coaching, both in teams and in team coaches that leads to this search for tools and techniques and what is it they are experienced as providing?

In this chapter we will explore our observations and the connection between tools and the management of anxiety. We shall draw on both relational and systems ideas to develop key premises of taking a more dynamic, relational-systemic view on team coaching in order to work with the team in the emerging 'here-and-now'. We will consider the evolution of team coaching as part of the wider "relational turn" taking place across a range of disciplines. We will end the chapter by naming some implications for the attitude of the team coach.

DOI: 10.4324/9781003325789-3

1.2   What we are noticing in the field of team coaching

In our experience, the requests we mention in our introduction are a common feature in our work. They can come in different guises. Allowing ourselves to be curious about this pattern, we arrive at some observations about our own work with teams, but also our teaching and supervision of team coaches.

There seems to be a real desire for what we call linear approaches to help make sense of the challenges teams face. Team coaches are asking themselves what models, tools and techniques they can make use of to understand what is happening in the team or intervene in order to make the team more effective. Team psychometrics (e.g. MBTI, Hogan, SDI, Insights, Belbin, etc. – see reference section for websites), theories around group stage development (e.g. Tuckman, 1965; Gibb, 1978; Schutz, 1958, etc.), theories on how to build trust in teams (e.g. Lencioni, 2002), are very popular. One function of using linear process models and input is to bring structure and containment to what might be complex and multi-layered team dynamics and presenting issues. This leaning towards linear and structured approaches is very understandable. Linear thinking, cause and effect logic has a long history, including the philosophy of Aristotle (Hankinson, 1998). In the scientific community, establishing the nature of causes and the relationship between causes and their effects is an often-used central approach to research (Bunge, 2017). It is these assumptions that underpin the evidence base of much scientific research and what gives rise to best practice and tried and tested strategies for intervening in the world, be it in fields such as medicine, psychotherapy, project management, coaching (de Haan, 2021) and consulting.

De Haan and Metselaar (2015) argue that using diagnostic tools firmly puts us as the coach in the role of the expert authority and that diagnostics are often used 'on' the team. This stands in contrast to an approach which involves allowing the coachee or team to use the coach to explore what is going on for them. We want to be clear here, we are not against linear process models per se. What we are noticing is that the team coach seeks and is seen to provide containment through a theory, model or tool, rather than through their presence, modelling a capacity to contain anxiety as it arises so that its meaning can be explored and understood, and working with the unpredictable, multi-layered, complex and dynamic nature of human relationships as they unfold and evolve over time.

At the same time, in many team coaching assignments, the focus seems to be on the task of the team (e.g. activities that the team needs to attend to, performance, deliverables), rather than the group dynamics and the inevitable relationship between task and group processes. Again, this task focus is often requested by the team, which many team coaches accommodate rather than be curious about, as attending to difficult or challenging interpersonal dynamics as they arise in the moment can be anxiety-provoking both for the team coach and the team. Yet many difficulties and obstacles to team performance which are visible at the task level (and are often why the team coaching has been commissioned) reside in the dynamics of human interaction. Our hypothesis is that often team coaches feel ill-equipped to deal with the moments, where difficult dynamics raise their heads in the team coaching work. We are certainly no strangers to feelings of anxiety when undertaking work with teams! It takes personal psychological solidity and grounding in ourselves and a clear sense of our own presence, capability and comfort with not knowing, to trust that we as a coach can be 'enough' to help a team facing complex challenges and the inevitable anxieties and at times challenging behaviours these give rise to.

Anxiety in the face of the unknown is a universal human experience (Phillips, 1997). Much has been written in the psychoanalytic tradition about the patterns of thinking and behaviour that develop as defences or ways of avoiding experiencing anxiety that might evoke feelings of overwhelm, powerlessness, confusion and fear (Hirschhorn & Barnett, 1993; Obholzer & Zagier Roberts, 1994). Isabel Menzies-Lyth (1960) describes ways in which these defences become part of an organisation's rituals and routines. Her main research took place in hospitals in the 1950s but remains relevant to our understanding of anxiety and its relationship to defences in human systems to this day. Medical staff face, on a daily basis, anxiety in the face of human fragility, disease and vulnerability. To protect themselves against feelings of sadness, grief as well as attraction and love towards patients, clinical staff would dehumanise them by referring only to their disease as "the liver in bed 14". On another occasion, she describes nursing staff waking up sleeping patients in order to give them a sleeping pill if this had been recommended earlier by a doctor. Whilst the medical profession has evolved somewhat since the 1950s, it is still possible to see in many organisations how strict routines, operating procedures, protocols, staff uniforms, deference to hierarchy in terms of decision-making responsibility can act as "institutional defences" against anxiety.

Against this backdrop of human anxiety and vulnerability it is possible to see how linear assumptions may soothe and appeal more than systemic assumptions. The linear and causal assumptions, rather like protocols and procedures, offer a clear road map, through the attribution of predictable causes and effects. They also offer the imagined security of being able to take clearly defined steps to arrive at a pre-determined destination whilst avoiding uncertainty, confusion and disorientation.

If we consider the perspective of linearity and consider for a moment what it implies, we can see how it finds its way into models and approaches that are all so familiar and valued in the field of team coaching. The Oxford English Dictionary offers us two major definitions of "linear":

1. arranged in or extending along a straight or nearly straight line

   • consisting of or predominantly formed using lines or outlines
   • involving one dimension only;

2. progressing from one stage to another in a single series of steps; sequential.

Considering these two definitions we can see that a linear approach can be very helpful and appropriate at different points and in different contexts of organisational life. When it comes to production, planning, structuring and changing concrete aspects like offices, brands or markets, then linear assumptions are usually fine and the laws of physics and economics broadly apply.

If we apply the first definition to teams and our work with teams, it would suggest a number of things, including that teams have clearly defined boundaries, that they are one-dimensional in the way they might attend to a task, relate to each other or to other teams within an organisation. An example of a presumed one-dimensional nature might be that a team following a clear, non-variable process imagines that it is solely responsible for a particular output without any touchpoints or inputs of other individuals, teams, external stakeholders and so forth. As many of us will know, organisational reality these days is very different and the contexts in which teams operate are complex, dynamic and unpredictable. Teams are often a messy collection of people who are usually also members of other teams (sometimes these can be temporary teams such as project teams). Often leadership is ambiguous and unclear. Team boundaries are porous and semi-permeable as a collection of different teams can all be responsible for specific outputs and deliverables.

The second definition offers even more apparent certainty both for how the team progresses through a task or even the work a team coach might do with a team. A linear view would suggest that teams can progress from one stage of development to another or attend to tasks in a clear and sequential order. This doesn't allow for the complexity that human beings can bring to the way we undertake our work activities and the human interconnectedness and dynamics that can get played out as we interact with each other every day including holding (and often competing over) different perspectives, ordinary and inevitable misunderstandings and disorientation in the face of the unknown. At the same time, if we applied the second definition to the work of a team coach, this would suggest that the team coach could somehow control and move the team forward in their work with each other, using a series of steps and processes to get them to a pre-determined outcome. Whilst an approach like this or the belief that this can be done might contain anxiety, this can risk leaning towards the coach manipulating the team and the team feeling "done to" rather than supported to make their own sense of their experience and assume responsibility for their actions. We might term this manipulation disguised as facilitation as "facipulation". In our experience, team coaching is a lot more messy, unpredictable and emergent than this approach to team coaching allows for.

> The linear causal model is (nevertheless) very useful as long as one is aware of its limitations and never forgets that this kind of linear cause-and-effect relationship does not actually exist, but is our way of simplifying a much more complex reality.
>
> (Compernolle, 2007, p. 39)

We want to be very clear that linear cause-effect models do have their place in the world, but can be less helpful in the context of the current complexity of our and our clients' environments and the issues they face. This is especially true where teams and their organisations are dealing with increasing unpredictability and are having to respond in agile and innovative ways on an ongoing basis to unexpected and unforeseen challenges. In this context linear assumptions about planning and control become less helpful and "best practice" increasingly limited or, as one of our clients once commented, "best practice is always yesterday's practice and is not guaranteed to be relevant for today's challenges".

Linear models can offer useful maps, if held lightly and tentatively by the team coach and the team. We would argue that the key is to extend our range as practitioners and not allow an overreliance on more linear models to dampen down what is emerging in the team or for the team coach. Linear process models have the tendency to clog up the space where surprising things could be happening that represent the rich tapestry of team life and that as team coaches we need to attend to and support our clients to attend to. It is in these unexpected moments of exploration and novelty that the potential for new discoveries and innovative strategies reside. We therefore want to make the case here for a relational-systemic approach, where the team coach with their presence and attention to the 'here-and-now' processes of teams is the basis for the work.

Case vignette: Part 1 – an invitation to help a team define their vision

I (Dorothee) was invited to work with a senior team in the charitable sector. The team had a relatively new and young leader. He had been promoted from within the team and wanted to bring the team together under his new leadership, spending a day revising the current vision, setting priorities and agreeing on a behavioural charter for the team and beyond. In initial conversations, the team leader reported that there had been some misgivings by sub-teams in the charity about the behavioural standard set by his senior team and that this was trickling down the organisation. The internal promotion of the team leader had overall been welcomed in the team, but had caused some shifting complex line-management relationships that certainly the team leader was keen to move beyond.

The invitation for this piece of work sounded quite straightforward to me and an agreement was reached that the team manager and I would co-design the day, following one-to-one inquiry conversations between each team member and myself. These conversations did not bring any new data to the design of the day: yes, the team wanted to work on their vision and priorities and discuss a behavioural charter. Everyone was in agreement that this was the work that needed to be done and there was nothing else important that they needed to attend to. At this point, I started to have some misgivings about what I had been invited to do. There was a very clear mandate to design and facilitate a process for the team to enable them to attend to their tasks better and more effectively.

However, somehow when I thought of the day ahead, I felt apprehensive. There seem to be something missing or unspoken. The complete agreement between the team leader and all the team members about the purpose and task of the day was somehow puzzling. No-one had raised any difference of opinion or issues within the team.

The day commenced as per the agreed design. The team leader opened the day and positioned the work. As requested, I offered the team a model to think about the task, process and desired 'climate' of the day and indeed their work. The first moment of tension appeared as a couple of team members started rolling their eyes in regards to the model offered as it was an often used model in work with teams and they had come across it before. Picking up the anxiety of the team leader to get through the agreed work and to the outcomes of the day, I pressed on with the designed process rather than attend to this moment of interest.

When the work turned to revisiting and refining the current vision, another moment of tension appeared in the form of an open challenge to me: a team member disliked the process I had suggested to review the vision. Could I not suggest a different process? A discussion followed in which different team members debated the value of the process suggested, whilst also requesting a new and innovative process by the team coach. When I attempted to encourage the team to think about what process they thought would work for them, this was turned back to me. I was told by the challenging team member that I had been hired for my expertise in facilitating this day, so I should suggest an alternative. The team leader made some attempts to encourage the team to stick with the work, but was largely ignored. I suggested a break, to allow everyone, including the team leader and myself to step back and pause.

Reflections: How did this piece of work get to this point? You will notice from the description of the case that I was invited to accept a particular one-dimensional way of viewing the work and the team. Applying some of our observations, musings and hypotheses from above, we conclude on reflection that I as the team coach was invited to perform a quite linear piece of work with a team that did not seem to pay attention to how it and its tasks and behaviour were connected to the wider organisational system. There also seemed to be little awareness within the team of relational dynamics between team members. There were some signs of this early on in the work. For example, the team leader mentioned the sub-teams' dissatisfaction about the behaviour of some of the senior team. The complexity of line management relationships that had been introduced by the promotion of the team leader was also raised by the team leader. As the coach I had been encouraged to take up the position of expertise by offering content (a model) and suggesting a process that would get the team to the outcome they wanted. What might have prevented me from sliding into the linearity of this piece, could for example have been to include the wider system early on in the work by holding some stakeholder conversations (including members of the sub-team) ahead of the day, contracting more clearly about my role as coach on the day and attending to my own physical experiences and senses and then sharing them both with the team leader and team members ahead of the day.

Shifting sands

A relational-systemic view of team coaching represents an evolution of thinking and team coaching and practice that is part of a wider movement of evolving perspectives on human development and growth referred to as the "relational turn". The relational turn has its roots in late nineteenth- and early twentieth-century humanistic movement (Buber, 1965; Kant, 1965; Levinas, 1989; Merleau Ponty, 1969; Nietzsche, 1966). At the heart of humanism was a move away from, and challenge to, the rationalist view which saw thinking and knowing as being the preserve of the individual mind and the application of logical thinking and reasoning. Humanism began to consider that knowing is not something that happens simply in the mind of the thinker who, isolated from others and their experience, seeing himself as the centre of his meaning-making universe, can ever only experience half of reality. Philosophers such as Buber (1965) and Levinas (1989) went on to consider the inextricable relationship between self and other in the processes of knowing and experiencing reality.

Buber makes an important distinction between two qualities of relating he refers to as "I-It" and "I-Thou" (1970). Orange (2010) referencing Buber (1965) describes how "in the I-It relation we can stand above or outside as observer, investigator or artist" (Orange, 2010, p.18) In I-It relating, the other is perceived as an object, reduced to an "it", dehumanised, acted upon, transacted with. It is our contention that linear and mechanistic approaches to team coaching might emerge from and risk leaning into an I-It stance. I-Thou relating, on the other hand, is a quality of meeting another person intimately as a fully human being, accepting who he or she is as an individual, without agenda – "I become aware of him, aware that he is different, essentially different from myself, in the definite, unique way which is peculiar to him, and I accept whom I thus see, so that in full earnestness I can direct what I say to him as the person he is" (Buber, 1999, pp. 79–80). Out of this quality of meeting, genuine dialogue and possibilities for development and growth emerge. For a relational-systemic team coach, this attitude of I-Thou relating supports a quality of being that can accept and work with "what is" in a team, as opposed to imposing a pre-determined structure in an attempt to control or shape a team in a particular way.

It is not possible to dwell permanently in an I-Thou stance and at times conscious and negotiated transacting might be appropriate, but it is this holding in mind the possibility of relating intersubjectively, human being to human being, that is core to a relational-systemic approach.

These humanistic ideas have found their way into what is now termed relational psychoanalysis (Mills, 2005) which, as a helping profession, offers perspectives which we believe are relevant to relational practice in the fields of coaching and team coaching. According to Mills (2005) the relational turn in psychoanalysis also reflects aspects of the post-modern era where rigid attachment to ideas related to scientific certainty, expert authority, objective measurement and universal laws to explain reality is now being met with an increased opening to multiplicity of meaning and subjectivity (Cavicchia & Gilbert, 2018). Western (2012) describes how in post-modernity "we have become sceptical about grand narratives, where there are no universally agreed beliefs ... where everything is therefore contingent" (p. 101). The questioning characteristic of post-modernism can offer tremendous opportunities for innovation and creativity whilst also increasing anxiety and uncertainty.

In the relational turn the emphasis is on the moment-by-moment processes whereby human beings interact. Human interaction is seen as the most fundamental process through which individuals come to know themselves, regulate anxiety and make meaning of the world they inhabit. The quality and dynamics of moment-by-moment interactions determine how people feel, think and act. These fundamental relational assumptions clearly have implications for how team coaches, feel, think and act as practitioners and will be expanded on throughout the book.

The relational turn has also influenced leadership thinking. The idea of what leading means and who a leader is continues to evolve from the lonely hero archetype, acting alone and achieving greatness through sheer charisma, inspiring followership, individual talent, extraordinary commitment and will, to seeing leaders and leading as a process of relating and orchestrating of relationships (Western, 2013). The complexity and scale of modern organisations mean that no one individual can know all that needs to be known to effectively lead an organisation. In this context, leading is seen to involve creating conditions for followers and organisation members to come together, develop themselves, relate, make sense of their collective goals and challenges and evolve their thinking and practice to deliver their strategic objectives and values, whilst responding and adapting to unpredictable shift, forces and constraints both inside and outside of their organisations (Western, 2013). This calls for leaders and team coaches to relax egoic attachments to fantasies of control and predictable successes and develop humility, creativity and responsiveness in the face of that which cannot be known, predicted in advance or manipulated.

A number of the assumptions associated with the relational turn can also be seen in organisation theory which has evolved (and continues to evolve) from the mechanistic assumptions of the early 1900s (Gilbreth, 1911; Taylor, 1911). Here organisations were conceptualised as machines and human 'capital' as units to be manipulated in service of organisational goals. For many years these models persisted and appeared fit for purpose due to the influence of, and compliance with, socially constructed and enforced assumptions about productivity, power and hierarchy.

Since the turn of the last century, organisations have also begun to be seen as complex fields of human interaction and social processes (Eoyang & Holladay, 2013; Oshry, 2007; Shaw, 2002; Stacey, 2001). From this perspective, meaning and resulting behaviour is being constantly constructed through the participation and conversations of organisation members. It is in these conversations also that different meanings about the purpose and nature of work are emerging. Younger generations of employees hold different assumptions about the place of work in their lives and the psychological contract they look for with their employers (Hobart and Sendek, 2014). A number of organisations are also asking questions about the nature of the bottom line and how to measure an organisation's value not simply in terms of profit and shareholder dividends. For some, contribution to the wider societies in which they operate, the well-being of employees and environmental sustainability are increasingly coming to be seen as values-based currency (Willard, 2012; Laszlo & Zhexembayeva, 2011).

The VUCA world

In the 1990s the acronym VUCA began to appear first in military and later organisational writing to describe environments where leaders and those who participate in organisational life are facing unprecedented volatility, uncertainty, complexity and ambiguity (Stiehm & Townsend, 2002). Past models and processes are no longer adequate to contain and navigate these challenges, and leaders are often faced with the dilemma of not knowing how best to proceed, having only ever partial information, but needing, nonetheless, to act. Adjusting to and navigating these challenges calls on individuals to know themselves better, manage their own feelings of anxiety, bear uncertainty, take up fluid roles, experience shifts in personal identity, and continue to be able to think, reflect, make sense and act under pressure (Kegan, 1998; Hirschhorn, 1998). Reliance on rigid processes, protocols and control mechanisms is no longer sufficient in many organisational contexts given the challenges they face, and in some, these mechanisms actually cause and perpetuate structural difficulties and less than productive behaviours (Schwartz, 1990).

There is now a greater need for individuals to come together, relate differently and effectively in order to create new ways of thinking, being, working and organising. This requires the harnessing of difference, fostering greater awareness of, and critical reflection on, the assumptions which underpin current thinking and action. It calls for paying close attention to the quality of connection and conversation between individuals, groups and entire organisations in order to develop the effectiveness, agility and responsiveness today's business, societal and global challenges call for (Lines & Schole-Rhodes, 2013).

1.3   Key premises of relational-systemic team coaching

The different contributors to this book will each explore different facets of what it means to take a relational-systemic view of team coaching. For now, and by way of orientation to the territory, we shall briefly propose some key premises of taking a relational-systemic view on team coaching, which can rise to the challenges of the VUCA world and which have clear implications for how we show up as team coaches, what we pay attention to and how we choose to intervene in the moment.

The first premise is a fundamental belief that individuals and teams do not exist in isolation. Both individuals and teams are embedded in a web of relationships and have a system around them. This sounds obvious, but has fundamental implications. If we hold this as a core belief, then the emphasis of our work moves towards exploring and creating heightened awareness of patterns of interactions between people and groups of people rather than focusing on individuals or teams being the 'problem' that needs to be 'fixed'. In keeping with the shift in focus of the relational turn, the space *between* people and teams becomes an important entity where both stuck patterns can be observed and also relational shifts can happen, rather than focusing on individual psychology, deficits or behaviours that might need to be changed. This in turn connects to the idea of interconnectedness and circularity, which sees more than two aspects of a system as connected. What this means in practice is that we need to move away from linear cause-and-effect thinking towards challenging ourselves to seeing all parts of a system as interconnected and mutually influencing each other in unpredictable ways.

A second key premise is a focus on the different levels of a system including the individual, the team, the wider organisational system, the socio-economic, cultural, political and ecological context. As team coaches we often focus on the level of individual or team as we feel that this is where our commission lies. However, particularly in stuck moments with teams, bringing in other aspects of the wider organisational system or the wider context for the team and organisation can be incredibly powerful, liberating and illuminating. Expanding perspectives in this way supports understanding of how individual experience and behaviour is often shaped by a host of systemic factors. This in turn reduces the tendency to personalise problems, blame and shame individuals and other teams. We have particularly, over the last couple of years, seen how relevant it has been to bring the wider societal context into our work with teams e.g. ecological and diversity issues.

Watzlawick, Weakland and Fisch's (1974) stark reminder that all behaviour is a form of communication in and of itself is, a third key premise when thinking about relational-systemic team coaching. This means, as team coaches, we cannot dismiss even the smallest gestures, moments or experiences *with* individuals, *between* individuals, teams or the wider system and need to be curious about them and encourage the team to also be curious about them. The late arrival to a meeting by a team member, the rather sharp exchange between two team members in a meeting, the unusual communication made by the communications department of an organisation, the curious sensation in us as team coaches that suddenly invites us to ask a particular question are all part of the rich tapestry of conscious and unconscious communication, mutual and reciprocal influence, that is there for us to inquire into. It also potentially reveals something about the complex patterns of interaction that are at play in the organisational system.

Another central and fourth premise underpinning relational-systemic practice is that human beings make meaning in conversations. Meaning and knowledge are seen as "socially constructed" (Burr, 2015), arising moment by moment in conversations and relationship. Although each of us comes to relationships with our individual histories and the meanings and behavioural patterns we have formed on the basis of past experiences, this inner experience is constantly being shaped, drawn out, or repressed in particular ways in the dynamic moment-by-moment relational interactions we participate in (Cavicchia & Gilbert, 2018). Neuroscientific research on memory (Slotnick, 2017) has demonstrated that memories do not exist as fixed units of knowing based on the past; instead when we remember something we are 're-membering': re-constructing and putting pieces of past experience together in a particular way in a particular context. What we remember, how we "re-member" is shaped by the context and how we are being shaped and impacted by it at both conscious and unconscious levels (Cozolino, 2006). This reality has important implications for human relating, team development and team coaching, for it signals that there is a dynamic, emergent quality and unpredictability to all human relating. This can raise anxiety as it inevitably involves the realisation that we cannot fully know what might happen next.

Individuals, teams and team coaches can defend against this anxiety by developing familiar routines and habits, imposing theory and unquestioned beliefs, cultural norms and protocols onto moment-by-moment experience. This results in experience being interpreted and negotiated based on a narrow range of beliefs and behaviour patterns. Whilst this confers a sense of safety in predictability, the price we and teams pay is in a reduction of creativity and innovation, which are so necessary if teams are to learn how to respond to complexity, unforeseen and unpredictable challenges.

The fifth key premise and, in our experience, one of the most difficult for team coaches to think about and feel at an embodied level, is the idea of viewing difference as information. These differences include individual perspectives, experiences, education and specialist training, working hypotheses, life experiences and the beliefs and assumptions that have been formed on the basis of these. Historically teams and organisations consciously and unconsciously develop spoken and unspoken norms and acceptable forms of thinking and acting to which individuals are expected to comply for fear of rejection from the system. Whilst this pattern can provide a semblance of order and surface agreement, it can also suppress differences in thought and perspective that might be required for creative resolution of intractable problems and leans dangerously in the direction of group think.

Embracing difference as information and always as a potential source of discovery and creativity is closely connected to the concept of joint meaning-making. As the individuals in the team – guided by the team coach's inquiry and interventions – make new connections and new information emerges in sessions, change is happening. We would argue that linear models and an over-reliance on habitual ways of meaning-making and familiar behavioural patterns and habits can often dampen down difference by implying people fit certain roles or behavioural categories or are expected to attend to tasks in particular ways, therefore disappearing complexity. Open and curious inquiry, such as the answer to the question "Is this conversation feeling any different to previous conversations?" can often be a sign as to whether the team is making new meaning together and therefore shifting their perception of each other or what has gone on before. This doesn't always require a very complex intervention from the team coach, but a simple trust in the idea that having a different conversation possibly even about the same thing does move the team forward as they are able to reframe situations and make new sense of what has gone on before.

In our final key premise, we want to say a little bit about the stance of the team coach, which we see as a key pillar of taking a relational-systemic approach. An attitude of curiosity and reflexivity in the mind of the coach is of utmost importance along with an "indifference" to a predetermined outcome which the client might have legislated for or the coach feels they need to achieve in order to look good or be successful. From a relational perspective, the capacity of the team coach to hold meaning and theory lightly and relax attachment to needing to be an expert or "authority" is key to being able to become a participant-observer in the team's process. Participant, because the coach cannot not be influenced and shaped by what is happening in the team at the levels of feeling, thinking and acting. Observer, because the coach needs to maintain perspective on what he is experiencing, be able to think about it and, without attachment to being right, offer new tentative perspectives back to the team. This allows us to hold multiple perspectives and see plurality of alternatives, bringing forth new meaning and enabling the team to make new connections as they work with each other.

It enables us to continue looking for different descriptions and explanations on an ongoing basis. Staying curious at all times is not an easy task, however we have found systemic hypothesising (see Chapter 3), working in pairs and supervision effective mechanisms to instil a discipline of an open and curious mind. Taking a stance of curiosity for us also includes an acknowledgement of the fact that as team coaches we are part of the system around the team, albeit temporarily. We cannot be a neutral entity that acts *upon* the team as we are both separated by our role, but also deeply embedded for the duration of our work. This will affect how curious and fresh in our minds we can remain at times.

Case vignette: Part 2 – an invitation to help a team define their vision

During the break, I checked in with myself. What was I feeling and sensing? A complex web of feelings around incompetence, stuckness, anxiety and anger emerged for me as well as a disbelieve that such a well-designed day could be going so wrong. I felt a sense of sickness in my stomach. I considered for a moment continuing with the design of the day, after all, this process had been designed with the team leader and agreed by the team. But I was aware that doing so would mean not attending to the data and information that had emerged during the morning and which, on reflection, had been there all of the time. I decided to take a moment with the team leader to take stock. I invited him to engage with what he was feeling right now rather than trying to get pulled into problem-solving the dilemma that presented itself. He echoed some of my feelings and spoke for the first time openly about his insecurity about managing some of the older and more established team members, one of whom had been his supervisor previously. Jointly, we hypothesised about what had been going on for the individual who had been dissatisfied with the process and what team dynamics might have been brought out during the following exchange. As the break drew to a close the team leader and I decided that he would open the second part of the day by sharing the feelings the episode before the break had evoked in him. I would then share my feelings and invite others to share what had been going on for them and what meaning they had made of the exchange.

As the team re-assembled, the leader spoke openly about the feelings that had been evoked in him, sharing some vulnerability by speaking to his transition to the leadership position. This was initially met with silence but at my invitation, other team members hesitatingly started speaking about their experience of the event and their experience of being in the team. To everyone's surprise, the theme that emerged from the conversation was that there were some concerns held by some team members about how different team members behaved towards each other and their sub-teams. Team members very tentatively began to challenge each other. After some debate, the team decided to continue as planned with the agenda of the day, but to use the time allocated to discuss the behavioural charter to continue the conversation.

Reflections: Often when a team member becomes challenging towards the team coach, it is easy to become defensive, give in to their request, challenge back or simply just carry on. In this case I tried to remain curious. Was it possible that this team member was consciously or unconsciously trying to express something on behalf of the team or wider system? Was she demonstrating a pattern that often appeared when the team was together? Using my feelings and sensations and trying to encourage the team leader to do the same, introduced difference into the conversation by moving away from the more 'heady' issue of trying to find a process to define the new vision. It also not only moved the conversation to the here-and-now, but also enabled the team to have a different conversation about an issue they had not felt safe enough to talk about outright.

1.4 Conclusion: implications for practice

In the various chapters of this book, different team coaches will introduce a range of theoretical and practice perspectives that illuminate and offer navigation aids for working with a relational-systemic orientation with teams. What all have in common is an invitation to the relational systemic team coach to:

- Orient to the dynamic and shifting processes of human relating in the present moment (see Chapter 6).
- Relax attachment to being the "expert" in order to equalise power relations to an extent, join with the team in collaborative exploration and resist the imposition of technique which can result in individuals feeling "done to" rather than related to.
- Adopt an inquiry-minded stance and become a participant observer in the team's process. This attests to the fact that, as is the case in anthropological research, the presence of the coach is a factor in determining what patterns emerge in the human system that is being inquired into.
- Cultivate ongoing awareness of their own and the team's meaning-making processes, seeing meaning as arising out of a process of social construction with emergent meanings being always partial and temporary.
- Hold meanings lightly so as not to overly fix meaning.
- Cultivate the ability to make use of their own subtle responses to being with a team, to offer perspectives and questions designed to raise the team's awareness of its own patterns of organising and meaning making.
- Cultivate a capacity to not know and learn to contain their own and the team's anxiety in the face of uncertain, and as yet unclear moments in a team's process without rushing to prematurely fix meaning or direct the team away from disorienting and potentially fertile moments of discovery. This in turn will enable the team members to feel contained in their own uncertainty long enough for new possibilities of thinking and action to emerge.

Chapter 2

Gestalt perspectives on relational team coaching

Simon Cavicchia and Ann Knights

2.1 Introduction

Gestalt psychology originated in Germany in the early twentieth century (Koffka, 1935; Wertheimer, 1944). Its focus was on how human beings perceived the world. A significant early discovery was the contextual nature of all perception, whereby something seen becomes 'figural' (stands out) in relation to something else, which then becomes background or 'ground' for short. Over the years these early ideas have been developed and refined to inform relational approaches to psychotherapy, organisational consulting, coaching and team coaching (Nevis, 1987; Gaffney et al., 2013; Chidiac, 2018; Leary-Joyce & Lines, 2018; Cavicchia & Gilbert, 2018).

Today, the focus of Gestalt psychology is primarily concerned with studying how individuals perceive themselves and the world, how they make sense of these experiences and how this sense-making informs choices and behaviour in ways that either limit or enhance development, effective living, individual and organisational performance and wellbeing.

2.2 The relevance of Gestalt principles to teams today

Contemporary theories about teams and team coaching (Leary-Joyce & Lines, 2018; Hawkins, 2021) recognise that teams have both task and process dimensions. Task refers to the function of the team in its context, what its role is as well as the specific tasks and actions it needs to implement moment by moment. Process refers to the human dynamics of the team, the ways in which individuals relate to one another and the wider context in which they are situated, how they feel, think and act together. These human system dynamics may not always be visible at the conscious level of the team. Rather, they may be out of awareness but will nonetheless make themselves subtly felt and have the potential to exert a powerful influence on how the team functions in relation to its tasks and situation. These moment-by-moment interactions and dynamics as noticed in the present moment are the main focus for the Gestalt-informed team coach.

Increasingly teams of professionals and leadership teams are faced with complex challenges which require them to slow down the rush to action in order to reflect

DOI: 10.4324/9781003325789-4

more on the situation they find themselves in and the nature of the challenges they face. Contemporary views on leadership emphasise the need for leaders to bring more of themselves to their work, learn to reveal more of their inner thoughts and feelings and unlock the collective intelligence of their teams and wider systems for responding in creative ways to these challenges (De Haan & Kasozi, 2014). The Gestalt approach, with its emphasis on relationship dynamics and how meaning emerges in relationship, is well suited to meeting this need.

We find that when teams encounter difficulties or obstacles impeding effective task execution that both the problem and the solution reside in the territory of the team dynamics. Being able to inquire into the team's group processes can generate awareness and insight in service of moving beyond what might be getting in the way (for an illustration of the process of inquiry in the presence of obstacles, see Figure 2.1).

Team coaching from a Gestalt perspective offers the opportunity for teams to reflect on the nature of, and relationship between, their tasks and human relationship dynamics. Gestalt shares the humanistic view that individuals and the teams, organisations and societies they co-create are intrinsically oriented towards wholeness, growth and wellbeing (Perls, Hefferline & Goodman, 1951). However, unhelpful patterns can form in teams, outside of individual team members' awareness. The nature of the individual team members and what they bring to the team, the team's context and how external forces impact the team, all contribute to shaping these patterns. They can interrupt the flow of the team's energy and activities in the direction of optimisation, leading to stuckness and sub-optimal functioning. In our view the *role* of the Gestalt-oriented team coach is to *observe the ways in*

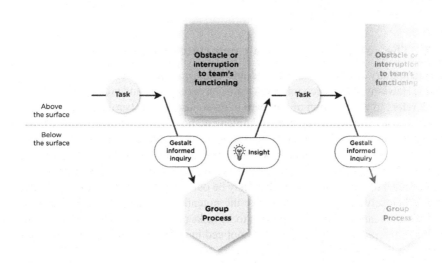

Figure 2.1 Team coaching as a series of inquiries in the presence of obstacles, challenges or interruptions.

*which team members organise themselves and their patterns of interaction and
to support the establishment of patterns that are more likely to be optimal for the
team's functioning.*

In this chapter we will explore six core principles of Gestalt and how they support this role in our team coaching practice:

2.3   The six core principles of Gestalt

Principle One. Awareness: the key to supporting growth and change

From a Gestalt perspective awareness, the ability to notice our feelings, thoughts
and the behaviour they give rise to, is key to supporting growth and change. Gestalt
sees human experience as a dynamic ongoing process as individuals respond to their
needs *and* to the ever-changing environment in which they are situated. The self,
who someone takes themselves to be, how they experience themselves moment by
moment, is conceptualised in Gestalt as arising at the boundary between the individual organism and the environment (Phillipson, 2001). Some Gestaltists use the
present participle "selfing" to denote the dynamic nature of this process. From a
Gestalt team coaching perspective, there is no such thing as a static "team" but an
ongoing process or dynamic of "teaming" as individuals organise themselves, and
their feelings, thoughts and behaviours in relation to their tasks, to one another and
at the boundary with other teams and the wider context in which they are situated.

The team coach works to support a team to develop and maintain a capacity for
awareness of how it is organising itself in ways that are effective or less effective
in relation to its task and context.

The team coach pays close attention to the levels of support and psychological
safety in the team and wider context in order to create conditions where awareness
can be cultivated, patterns can be named and team members can become increasingly able to speak their own minds without feeling overly exposed or at risk of
shaming one another or being shamed.

As Gestalt-orientated team coaches, we help teams to develop their awareness by modelling and inquiring into what comes up live, in the present moment,
as we work with them. This helps to develop the team's own reflective practice
and after time, in the supported team coaching environment, team members may
become more aware of their own experience and that of the team as a whole. But
noticing and naming physical sensations, early unprocessed feelings and thoughts
and inviting others into a conversation about these without judgement, is not usual
practice in most organisations, or indeed wider society. Learning to track how team
members make sense of their current situation together and choose how to respond
is a vital capability in today's challenging organisational environments. Our belief
is that teams need to practice this – and not only when they are in the protected
environment of the team coaching setting. With this in mind, we may sometimes
offer a simple framework, to help clients to practice in their day-to-day interactions

with each other. They can then use the team coaching session to reflect on their awareness practice as a team.

> **Case vignette:** I (Ann) was working with a senior team. One of the intentions for the work was for the team to be able to be more effective in working collectively. They had a hunch that they needed to become more reflective about their working relationships with each other and with the wider organisation. They were a team of talented, task-driven individuals, but spent little time together beyond very operational leadership team meetings. During the team coaching sessions, I had introduced the team to two key practices to support their reflection as a team:
>
> "Phenomenological noticing" which I described as being aware of what is actually happening – what they feel, sense, experience before jumping to meaning making or action, and "Co-Inquiry" (short for collaborative inquiry) – sharing and inviting others to share what they notice and then to engage in shared sense-making about that experience.
>
> Intellectually curious and keen to engage, the team members were challenged, intrigued and sometimes irritated by my naming of patterns of relating in the team, and my inquiry into small gestures and responses, and into the sensations and feelings that accompanied them. This had started to unveil some of the hidden difficulties in the team relationships and differences in perspective that had been undiscussed. Yet this was an alien and somewhat challenging way of being together, and I felt it might be helpful to make explicit the noticing and inquiry process they engaged in during the team coaching. I helped them to map the process as it unfolded. What was interesting (and challenging) for the team was to stay longer with the Notice, Name and Inquire stages of the process, instead of leaping to their own private sensemaking and individual action.
>
> After some initial discomfort, which always accompanies a new practice that takes a team beyond its familiar patterns of behaviour, the team took the "Team Reflective Process" map (Figure 2.2) into their usual gatherings as a leadership team. As one team member put it "It gives us the framework and the permission to talk about what is really going on".

Principle Two. Emergence: the requirement to balance structure and space

Put simply, emergence in Gestalt means pattern formation. Human beings naturally perceive patterns and this is a very dynamic and lively process. We can shift our attention between one emerging pattern and another, but we find it very difficult to see more than one at the same time. For team coaches, working with emergence means that we need to be alive to (and help the team to be alive to) what patterns are arising and fading, and be aware of what data, information and experience is influencing what emerges.

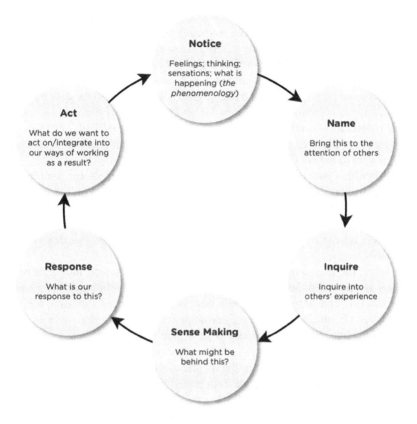

Figure 2.2 The team reflective process map.

In Gestalt terminology, we talk about a 'figure', the current focus of interest, which emerges and takes shape from the 'ground', in essence the background both in the current organisational melee (Harris, 2001) and also the past experience of the team. Ground evolves from past experiences, 'unfinished business' (for example past tensions that that have not yet been resolved and which haunt the team's patterns of interaction), and from the flow of the present experience – both for the individuals in the team and the team as whole (Polster & Polster, 1974). The relationship between figure and ground is dynamic. In Gestalt this process is considered optimal when something emerges and takes form (becomes 'figural') and demands attention, is consciously attended to (or not) and fades back into the ground as another figure emerges.

The team coach can help the team to create a figure based on data and information available to them in the moment and also to notice what is emerging live in the work. In this way the team coach works with what emerges and may also play a role in calling the team's attention to data and information in the moment which helps figures to take form.

I (Ann) was working with a transport organisation that was going through a huge shift in ownership, structure, and culture, whilst at the same time needing to keep their tens of thousands of daily passengers moving safely. The leadership team flitted from figure to figure (from worries about the new Health and Safety challenges in the new infrastructure, to consultations on redundancies, to a personal conflict within the team), and repeatedly asked for external expert advice to help them respond, only for another series of problems to emerge and indeed for old problems to return. They rarely stayed with one thing long enough to explore all the knowledge and perspectives in the team before handing it over to the outside experts.

When this pattern emerged again in a session, I made some simple interventions to bring it to awareness for example "What do you notice as you end this conversation about the safety brief?" Some members of the team wanted to say more and felt some key aspects of the issue were missed, another was relieved, one was satisfied and keen to move on, two noticed that they felt inexplicably angry.

When the team explored these different responses further, they noticed that this was very often the range of responses in the team to their discussions about the tasks of transition. This led to a new, shared figure for the team, the sense of loss and confusion about the organisational restructure – their own as well as that of the hundreds of employees in the organisation.

In our view this experience highlights one of the core tenets which differentiates relational team coaching work from expert consulting or expert-led facilitation down a pre-determined path. For the transport organisation leadership team, there were very many calls on their time and energy, and these would leap up and take their attention, then fade (probably only temporarily) into the background as another emerged. Advice from experts might emerge as important for the team at a given moment, but as team coaches, we are more interested in how team members engage with such expertise, rather than providing expert input ourselves.

Many of team coaches' plans and designs for team coaching are attempts to "preconfigure the field", meaning they impose pre-existing ideas, theories and models onto reality, often in the (misguided) belief that they can control it. Sometimes this is helpful – for containment, for framing work or for offering new data. However, any preconfigured process needs also to allow for creativity in the moment with what emerges, which cannot be known in advance.

For some this might mean starting with clear intention for the work, some agreement on ways of working and some light process design. For example, the team coach may have a process in mind with which to support the emergence of new information and experiences. But the trick is always to be prepared to let go of preconfigurations in the service of recognising what is actually happening.

This means that most of the team coach's preparation is in continuously grounding oneself in a phenomenological stance, where we open up space for observation and protect this space against jumping to conclusions or judgement. This phenomenological idea was first introduced by Husserl (1912–1929), who spoke about *bracketing* (*Einklammerung*) to indicate an act of suspending judgment about the natural world. After creating this open, free space for the team through bracketing, one might continue with *horizontalisation*, which is a deliberate act of allowing everything to be potentially relevant until further notice (Husserl, 1912–1929). Horizontalisation deliberately treats each item of observation or description as having equal value or significance. Therefore, you decide that all that happens or that occurs to you is important or may be important, until a different understanding emerges within the team.

Principle Three. Making room for "whole person" experience – balancing safety and exposure.

Lose your mind and come to your senses. – attributed to Fritz Perls

Gestalt is considered to be "experience near" as a philosophy and methodology (Naranjo, 1993). Cultivating awareness not only of our thoughts and concepts, but also our bodily sensations and emotions is key to the Gestalt approach. This can be challenging in corporate contexts where thinking and conceptual knowledge dominate (Cavicchia and Gilbert, 2018). Nevertheless, advances in neuroscience have amply demonstrated that the human nervous system processes vast amounts of sensory information which in turn shapes thinking and the thoughts that come to mind (Damasio, 2000). Therefore, when beginning work with a team it is helpful to orient team members to a number of key Gestalt concepts and then make space for clients to experience more fully what these point to in terms of human experience. This helps to create a sense of safety for this "unusual" whole person work.

> **Case vignette:** I (Simon) was asked to work with a team that was considered by organisation stakeholders to be underperforming. It was seen by the wider organisation and by its leader to be a collection of individuals "doing their own thing" with an undeveloped capacity for the dialogue, coordination and collaboration deemed necessary for delivering on an ambitious strategic agenda for the business. At the first meeting with the team the leader took time to describe the context for the team coaching intervention, the feedback that had been received and his views on the team and perceived need to improve on current performance. I sensed anxiety rising in the room, a heavy silence descending with body language such as sideways glances and shuffling in seats indicating mounting discomfort. All developmental feedback can evoke narcissistic injury in the form of team members having their self-esteem and positive perception of themselves and the team challenged. I acknowledged these challenges as a way of normalising them and, as an antidote to ego defences and the possibility of shame, I intervened to say that, although the team had received challenging feedback, it might be helpful to view the intervention in the context of lifelong

learning and continuous improvement, not as something broken that needed to be repaired. I acknowledged the fact of there being much collective wisdom and years of experience in the team and a curiosity as to whether this might be fully utilised in the current ways of working that had become norms for the team.

I introduced the concept of awareness and the role of emotion and sensation in human experience and sense making (Gendlin, 1997) and invited the group to break into pairs to discuss the impact of hearing the framing of the two days. I invited people to pay attention to the thoughts that they were having as well as any feelings, energy, or lack thereof, they were experiencing. Nevis (1987) suggests that one of the roles of the Gestalt-informed consultant and team consultant is to model those capacities which are, as yet, undeveloped in the system and which might need to be cultivated in order to develop the skills and resources for greater human connection, dialogue and meaning making. I chose to model what I was inviting the team to do by sharing some of my own feelings and thoughts upon beginning to work with the team including some anxiety about whether I would be the right coach for them and whether we might be able to create together a meaningful and fruitful working relationship. I also said that, after the pairs work, we would create a space for people to share any experiences or insights they may wish to but that this was not compulsory. Offering permission for individuals to choose their level of participation paradoxically can have the effect of supporting greater dialogue as individuals are able to set the pace and remain in control of what in Gestalt is referred to as the personal "exposure boundary" (Polster & Polster, 1974).

As might be expected at this early stage, when people returned to the group many individuals chose to disclose mainly the thoughts they were having, not yet feeling safe to reveal more of themselves. I intentionally acknowledged each contribution and shared my genuine appreciation for people finding a way to engage with the inquiry. The point here was not to achieve a desired outcome by insisting on particular outputs, as might be the case in more linear and solutions focused orientations to coaching, but to model curiosity, receptivity, permission and respect for each team member and their right to find their own level of participation. My interventions had also introduced some basic Gestalt principles to establish some common understanding which I could refer back to and use to work, over time, to increase the team's capacity to acknowledge the interplay between feelings, thoughts and the actions they give rise to.

Whilst establishing supportive and enabling conditions for relating and reflecting together is extremely important in the early stages of a team forming or of an engagement, the coach will monitor levels of support on an ongoing basis. Every time a team steps to the edge of naming or confronting an issue which may feel challenging or exposing, the coach will attend to how to co-create sufficient support for the team to take the next step, for example in naming unhelpful behaviour among team members without shaming and learning to give direct and honest feedback to one another.

Principle Four. Experimenting: a way of exploring experience and trying on new ways of being

Working with that balance of safety and exposure, the Gestalt-orientated team coach encourages the team to experiment live to explore their current experience and 'try on' new ways of being, rather than spend time planning action for later. With this in mind, the coach co-creates opportunities for thinking and acting differently and experimenting with new perspectives. As such, creativity and experimentation form a large part of the Gestalt team coach's repertoire. The coach co-designs exercises and experiments with the team to support awareness and the development of required skills in noticing and making meaning from experience. Experiments can be opportunity to pay more attention to something that is pressing for attention and needs to be understood.

Experiments are informed by, and arise from, the specific moment-by-moment processes and particulars of the team in its current context. Often, they arise as a response to a pattern that is considered to be limiting or sub-optimal in some way by the coach and/or the team.

When suggesting and co-creating experiments with a team it can be helpful to consider the following:

- What is becoming figural in the team that might need attention and how might the team explore and develop the figure?
- Does the experiment make sense to the team and its stated goals and learning and development objectives?
- Is there sufficient interest, curiosity and energy in the team for the experiment?
- Is there sufficient psychological safety and support for the experiment and how might the coach work to establish sufficient support for the team to risk doing something novel and out of the ordinary, moving beyond their comfort zone?
- How might the team coach "grade" or calibrate the experiment to respond to the sense of readiness (safety, energy, etc.) in the team for the experiment?

This latter point often takes the form of exploring with the team individual perceptions of safety and exposure in the team and what concerns team members may have about the experiment. From a Gestalt perspective, change only happens when we encounter something novel, a new experience of some kind, which forces us to discover new ways of responding (Perls, Hefferline & Goodman, 1951). Exposure to the novel is always anxiety provoking as it involves facing into the unknown. Perls famously referred to anxiety as "unsupported excitement" (Perls, Hefferline & Goodman, 1969) in that anxiety and excitement are physiologically identical in experience – a fluttering in the chest, shallow breathing and knot in the stomach. It is the degree of "support" and psychological safety available that converts anxiety into excitement. For this reason, it is important that the team coach work to calibrate levels of support and exposure with the team. Too much safety and the team will remain in its comfort zone. Too much exposure and the team will retreat from the experiment. This balancing act is referred to as the "safe emergency" in Gestalt (Perls, Hefferline & Goodman, 1951). The balance of safety and "emergency" which refers both to the feeling of anxiety and the emergence of new perspectives and possibilities that experiments can provide. The golden rule here is never to push a team beyond what it can safely experiment with. Even very small experiments can reveal something significant and lead to small breakthroughs for the team. They can also feel quite exposing and disruptive (both in a positive and challenging way).

> **Case vignette – a very small experiment:** As part of a two-day long OD intervention in a management consulting firm. I (Ann) coached the leadership team of one of the regions for an afternoon. I had had short introductory conversations with each of the team members prior to the session and had been part of the work in the larger group. For the afternoon session with the team, I had set out our breakout room with a circle of wheeled chairs, and the team was settling into the circle. I noticed that Carsten, who was next to me, kept his chair slightly out of the circle, I became aware of my feeling isolated, so I wheeled my chair closer. He ever so slightly moved back. "You moved your chair ever so slightly back", I said. He replied that he was more comfortable slightly further back; I was interested, but wanted to attend to creating a learning space for the whole team. I was also carefully calibrating my presence, not pushing too much.
>
> Later as we checked-in in the group (I'd asked – "how are you arriving in this smaller group at this time?") Carsten reflected that this small movement of his chair had brought to mind his pattern of always sitting on the outside; he wanted to experiment with immersing himself in the team. I encouraged him to notice what small experiment he might make now with that intent in mind. He shifted his chair so that he was part of the circle.
>
> I asked: "What are you aware of – as you sit in the group now?"... (staying with phenomenological tracking) "I am nervous, but exhilarated ... I feel I am leaning in ... I see you all differently", he said.
>
> Interestingly, later in the session, one of the team members, Christine, reflected that I appeared to have "got stuck in" without any explicit contracting. I agreed, I had started to talk quite directly about what I noticed in the moment, as we checked in in our chairs. In her reflections after the session she noted, "In the beginning I was a little surprised by the assertiveness and how you very directly addressed what you observed". I am reminded of the power of phenomenological noticing, and how counter cultural a willingness to be in contact, close connection without holding back, is for most organisational settings. I am also reminded that good contact needs to emerge from being well supported and feeling safe enough.

Noticing and describing what captures our attention simply to raise awareness, without knowing where it might lead may seem counter-intuitive when set against linear assumptions and a belief in a pre-determined direction. Fritz Perls described Gestalt as "the therapy of the obvious" (Perls, Hefferline & Goodman, 1951) whereby the practitioner draws attention to what is observed and then explores what (if anything) emerges in collaboration with the client.

Principle Five. Field theory: everything is interconnected

How individuals feel, think and act and how teams function are shaped in and out of awareness by the context or field in which they are situated. The goal of Gestalt is to support healthy and effective living/functioning in the face of shifts in contexts and what these call forth as being optimal responses. From an existential perspective, responsibility for one's choices and actions in Gestalt is seen as depending greatly on individual and collective *response ability*. Change is seen as constant and how individuals, teams and whole systems respond to this constant is a primary focus of Gestalt. This is a particularly useful approach when working in volatile, uncertain, complex, ambiguous and challenging contexts.

The coach holds in mind, and is curious with the team about, how events in the wider context are shaping how team members feel, think and choose to act. The coach names patterns and invites the team to notice and reflect on their experience as individuals and as a team.

Given the interconnectedness implicit in Field Theory, change in one pattern or aspect can bring about change in other areas of a system, but these cannot be predicted in advance as there will inevitably be a multitude of factors shaping a given moment, set of behaviours or patterns.

Working from this field relations perspective, the Gestalt team coach is well placed to work with the team on its interactions with others in its context. At the heart of Field Theory is the notion that as we are involved in an ongoing process of interrelating, we are at the same time shaping and shaped by the current situation – which includes people and groups (and their "drives, tensions and thoughts"), as well as wider contextual factors. Field theory holds that only by paying attention to the specific 'dynamics' of a phenomenon in its context, can it be fully understood (Lewin, 1951). This means that for a team, it is rather pointless to consider what is going on in the team in isolation from their context and current situation.

Very often, team coaches are working with relatively senior teams, where team members are themselves leaders of other teams. These teams also interact with other stakeholders, including potentially a Board, customers, investors, politicians and so on. Sometimes, work on external relationships is explicitly part of the team coaching brief. But whether explicit or not, team members or the team as a whole, carry their experience of relating with others into the team coaching space. Here the team coach can support the team in becoming aware of how they talk about other important relationships and groups, what narratives or assumptions are present, or what patterns seem to repeat (such as in the Engage mode of the Talik model described in Chapter 9).

In one senior team I (Ann) worked with, which was facing some challenging shifts in its market, members often complained that they did not get the kind of creative and strategic thinking they wanted from the directors reporting into them. Directors in turn complained (via a survey) that the top team was not visible and felt that the senior team had fixed views on what they wanted, but did not communicate these clearly. In this case, senior team members noticed that they had fallen into a pattern of glossing over gritty issues and passing on unclear requests to their reports. They usually invited Directors leading projects to join their senior team meeting, for very short sessions usually of 30 minutes or less to report on progress and receive input and feedback. I helped them to notice and name their patterns of interacting with their direct reports and then to explore in the moment their own struggle with thinking together (as opposed to their current habit of each sharing their pre-thinking), in the context of the significant volatility and uncertainty in the field. They devised an experiment with some of their direct reports to disrupt the psychological game they felt they (along with all their market competitors) were playing. They called their game "We know what to do … don't you?".[1] They invited Directors for a day-long session to think with them about framing the problem (in leading the organisation's response to their shifting market) where the invitation was "Nobody knows what to do, let's work it out".

This is work in progress, but if we take field theory seriously, we might expect this shift in a way of relating to lead to other changes within and outside the team.

Principle Six. The cycle of experience as a "process" map

One of the best-known maps of Gestalt theory is the Cycle of Experience. First developed at the Gestalt Institute of Cleveland and refined and adapted since, it seeks to describe the process whereby individuals make sense of their experience and get their needs met by taking action at the boundary between their organism and the environment.

The Cycle can also be represented as a wave as we have done here, in Figure 2.3, to denote the ongoing flow of experience from identification of need to the satisfaction once a need has been met.

From a Gestalt perspective we first become aware of a need on the basis of sensation, we feel something. We then enter the awareness or recognition stage of the cycle where we make meaning from our experience. We might feel a gnawing ache in our stomach and recognise this as a sign of hunger. In mobilisation we begin to orient towards taking action appropriate to our identified need. We may begin to move towards the kitchen and then prepare a sandwich. Contact is where we fully immerse ourselves in the action that is designed to meet our needs, in this case eating the sandwich. So, contact is the difference between wolfing the sandwich down thoughtlessly at your desk whilst doing your emails (for example) and stopping work to really experience eating the sandwich. In the former you hardly notice that

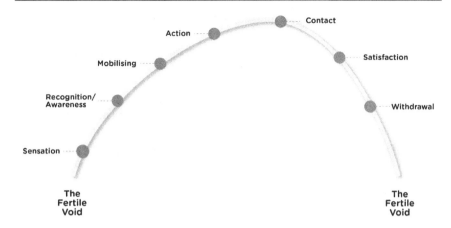

Figure 2.3 A representation of the cycle of experience as a wave from the identification of a need to the satisfaction of the need.

you've eaten, and so are unchanged by the experience – still hungry. In the latter you make contact with your experience and are changed by it.

Then, having correctly identified the need and taken appropriate action, we enter the stage of satisfaction. Savouring the sandwich and having allowed our experience to be changed by the action we have taken, we go from feeling hungry to feeling satisfied and nourished. We then enter the stage of withdrawal, where the energy we had invested in meeting the need of hunger is now withdrawn from that task and is free to be invested in whatever next needs attending to. Hunger is an example of a physiological need, but the same process also applies to meeting psychological needs as well as team and organisational tasks.

Given Gestalt's roots in existential philosophy which sees human beings as motivated by making sense of experience and finding meaning in their lives, the Cycle/Wave implicitly offers a map for tracking and paying attention to the process by which this happens.

Notions of health and well-being in Gestalt are predicated on being able to move fluidly through each stage of the Wave which is then likely to result in appropriate action being taken to resolve the presenting need or issue that an individual or team is facing.

In team life, team members go through their own waves of experience, with more or less awareness and more or less flow. They are also members of the collective team experience. Teams, like individuals, might inhibit their ability to move through the Wave smoothly and thereby limit their potential for a full, vibrant and impactful existence. These inhibiting patterns are referred to as moderations to contact and they can occur at any point along the wave. Our role as coaches involves paying particular attention to ways in which these moderations inhibit the team's flow and effectiveness.

In the context of teams these moderations can include:

- Desensitisation – Difficulties in sensing and being able to identify needs or form clear foci of attention or "figures of interest" in individuals and the team as a whole.
- Introjection – Internal messages which might prevent an individual saying what he or she really thinks. In teams this can be as a result of organisational culture and/or team norms which permit and welcome certain patterns of behaviour and discount or punish others. Teams in the grip of norms around politeness and not embarrassing or shaming other team members will struggle to give direct developmental feedback, even where this might be vital to ensure the team can make necessary course corrections and deliver against its objectives.
- Desensitisation to needs and cultural norms preventing the acknowledgement of vulnerability and not knowing can lead to a lack of support for facing the inevitable disorientation that arises at individual and collective levels when faced with needing to experiment with a way of being or behaving that is new and unfamiliar. This is particularly relevant in the context of teams and organisations developing the agility and innovative orientation needed to respond to unforeseen and hitherto unknown challenges. This gives rise to the tendency in teams to rush from sensations such as anxiety in the face of overwhelm or complexity into activity as a way of discharging anxiety. This often results in a fragmentation of the team into individual "headless chicken" behaviour where action is not aligned or adequately co-ordinated.

Teams and organisations which can be aware of their patterns and reflect on them are implicitly more able to move smoothly through each stage of the Wave. This is likely to result in action that is grounded in more of the elements of the context and ensures alignment between team members in relation to action.

Case vignette. In a team I (Simon) was working with, which had a strong bias for action, the team would typically structure meetings tightly around delivery priorities and information sharing. Energetically the climate of the meeting was often characterised by one person presenting in a rather droning and monotone voice with the rest of the team seeming flat and appearing to be entranced by staring at a Powerpoint presentation.

Every now and then a person would ask as a question to understand more the context or implications of the presentation for their part of the business. At this point the group would become animated and a lively discussion would ensue with people sharing different perspectives, reservations, questions. Eventually someone (and it was a different person every time) would say "hey folks we are going down a rabbit hole" and the group would return to its trancelike, flat state. As this happened a number of times I decided to name what I was seeing.

In a neutral tone I said "I have noticed that occasionally one of you will interrupt the presentation to ask a question, the conversation then gets animated. After a short while one of you will say 'we are going down a rabbit hole' and you go back to being quiet and watching the screen – what do you make of this?"

A silence ensued, which often happens when a coach names a pattern that has been out of awareness and takes people to an edge of feeling slightly exposed. Then individuals began to acknowledge that they had noticed it too. They were able to see that when asking questions and talking to each other they felt more energised, but soon they realised they had different views and they began to feel confused, anxious and unsure about how to respond to their differences. They were also able to see that they were in the grip of some powerful beliefs, as well as their organisation's norms, that performance was related to doing things rather than talking about things. This core belief was driving their behaviour in relation to listing all the activities they were doing as individuals via the medium of presentations. The particular moderation of contact of 'deflection' (Perls, Hefferline & Goodman, 1951) was in play here as team members moved away from their mounting discomfort by returning to a familiar, safe yet unproductive pattern. "We are going down a rabbit hole" had become code for "this is all rather interesting but a little overwhelming as this feels like uncharted territory and we don't know what to do next so let's go back to our Powerpoint ritual".

This was a team that historically had been very poor at acting in a coordinated and consistent way in relation to the team objectives and strategic direction of the business. Together the team and I were able to explore the differences in the team, which had fuelled the inconsistent behaviour, explore and understand the different perspectives people had and attend to aligning more overtly. They were able to experiment more with interrupting the passive pattern of listening to Powerpoint presentations and become more active in engaging with one another and the tasks of the team. As a result their performance and contribution to the wider business improved considerably.

2.4 Supporting response-ability in teams

A common pattern in many organisations given the emphasis on doing and taking action, is that teams become "reactive" moving quickly from identifying an issue to action, bypassing the crucial stages of exploration, exploring options and committing to action (as illustrated in Figure 2.4). This can result in uncoordinated behaviour which is less connected to the richness of information in the field about what action might be optimal. It is more likely to be driven by the different motivations, needs and perspectives of different individuals than any shared understanding or commitment to a common set of goals. When individuals and teams are feeling anxious, the primary individual response is to find any way to relieve anxiety, and this often results in a withdrawal into individual activities or silos and a retreat from dialogue and relating.

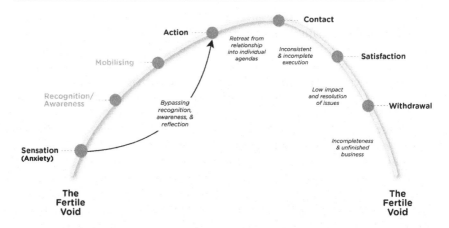

Figure 2.4 The cycle of experience when bypassing crucial stages of exploration.

An added dimension here is that individuals in a team can be in different places on the Wave at any one time and so it is necessary to slow down the rush to action to ensure that all team members can arrive at the action phase simultaneously. Otherwise individuals may publicly agree to something in order to move things on but then will not follow through, as privately they may not be at a stage where they can wholeheartedly commit to what has been decided publicly. When this happens, it might be construed as resistance to change or doing something new.

From a Gestalt perspective resistance is viewed as "multi-directional energy" (Nevis, 1987) given the different stages individuals might be at. The Gestalt-informed team coach will pay attention to the different energies of individuals and seek to support sufficient alignment for a team to take co-ordinated and committed action where this is required. This includes individuals acting alone with the team's support. Without alignment, individual activity can easily undermine collective action.

The role of the coach is to support the team in attending to all stages of the Wave, by creating the conditions for reflection in the team (as illustrated in Figure 2.5). This process of thinking together and creating new perspectives and possibilities is also key to supporting innovation and creativity adjusting to the complexities of situations teams are increasingly operating in.

2.5   In conclusion: the core practices of the Gestalt-informed team coach

In this chapter, we have explored the elements of Gestalt which are most figural in our practice as team coaches.

At the heart of our approach is the stance of being a participant observer (Barber, 2007). This use of self is core to the practice of the Gestalt coach. The

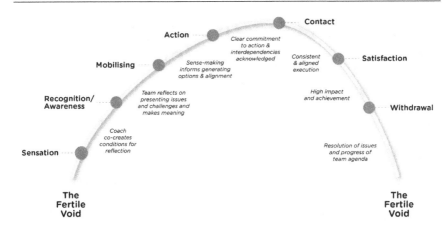

Figure 2.5 Contributions of a team coach at every stage of the Gestalt cycle of experience.

coach observes and describes what they notice. Interventions are seen as gestures or offers to discover what happens next. The coach pays attention to the response of the team and the meaning they can make from the intervention if any. In this way meaning, learning and possibilities emerge from the in-between of the co-created relationship between the coach and team members. The coach works first and foremost in service of raising the team's awareness in the context of their primary task and purpose in their organisation.

Note

1   For more on psychological games see Eric Berne's 'Games People Play' (1964).

Chapter 3

Systemic perspectives on relational team coaching

Dorothee Stoffels

3.1 Introduction: my own journey

In order to get into the subject of systemic perspectives on relational team coaching, I want to start with my own journey and history. More than 15 years ago, I trained as a systemic family therapist, working in the field of Child and Adolescent Mental Health. The four-year clinical training changed not only my outlook on families and mental health and mental health interventions, but indeed my outlook on society, life and how 'problems' and 'solutions' were constructed by us as human beings. It challenged my view that there was one link between cause and effect that needed to be established and worked with in order to achieve change.

What was striking for me at the time in my systemic work with families was how organisations involved with them were their own little systems, who were constantly interacting with other organisational systems and indeed the family system. I became curious and interested in this phenomenon and decided to leave mental health work to embark on a career in Organisational Development and Team Coaching. Very quickly I noticed that not only my systemic and relational thinking (laid out in Chapter 1, co-written with Simon Cavicchia) was helpful in making sense of organisational and team challenges, but that there were also a number of ideas or 'disciplines' from the world of systemic family therapy that would be helpful when intervening with organisations and teams.

The field of systemic family therapy is very wide and has its own traditions and history, including influences from anthropology, cybernetics as well as constructivism and social constructionism. It is beyond this chapter to detail them all and I have therefore selected a few key ideas. An early influencer to the field was Ludwig von Bertalanffy, a biologist, who proposed general systems theory. He believed that the whole is greater than the sums of its parts, a key idea across all family therapy traditions (Carr, 2008). Gregory Bateson (1978), an anthropologist and ethnologist, introduced the notion that the family could be viewed as a cybernetic system, where communication happens on multiple levels. He also viewed the behaviour of each family member and each family subsystem as determined by the patterns of interaction that connects *all* family members. Gestalt psychologist Kurt Lewin's work on work group dynamics added another dimension to early family

DOI: 10.4324/9781003325789-5

therapy thinking. Similarly to Bertalanffy, he saw the group as greater than the sum of its parts, however he also noticed that group discussions were more effective than individual instruction in changing group behaviour. He was interested in how groups developed a quasi-stationary equilibrium and that this force has the ability to resist change (Carr, 2008 and Dallos & Draper, 2002). These influences and key ideas not only lead to different schools of family therapy developing including Structural, Strategic, Milan, Narrative and Solution-focused approaches (Carr, 2008 and Dallos & Draper, 2002), they also had a significant influence on the field of organisational development.

In this chapter, I want to particularly draw on the work of the Milan Team, which practiced in the 1970s in Italy and developed a particular approach, known as the Milan approach. The team consisted of Selvini, Boscolo, Cecchin and Prata, four psychiatrists, who were in their thinking heavily influenced by Gregory Bateson. Their ideas in relation to circularity, systemic hypothesising and circular and reflexive questioning, which all build on each other, are particularly useful and relevant to working with teams in organisations. Before I develop these ideas further, I want to encourage the reader to re-familiarise themselves with the five key premises mentioned in Chapter 1, as their systemic nature provide the grounding for this chapter. I also want to highlight that one key assumption of this chapter is that the team coach is part of the system (albeit temporarily) with some level of neutrality and not an entity that acts 'upon' a team. The idea of 'neutrality', originally coined by the Milan team, means in this case that the team coach although they don't have the same organisational attachments as team members is not a completely blank page with no views or mental and emotional affiliations. The coach should therefore attempt to avoid the position of privileging one view or position on the presenting issue over another and seeing it as more correct (Cecchin, 1987).

3.2 People are not a problem to be fixed: ideas around circularity

One of the key premises of systemic thinking and work with families and teams is that there is an emphasis on exploring and creating heightened awareness of patterns of interactions between people rather than focusing on individuals being the 'problem' that needs to be 'fixed'. In my practice, I have become aware of the tendency of team members to select another team member or indeed the team leader to be 'the problem that needs sorting out'. In the systemic field this person would be called 'the assigned patient'. If only the leader/team member was more present, more consistent or more professional (any word can be inserted here), then the woes of the team would disappear. This world view or view of problems is very common and very human and denotes a linear cause-effect thinking of relationships and problems. It assigns responsibility to one person for the existing difficulty. The feeling is that if one thing or person can be changed, then the problem is solved, we feel happier and the effectiveness of the team is restored. This is challenged in a systemic view on teams –in fact it is the interplay between all parts of the system or all team members that is key to success.

Circularity means not only that we consider all parts of a system interconnected, but also that we see circularity in the information that we gather from different team members. Information is viewed as news of difference. This means that as the individuals in the team make new connections and meaning and new information emerges in sessions, change is happening (Selvini et al., 1980). Essential for this is a state of curiosity in the mind of the coach. Holding the stance of curiosity helps to see plurality of alternatives. It enables us to continue looking for different descriptions and explanations all the time.

Case vignette 1: Opening the doors to multiple realities in a regional sales team:

A number of years ago, a colleague and I worked with a regional sales team of a manufacturing business. We had been 'called in' by a senior manager as there was trouble in the team. Trust was low, returns not satisfactory, there was high staff turnover and many interventions that had been internally and externally tried had failed. The sales team consisted of sub-teams, each responsible for a certain sales area. A much-loved manager had left the team three years prior and a new manager had been appointed and things had just not been the same since then. In our initial meeting with the senior manager, it became evident that both in senior management and in the team a story existed that the current manager was the problem that needed to be sorted out. He was seen as unreliable, would often disappear on his own sales missions, leaving the team without a point of contact. In team meetings, his behaviour was described as confrontational, blaming and attacking, when individuals and sub-teams did not deliver results. His connection to other parts of the organisation and external stakeholders was not seen as successful. The perfect solution seemed to be to either let him go or change his approach and behaviour, which the organisation had considered doing by offering him individual coaching, with little success. The organisational fantasy was that this would lead to the end of the trouble in the team.

The commissioning senior manager however, had a small inkling that this simple cause-effect thinking was not the answer and that there were other aspects to this situation that needed attention, hence the desire to engage team coaches. Through our stance of not accepting a linear view of the situation and our curious questioning, we encouraged her to give voice to the other interconnected aspects that she saw in the team and across the sub-teams. Suddenly a complex web of stories and relationship issues across the sub-teams pre-dating the current manager emerged. This helped us to define with her and the current team manager what the work with the team could look like. We embarked on a series of one-to-one conversations and then sub-team conversations as it was felt that it would not be helpful to bring the whole team together at this point. Other facilitated whole-team meetings had resulted in an entrenchment of the current pattern of blame. The one-to-one conversations focused solely on enabling every individual to express their own reality within the team, exploring history and relationships, issues of equality, diversity and inclusion, challenging the view that the team manager was the problem in the team. We gently introduced the idea of multiple realities that co-existed into the thinking and stories of the different team members. Feeding back the collated themes from these conversations was the next important step. And although the work with the team did not progress much beyond the point of sub-team meetings that allowed collective sense-making of the feedback, an important inroad had been made by starting to shift the mindset of both individuals and the team to a more interconnected and circular view of the challenges it faced.

3.3   The discipline of systemic hypothesising: how to use your hunches

An important pillar of systemic team coaching practice is the discipline of systemic hypothesising. But, what do we actually mean by a hypothesis in the context of working systemically with teams?

The Oxford Dictionary definition suggests that a hypothesis is "a supposition made as a basis for reasoning, without reference to its truth; as a starting point for an investigation". The key aspect here is the phrase 'without reference to its truth'.

In systemic practice with families or teams the hypothesis is seen as a starting point for a piece of client work with a team or a particular session (Selvini et al., 1980). It is not concerned with finding the right story or description about the team, but rather it is considered more or less useful in guiding the activities and choices of the team coach. It is based on assumptions of circularity and can support tracking relational patterns. It is seen as a building block for curiosity. Hypotheses can be based on written information, observations or our felt experience of the team. Often, we are not even conscious about how much information we already hold about a team and the system around it. The way we receive the commission, from whom, in what form, our experience of the organisation as we attend a pitch or initial meeting all form part of the rich fabric of information that we gather as soon as we become aware of a piece of work. All this data, whether it is cognitively thought about, felt in our body or expressed in emotions that we feel, will ultimately contribute to hypotheses that we are developing about the team. Our job is to track and observe what is being evoked in us as part of the hypothesising process.

But what is the ultimate function of a systemic hypothesis? We often consciously and unconsciously hold hypotheses about individuals and teams that we are working with. This informs what questions we ask and what interventions we make. The discipline of *purposefully* hypothesising helps to open our mind as coaches to different possibilities about what might be going on for the team and will guide our questions and interventions with the client (Cecchin, 1987). It helps us to stay curious.

A systemic hypothesis should attempt to include all parts of the system in and around the team. This would include the leader, different team members, senior management, key stakeholders of the team, other key business areas that the team interfaces with or even societal, environmental, financial, economic considerations. Paying attention to all parts of the system will help track relational patterns that might be going on in the team. If we are struggling to hypothesise or to keep the hypothesis systemic, it is often useful to ask oneself, who else or what else might be included in our sense-making of the team and the work at hand (primary task).

One pitfall we can experience as coaches is that we get wedded to our hypothesis. We feel that we found the grain of truth and we stick to it. When this happens, we can lose all curiosity and become stuck with the team in one place. It is therefore essential to regularly revisit our hypothesis or hypotheses, to inquire with colleagues, the commissioner of the work, the team leader and team members as to what *their* hypotheses about the team, its challenges, relationships and effectiveness are. In fact introducing the idea and language around hypotheses can be very powerful for a team as long as we encourage them to hold their views tentatively. "What are your hypotheses about what is going on in your team at the moment?" can be a key question to help the team become more conscious of their own sense-making and what guides their actions and behaviours with each other and in relation to their task. It helps the team appreciate multiple ways of constructing a situation.

There are a number of things that we can hypothesise about. They include:

- People and relationships (this includes their relationship to their individual or the team's work or task at hand);
- behaviour, beliefs and intentions and meaning that team members make;
- feelings (this includes feelings that get evoked in us as team coaches as we attend to the work);
- situations and events; and
- time.

Not all of these might be relevant at all times, but again extending what we pay attention to as a team coach, will help us to remain curious and open up possibilities in our minds what might be going on and how we might want to intervene.

In summary, here are some guidelines that might help team coaches embrace the discipline of systemic hypothesizing. A systemic hypothesis should:

- connect the team members' behaviour with meaning;
- be useful in that it guides your questions and interventions;

- include all components of the system;
- relate to the team's concern or challenge;
- be different from the commonly accepted hypothesis in the system;
- be discarded if it no longer feels useful; and
- evolve in response to feedback.

Case vignette 2: Systemic hypothesis about working with the executive team of an international engineering company:

We were asked to work with the executive team of this global business because the CEO recognised that there were tensions in the team that stopped them from working effectively together. There were also concerns that they were not leading their functions properly, which resulted in unsatisfactory cross-functional collaboration. The company was a family business that had been run by generations of the same family, always handing the role of the CEO down to the oldest child.

We created this initial hypothesis, based on information from the initial written commission, contact and conversations with the HR director, executive team members and the CEO. We also used our felt sense of the conversations (one of the team coaches experienced an acute sense of anxiety in a number of conversations) to add to our tentative hypothesis. We developed further hypotheses based on what we learnt about and experienced with the team throughout this piece of work.

Initial tentative hypothesis:

> The family member had – possibly quite reluctantly – taken on the CEO role a few years ago, being under pressure from her family and stakeholders of the company. Being from an engineering background she seemed most happy in the detail of the actual work and probably felt inept attending to the leadership aspect of the CEO role. As a result she did not take kindly to people challenging her or her leadership and fired people from her executive team very quickly when disagreements arose. This seemed to create a feeling of fear amongst executive team members, who, as a result, appeared not to trust each other and were undermining each other in interactions and meetings. This had a huge impact on how they led their functions, where staff was possibly given the unconscious message that collaboration was not desired and one had to protect one's function, which in return led to not sharing decisions and keeping information secret.

This initial tentative hypothesis led to us designing a first away day with the executive team that focused on rotating pair work. The aim of the pair work was to give each other feedback and build trust, with the result that team members started to express how they felt being part of the executive team. First tentative attempts were also made to speak 'truth to power', with some gentle challenges to the CEO. The intervention started to break up the patterns of communication between team members and the team and the CEO.

3.4   Intervening with Circular and Reflexive questions

The term circular questioning was originally coined by the Milan team (Selvini et al., 1980) and describes a particular interview format used with groups and families. Its aim was to create a context in which families, groups and individuals can explore and think differently about their problems and concerns. Systemic hypotheses tend to inform what circular questions the team coach uses in their work e.g. what they ask questions about.

Circular questions are not so much concerned with finding out more about what is happening but rather focus on what other people are doing when something is happening. These questions assume that the behaviour of one person is shown by implication to be connected to another. In the context of a team, for example, one team member might speak in a team meeting at lengths about their part of the business, repeating information time after time. This leads to a number of other team members taking their laptops out and 'switching off', feeling bored and frustrated as they feel they have heard it before. This in turn leads to the team member speaking even more and reiterating his point again and again as he doesn't feel heard by his colleagues. Circular questions help team members to make connections and broaden their understanding of their contexts. Through circular questions, new information tends to be released, which in return encourages new ways of viewing team challenges and effectiveness.

The premise behind circular questioning is that information comes from difference and that difference implies a relationship (Brown, 1997). The idea is to explore issues and challenges in detail and the questions tend to be categorised into questions that create *difference* and questions that create *connections* between people in the team and the wider organisational system. Questions that create difference tend to focus on changes in an issue over time, between people and between situations. On the other hand, questions that create *connections* tend to be asked about behaviours, feelings, beliefs, meaning and relationships. Questions can often be directed to a third party and encourage them to comment on what is happening between other people.

Karl Tomm (1988), another systemic thinker took the idea of circular questions further and developed a framework around questioning, which includes the assumptions and intent behind it. This has been depicted in Figure 3.1. He named four categories of questions (lineal, strategic, circular and reflexive), but particularly emphasised the category of reflexive questions in his framework. Reflexive questions assume that every question is an intervention that can be helpful. At the same time people are viewed as autonomous individuals who cannot be instructed directly. The intent behind reflexive questions is to trigger reflexive ability in the

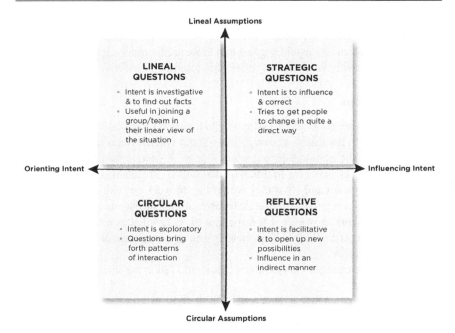

Figure 3.1 A framework for distinguishing four major groups of questions, as proposed by Tomm (1988).

group or team's pre-existing belief system and therefore open up space for new possibilities and perspectives.

Saying this, Tomm (1988) argues that all types of questions have their place and usefulness, but the impact is different.

When asking questions, the coach might hold, often unconsciously, different assumptions about the issue and the team at hand. Lineal assumptions might be associated with linear reductionism, judgemental attitudes and cause-and-effect thinking, whilst circular assumptions are more associated with holism, neutral attitudes and interactional circular principles (Tomm, 1988).

All questions that team coaches ask may be assumed, consciously or unconsciously to have some intent (Tomm, 1988). This can be either to orient oneself e.g. find out more information, explore and track patterns and relationships (Lineal and circular questions) or to influence the team or group with the questions one asks either by making suggestions imbedded in a question, offer reframes or influencing in a more indirect manner (strategic and reflexive questions). Strategic and reflexive questions have the ability to trigger deeper change. Intent is obviously not always very clear cut as a question asked with an orienting intent, may well influence the team in unexpected ways.

I will explore the four quadrants in a bit more detail below and offer some examples. The section for circular and reflexive questions will contain a lot more detailed information as I would suggest that these are far more useful and effective questions to use with teams from a relational-systemic perspective.

Lineal questions

Lineal questions are generally investigative in their intent and establish facts. They tend to bring forth the team's existing view of their current status quo and are very useful in joining the team in their current thinking. Lineal questions are often asked by team coaches as part of a traditional 'diagnostic', to establish what has been happening in the team and what they would like to work on with the coach. They are therefore necessary to develop a clear focus of the current situation and engage the team in the work, however it is important to ensure that as a coach we do not inadvertently entrench the existing view of the present situation and encourage judgemental attitudes.

Here are some examples of questions that would fall in the lineal category:

- "What made you engage a team coach?"
- "Why do you feel you have an issue with communication and effective execution in your team?"
- "How long has this been going on?"
- "Do you struggle getting your voices heard in meetings with the sales team?"

Circular questions

The intent of circular questions is exploratory and to bring forth and raise explicit awareness of patterns of interactions and behaviours. The key is that other team members listen to the answers of the questions and therefore start making their own connections. By doing so, they will also become aware of the circular nature of their issues, e.g. through a series of behavioural effect questions (see below) a team leader might become aware of the fact that his consistent checking of team members' work does in fact foster their dependency on him for detailed decision-making and as a result constant demands on his time. One risk with circular questions is that larger and larger areas of team interaction might be explored, which might have little to do with the team's main concern and the work starts to have the sense of drifting. There are different types of circular questions and I will show a selection of them below and how they might be applied.

Types of circular questions and their purpose and effect

In this table four different kinds of circular questions are described and their purpose and effect highlighted. The examples given are based on case vignette 2.

Type of questions	Purpose & Effect	Examples
Problem definition questions	• Finding out different team members' hypotheses about the situation • Explore perceptions & explanations of the problem	*"What do you feel your team is struggling with currently?"* *"What sense do you each make of this situation?"* *"What explanation do you have about why this problem exist?"* *"How would you know that things have changed?"* *"Who agrees with whom that this is an issue?"* **Note:** Ensure that each team member has been asked and been able to respond in order to create awareness of the circular connection around the problem in the team. You can also invite team members to imagine what other team members might say in response to the questions.
Sequential questions	• Tracking & inquiring into interactional sequence & patterns	*"When your CEO decides in your meeting she is going to make the decision by herself without consultation, what do the rest of the team do?"* *"And what happens after that?"* *"What do you do then?"* *"How do you respond?"* *"Who agrees/disagrees that this is how it happens?"* *"When you see X do this, what meaning do you give it?"* *"How is what happens now different from the past?"* **Note:** Try to track a full cycle of interaction around a situation or issue. It is not just useful to track the interactional sequence but ask each team member for an explanation of another member's behaviour to start exploring the meaning people attribute to other people's part in the pattern.

(Continued)

Type of questions	*Purpose & Effect*	*Examples*
Classification (ranking)/ comparison questions	• Draw out similarities & differences • Rank team members' responses	*"Who noticed first that trust seems to be lost amongst you as a team? And who after that?"* *"Who is most upset about not being consulted about this decision?"* *"Who do you think is closest to the CEO in this team? Who is closest after that?"* *"Who feels fear the most in this team?"* *"Who spends most time working with whom in this team?"* *"Who else feels this way?"* *"Who agrees/disagrees with this statement most?"* **Note:** Exploring difference in past and present as well as the imagined future can be helpful here and enables team members to see that their relationship to the problem and each other is connected in a circular manner.
Triadic questions	• Invite one team member to comment on the thoughts, feelings, beliefs, relationships of other team members (in their absence or presence)	*"If the CEO were here, what do you think she would think about this discussion? How would she feel about it?"* *"What do you think is going on for your colleague in x department, when he has to go through the CEO to get a response from you?"* *"What are your thoughts about the nature of X's relationship with Y?"* *"What do you think X's underlying belief is when he decides to make the decision without consultation?"* **Note:** Triadic questions are particularly powerful in enabling team members to witness the circular impact they have on each other. They can also be used to 'bring' absent parts of the system into the room.

Strategic questions

When using strategic questions, the team coach tries to influence the team in a more direct and lineal fashion by using their own judgement of what they would consider more effective or 'correct' for the team. As team coaches, a clear sign of asking a strategic question is if the question contains an implicit suggestion. The use of strategic questions can lead to the team feeling guilt or shame that they haven't done certain things 'properly'. As team coaches we need to be aware that we are often invited to be the expert on the team's issues, so we might be continuously invited to make strategic interventions or we feel we need to discharge our duty as an 'expert' by making inadvertent suggestions. Team members then in turn might say what they think the team coach wants to hear. On the other hand, the occasional strategic question as part of the coaching process can be very helpful by challenging problematic patterns and behaviours in the team without resorting to direct statements or commands, particularly if sensitively, but firmly worded.

Below some examples that fall in the category of strategic questions:

- "Wouldn't you like to spend more time together as a team reflecting on your work?"
- "What would happen if you had a 15 minute check in at the next team meeting?"
- "Have you noticed that every time someone makes a suggestion in this workshop, nobody responds to it and the discussion just moves on? What would it be like changing this?"

Reflexive questions

Reflexive questions influence in an indirect manner. Their intent is to be facilitative and open up new possibilities. They are therefore generative for the team. As relational-systemic team coaches we are guided by a firm belief in the autonomy and competence of individuals and groups. Rather than being directed by us, reflexive questions invite teams to discover new views and paths for themselves and open up space for dialogue. Circular and reflexive questions are often viewed as very similar and on some level reflexive questions are also circular as they are based on circular assumptions, however the key difference between circular and reflexive questions is that there is a much stronger leaning towards achieving change in the team by influencing the team and its view of the problems and challenges. This could be done for example by helping people to become conscious of the pattern they are enacting, the process of a particular interaction or by embedding a reframe in a question. The one downside of reflexive questions is that generating multiple possibilities and views can be frightening and disorienting for team members without enough holding and sense of direction by the coach.

Types of reflexive questions and their purpose and effect

In this table, four subcategories of reflexive questions are described and their purpose and effect highlighted. Questions in the example section are based on case vignette 2.

Type of questions	Purpose & Effect	Examples
Observer-perspective questions	• Enabling people to become the observer of a phenomenon or pattern. This is often the first step towards helping them to act in relation to it • Raising self and other awareness	*"How did you interpret the situation in the team meeting that triggered those feelings in you? How do you imagine others in the team interpreted it?"* *"When you responded the way you did, how did you feel about your reaction? How do you think others felt?"* *"What do you imagine X experiences when the discussion in the team meeting becomes focused on this topic?"* **Note**: What makes these questions powerful is that everyone can hear the response as the question is asked in the presence of everyone. They also dive into individual and collective meaning-making.
Embedded-suggestion questions	• Suggesting a reframe or alternative action	*"If you were to view his behaviour as an attempt to protect his team rather than be competitive with you over the CEO's affection, how might you react differently?"* *"If instead of staying silent in the meeting you were to openly offer your thoughts, how might the rest of the team react?"* **Note:** Reframes are often a very helpful tool in the team coach's repertoire particularly when they are offered tentatively through a question. Although these questions sound very individually orientated, the key here is that the question and response is witnessed by others and possibly asked of several if not all team members.

Type of questions	Purpose & Effect	Examples
Process-interruption questions	• Remarking upon the immediate process of a session	*"When you have time together as a team, do you spent as much time as at the moment talking about the CEO?"* *"When you usually get together do you speak as openly and truthful to each other about your feelings as you have done just now?"* **Note:** The tone of voice in which these questions are ask can be key here. Process-interruption questions can be experienced as very confrontational even though the intent is to influence the team to think about its patterns of interaction.
Future-oriented questions	• Helping a team to envisage a different future together • Not getting stuck in past or present difficulties	*"What is your future goal for your relationships with each other?"* *"When you have achieved your collective goal, what different behaviours will you see in this team? How will everyone feel?"* **Note:** Moving the focus into the future can be very liberating for a team that might feel very stuck with each other in the here- and- now.

In summary, lineal, strategic, circular and reflexive question all have their place in the repertoire of the team coach. However, my encouragement here is to increase one's use and skill in the area of circular and reflexive question. My suggestion is not to become too preoccupied with the 'correct' type of question or how to exactly phrase it 'right', but to be clear about your intent when conducting an inquiry or undertaking coaching work with a team. What are you trying to achieve in this moment in time with the team and what question might release new and different information into the system? Your systemic hypotheses will support your questioning choices. It is not advised to aim at using all the different types of questions, but a few well-placed circular or reflexive question can often achieve real change in a team. They can also be effective in introducing circular thinking in individuals and could be used in one-to-one conversations ahead of the whole team work in order to lay foundations for systemic group sessions.

One thing to note is also that using different kinds of questions also has an influence on the team coach e.g. lineal questions might keep the coach stuck in the team's thinking, whilst circular and reflexive questions would enable the coach to remain more curious and creative in their approach to the work.

Case vignette 3: Using circular and reflexive questions with a technology team

A technology team within the finance sector was given the challenging task to lead the institution into a new 'technology era', which required a lot of buy-in across the organisation. The team had been tasked with leading the organisational change, which was causing a lot of anxiety both in the team as well as in senior management. The team leader had asked for some team coaching to prepare the team for the task ahead. During the session with the team, my colleague and I became aware of a particular dynamic between a team member and the leader. The team leader's positive and future-oriented statements were generally met by cynical, pessimistic and disheartening comments from this particular team member. Initially, the leader did not react to this, but carried on, but at some point he stopped and openly challenged the team member. The effect on the team was staggering: Most team members became very silent, some withdrew completely, looking at their phones. No-one joined in the discussion.

My colleague and I used the opportunity to pause and use some sequential questions to explore the pattern around this interaction. Questions that we asked included:

> "When the leader speaks so glowingly about the technological future, what tends to happen? Who supports him, who is more hesitant?"

We quickly established that there was a particular interaction loop that seemed to happen between the leader and this particular team member that would often result in a more open confrontation. Rather than tracking this particular interaction, we then tried to introduce a more circular view by asking a classification/comparison question to the whole team:

> "Who is most upset or silent when the discussion between the two erupts into an open argument? Who after that? Who after that?"

This resulted in different team members speaking movingly about how disabled their felt by the interaction (rather than by the team leader and the team member's individual behaviour) and why this impacted them so much. After some conversation about this we used an embedded- suggestion question to reframe the interaction and the behaviour of the colleague who had been so negative as something that might be representative of the wider system:

> "If you were to view your colleague's behaviour and the confrontation between team leader and your colleague as an attempt to demonstrate the resistance that you might encounter in the wider organisational system, how might you view the situation and react differently? What might you as a team learn from this and transfer into how you will lead this change?"

This question enabled the team and the team leader to speak about their intrinsic anxiety about the task at hand, the massive technological shift and the pressure that they felt placed under by the institution to lead this change. There was a clear fear that if they were not able to succeed the organisation would not be future-proof and falter. The team was able to articulate this with the help of our questions.

3.5   Conclusion

A circular view on teams, the discipline of systemic hypothesising and the use of circular and reflexive questions add to the rich fabric of ideas, concepts and approaches that team coaches can draw on in their work. It requires us to adopt a particular view of the construction of problems and challenges within teams in line with a relational-systemic approach and gives us tools to intervene. It encourages us as team coaches to always remain curious and see pluralities of views and experiences. It easily co-exists with other approaches offered in this book and complements different ways of thinking about and intervening into teams.

Chapter 4

A systems psychodynamic perspective on relational team coaching

Andrew Day and Judith Bell

4.1 Introduction

Experience teaches us all that groups and teams have a life of their own. This can be exhilarating, rewarding or energising and at times troubling, bewildering and perplexing. Indeed, Sigmund Freud (1921) observed that: "Something is unmistakably at work in the nature of compulsion to do the same as the others, to remain in harmony with the many" (21). In this statement, Freud is directing our attention towards the unconscious forces that exist in groups. These affect a team's functioning and capacity to perform its work. In this chapter, we will explore how we can understand the unconscious life of teams and consider what this means for the practice of team coaching. We begin with a description of concepts that are relevant to team coaching and core to a systems psychodynamic perspective, we then outline how these concepts might be applied in practice and illustrate throughout with vignettes from our own work as team coaches.

Even though we *know* about dynamics such as competition, attraction, rivalry and envy, we find it hard to recognise their presence and influence when we are at work in a team. Psychoanalytic theory argues that this is because the team wants to keep disturbing emotions and thoughts out of their conscious awareness (see, for example, Obholzer and Roberts, 1994). They do this by enacting a range of defence mechanisms, such as denial, avoidance, and projection, that prevent them from experiencing and accepting the unwanted thoughts or feelings. Much of significance that is happening in a team tends therefore to be unspoken.

The idea that unconscious processes influence what goes on between people and in teams is the essence of a psychodynamic perspective. A team coach working from this orientation draws the attention of the team towards such processes when they appear to be impacting its work. The coach will also be affected by the emotional tenor of the team and a central feature of this approach is that the coach will use their awareness of how they themselves are experiencing the team to understand what might be going on for the team. If we accept that much of what is happening in a team has its origins in unconscious processes, then this influences what we observe, listen to and hear; how we make sense of what is happening in

DOI: 10.4324/9781003325789-6

the team and within ourselves; the role we take up as a coach and what we do by way of intervention. To give an example:

> The leadership team of a newly formed business experiences difficulties making decisions. They find it difficult to reach agreements and apparent decisions fall apart. Each member of the team expresses their frustration with this struggle, but this seems only to exacerbate the difficulties rather than resolve them. Clearly something is getting in the way of the team's function but what is "it" and how to help the team recognise "it"?

4.2   Core concepts: making sense of life in teams

4.2.1   Our internal world

Central to psychodynamic thinking is the idea that we all have a lively internal world of feelings and thoughts that may be outside of our everyday awareness.[1] This internal world is made up of emotions that derive from our experiences in life, beginning with the very earliest relationships of our babyhood. Such feelings are, for most of the time, 'hidden from view' but re-enter our awareness when triggered by current circumstances. How we think, feel and behave towards people we encounter in the external world is, at least to some degree, influenced by these early experiences. In teams our experience and role in our family of origin, whatever form this took, can influence how we relate and engage with a team and its members.

> **Case vignette.** A team leader had difficulty in delegating to one of his two deputies, an older man, highly competent and experienced who had been in post for many years. The leader had no trouble in delegating to his other deputy, a younger woman. The male deputy pushed back and the two men were locked in a tense, unproductive relationship. Trust was an issue here, which in his coaching the leader came to understand related to early experiences of being let down by paternal figures, which had resulted in a difficulty in trusting that older men could deliver.

4.2.2   The primary task

Wilfred Bion (1961) first observed that a team or workgroup exists to perform an overt purpose. In other words, it meets to do something (Rice, 1969). This, Bion called its primary task. It is the task the team needs to achieve to survive (Bion, 1961) and thrive (Lawrence and Robinson, 1975). To perform their task, team members need to take up roles and form relationships with each other. Unconscious (and conscious) assumptions and emotions both help and hinder a team in their work.

The heuristic of the primary task helps us to understand a team's dynamics. First, it helps us to understand why the team exists and what is its purpose. Second, it helps us to judge at any moment whether the team is performing its work effectively or not. Finally, when we observe that the team is not doing 'work' then we need to be curious about what it is engaged in or what it is doing instead, and why might this be the case.

Teams require a sufficient degree of authorisation to fulfil their primary task. That is, they must be authorised by senior leadership to take up the task. This requires explicit sanction and appropriate resourcing. Their authorisation must be clear to other teams and groups within the organisation. A lack of clarity may result in uncertainty about how to go about the task and ambivalence about the roles necessary to achieve the task.

4.2.3 The influence of context: a systems perspective

Kurt Lewin (1947) and, later, Miller and Rice (1967) applied systems thinking to organisations and teams. This work has been extended by other systemic thinkers, e.g. Campbell and Huffington (2008). The central idea is that teams must interact with and adapt to their environment. Furthermore, what is happening in the team is linked to its context. No team therefore exists in isolation. In a similar way to a biological system, for organisational systems to survive a dynamic interaction with the environment in which they exist is essential. (See Chapter 3 by Dorothee Stoffels for a more detailed account of systems thinking). Conceptualising a team in this way draws attention to its boundary and the systems that regulate the boundary. Within the boundary the task needs to be accomplished with the resources allocated. Responsibility for this lies with the manager. Some contexts can make it challenging for a team to function and to perform. For instance, a marketing team that is part of a matrix structure must be able to relate to the sales force, it needs close and collaborative relationships with its customers and may also have responsibilities to other marketing teams globally. Some of these demands may be conflictual, resulting in a complexity that may be denied or avoided by team members or otherwise defended against.

Every organisational system consists of a series of sub-systems, formal and informal, each with their own managed boundaries. Some sub-systems will be operating fully in the service of the task and some may be off-task. Equally, unconscious dynamics and communication exists between sub-systems. In the above example, the marketing team may struggle with projections of incompetence from the sales force which affect its capacity to develop confidence and trust its work.

In establishing a contract for team coaching it is important to consider whether the team is the most appropriate level for an intervention. If a team has been identified as 'problematic' we must ensure that the issue of concern is legitimately at the level of the team. A team can be failing, not because it is ineffective but because the problem lies at the level of the wider organisational system, for example with leadership, strategy, structure or resources. If the parts of a system become detached from the whole then overall effectiveness becomes compromised. Similarly if the sub-systems within a team seek an autonomy from the team, then team effectiveness is compromised (Campbell, Draper and Huffington, 1991).

4.2.4   Primitive anxieties and defence mechanisms

When teams form and work together, they experience a range of intense and primitive emotions, some of which may have their origins in early anxieties of family life. They include issues such as competition and rivalry, power and control, competence and incompetence, frustration and learning, emotional intimacy and distance, inclusion and exclusion, jealousy or envy, and so on. These arise because of the conflicting emotional needs of the team members and their anxieties about group life (i.e. membership, participation and influence), their anxieties about their work, and because of realistic and imagined threats to the team's existence (see also Chapter 5 by Charlotte Sills). Teams also tend to act like sponges absorbing the emotions and anxieties from their environment (Cardona, 2020). These relate to the nature of the team's task and the work of the organisation. In healthcare these anxieties relate to death and dying (Obholzer & Roberts, 1994); in social care they tend to be about dependency and vulnerability; in industries, such as nuclear or construction, around safety and risk; whereas in an investment bank they will be more related to the uncertainty and risks of investment decisions. A team's dynamics will therefore in some way or other relate to what is happening in the work of its organisation and its relationships with other groups and teams.

> **Case vignette.** An internal organisation development team for a mental health trust found itself overwhelmed and pulled and pushed by demands for their services from both the leadership of the organisation and teams across the Trust. At one of their regular team sessions, one of us as their team coach wondered whether there was a link between the demands on the team and the work of the Trust. One of the team members observed that the organisation was faced with a "gaping hole of need" that could never be filled. This insight helped the team recognise how they, like many of their internal clients, were trying to satisfy every demand that was being made of them. Having made the link, they started to appreciate that meeting every need and addressing all the major difficulties within the Trust was an impossible task. I helped them to explore how perhaps they were identifying with the anxieties of their clients because of the guilt they felt about not being able to help and, at the same time, their anger at the demands that were being made of them. This helped them to become more aware of the emotional influences on them which helped them to think and reflect on their experiences of their work. By asking them to clarify their role in the organisation, I opened up a conversation around how they made decisions about what projects to prioritise and how they could say "no" to requests and at the same time manage expectations.[2]

When the emotions or feelings that arise in the team become too disturbing or threatening, then teams find ways of keeping them outside of their conscious awareness. The team however needs to find a way of ensuring that the issue in question (a) does not surface and (b) does not trigger excessive anxiety. The underlying issues do not go away and may continue to exert an influence on the team. Colloquial expressions such as the 'elephant in the room' indicate that this idea is widely accepted in organisations.

Teams and their members use a range of psychic processes or defence mechanisms to keep such unwanted thoughts or feelings outside of their consciousness. These include:

- *Denial*: whereby the team rejects particular or all difficulties by denying their existence. Eg. "We don't need to worry about junior staff feeling overwhelmed, they're lucky to be working here and won't leave such a prestigious company."
- *Avoidance*: whereby the team evades difficult topics or decisions. For instance, a team creates a packed agenda and in doing so has no time to open up contentious issues on which individuals disagree with each other.
- *Intellectualisation*: whereby the team uses distant and abstract language to avoid disturbing feelings or emotions. E.g. a focus in meetings on spreadsheets or Powerpoints with dense text.
- *Confusion*: being confused and struggling to see the point or issue. E.g. team members acting confused about what is happening and why. Remaining in a state of confusion might avoid a painful reality.
- *Splitting*: whereby the team divides the world into 'good' and 'bad' to externalise painful or disturbing feelings. For instance, a team might consider themselves to be competent and see a rival team as being utterly 'incompetent'.
- *Projection*: whereby the team gets rid of 'bad' feelings by attributing them to other people or other teams.
- *Competition*: whereby the team feels superior to others to avoid feelings of inadequacy.
- *Projective identification*: where unwanted difficult feelings are projected into others who come to own the feelings and behave in a corresponding manner. This phenomenon can be seen clearly when teams are deliberately positioned in competition with each other.
- *Acting Out*: where team members might respond to difficult feelings by acting them out in their behaviour. They may, for instance, attack others (directly or passively) without awareness of where their anger originates.

Such defence mechanisms reduce the team's anxiety by creating a version of the world where difficulties are not faced, however this comes at a cost; avoidance of the task or at worst a distortion of reality that seriously impacts relationships and team functioning.

4.2.5   *Work group and basic assumption mentality*

Bion (1961) posited that a group can inhabit two different states of mind, work group mentality and basic assumption mentality. Work group mentality represents the conscious, overt, rational level of group life. In this state of mind groups are in touch with 'reality' and can manage the task in hand, unconstrained by defensive behaviour. There is cooperation by members, who hold in mind the whole group and its interconnectedness with other groups. Groups operating in work group mentality recognise difference and their own need to learn and develop.

By contrast, basic assumption mentality is a state of mind where a group is unconsciously preoccupied with activities that distract from the primary task, mainly to avoid dealing with difficult feelings that may arise through the work or through relationships in the team or with others. In such a state of mind groups behave 'as if' they were working to another task completely, as though there is a shared assumption that the team is there for another (unconscious) purpose, such as critiquing proposals for change or criticising management.

Basic assumptions are ways of being in a group that are essentially defences against intolerable feelings or feelings that might disrupt the functioning of the group if brought to awareness. Bion himself (1961) described three different types of basic assumptions, each of which is associated with different emotions and behaviours. These he named as 'fight-flight', 'dependency' and 'pairing'. Since then, two more basic assumptions have been described – 'oneness' (Turquet, 1975) and 'me-ness' (Lawrence, Bain and Gould, 1996). Group behaviour can fall into one or more of these defensive patterns; noticing this, a group coach can better understand why groups and teams fail to manage themselves effectively in relation to their task and may not achieve their objectives.

- Basic assumption fight-flight (baF)[3]
  Fight-flight mentality emerges as an unconscious attempt by a group and its members to deflect engagement with a difficult task or situation. In fight mode the group may be characterised by hostility or aggression and there may be talk of challenge and confrontation. In flight mode members may cancel meetings or arrive late, engage in irrelevant conversation and generally avoid addressing the task in hand. For example, a team tasked with designing a major organisational restructure may become preoccupied by the impact of this on colleagues and instead spend their time designing elaborate consultations. This behaviour serves to unify the group, protecting it from the pain of engaging with the task and the possibility that the implementation of the restructure may result in division and conflict between them. In a similar way a team in fight mode may rise to anger at some organisational injustice, which again allows them to avoid the task.
- Basic assumption dependency (baD)
  In basic assumption dependency members rely on the leader of the group (who may or may not be the designated leader) to such an extent that they may act

as if they have no ideas of their own, deny their capabilities and fail to take initiatives. It is as though the group has lost the capacity to think and surrenders its own authority. Leaders will be familiar with 'dependent' behaviour which typically includes people asking for information they already have, unnecessarily looking to the leader for support, and avoiding responsibility for the task. Extreme dependency prevents development. Such groups do not manage their agendas or engage in decision-making. This behaviour spares members the experience of confronting their abilities or responsibilities when they are perhaps feeling disabled or without capacity. Rigid hierarchical structures can encourage dependency; a risk in organisations where a degree of dependency is normally present, for example in health or education services.

- Basic assumption pairing (baP)
  Basic assumption pairing mobilises an unconscious wish to bring two people together, or perhaps for a group member (who may or may not be the leader) to join with an external individual to 'save' the group. All hope is invested in this pairing and the membership is preoccupied with the future and the anticipation that an ideal, almost messianic, solution will arrive, thus avoiding attention on the present or the task in hand. Typically, decisions are not made and members are left with a sense of dissatisfaction and time wasted. There may be statements about new ideas or possibilities, but nothing actually happens. A team in baP might discuss planned changes but be unable to make decisions until some future date after which an imagined crucial requirement is in place, e.g. new staff appointed, new equipment available, but without the application to make such things happen.

- Basic assumption oneness (baO) (Turquet, 1975)
  In this type of group, members behave in an undifferentiated fashion. Agreement is high and individual differences of perspective cannot be tolerated, resulting in an impression of unanimity. This is akin to the concept of group-think (Janis, 1972). As a case vignette to illustrate this idea, Janis used the decision-making by the US administration that led to the invasion of the Bay of Pigs in 1961. The Kennedy government had accepted uncritically the CIA proposals for invasion and while some members of the team had initially raised objections they then censored themselves in order to preserve a consensus. Clearly the stakes were very high and the anxiety about being an 'outlier' had to be minimized by becoming part of the group. Similarly, in staff group settings, this behaviour is not uncommon and seems to represent a fear of exposing differences. BaO suggests that the group is avoiding any competition, conflict or feelings of rivalry or envy that may be present, or the wrath of an individual. The discomfort of feeling outside of the group (for example by having something unique to offer) disrupts the capacity for rational thought.

- Basic assumption 'me-ness' (baM) (Lawrence, Bain and Gould, 1996)
  In baM members of a group retain an individual perspective at the expense of any desire to understand or to take into account the position of others. There is resistance to participation in a collective enterprise as if the act of joining with

others may result in something that can't be managed. The prospect of belonging to the group is experienced as persecutory so members retreat to their individual perspectives and silos to avoid the feelings that are aroused by coming together. At an unconscious level, this may be a fear of exposure, change or development. For example, in practical terms, it may be difficult to assemble professionals to work on a challenging change or integration project and as a group they may appear emotionally resistant to collaborating as a team, with the effect that joint projects do not get off the ground.

4.2.6 Valency

Individuals in groups may display a propensity to be pulled into particular patterns of behaviour; for example, 'the one who always puts a spanner in the works', 'the one who tries to keep the peace'. Bion (1961) described this susceptibility to being pulled into a particular way of behaving as 'valency'. It is a powerful determinant of how and why we take up familiar roles in groups and may link to the dynamics of our family of origin. Coaches need to be aware of their own valency – perhaps as a helper, parent, problem solver and to be able to take a step back to consider what is influencing their move to that position. For example, a team coach may have a propensity to 'hold the floor' and offer suggestions to the team. Being activated in this way means they are no longer open to the unconscious dynamics of the team. Charlotte Sills explores this in Chapter 5.

4.3 Practising from a systems psychodynamic perspective

The role of a psychodynamically informed coach is to help the team to become aware of how it engages in a wider system beyond its boundaries and how its dynamics help and hinder its ability to perform its role in this wider system. In other words to reflect on how the team works together to achieve its aims. To do this the coach needs to take up a position on the boundary of the team, listening for the conscious and unconscious meanings of what is happening without getting overly involved in the work of the team. The core belief being that by making what is unconscious conscious the team shifts from enacting a dynamic to talking about it. In time, a second aim can emerge which is to develop the team's capacity to notice and explore its dynamics for itself.

4.3.1 Preparation: creating a 'safe enough' container

For a team to feel safe to explore their dynamics certain minimal conditions need to be established. First, the team needs to agree that it both needs to and is willing to work on itself. This usually means they have recognised that they need help of a particular form. Second, clear boundaries of membership, place and time are required to create certainties and clarity around issues that members may feel uncertain about. This helps to create a safe container for the work. Third, a basic agreement is required around the purpose and form of the coach's work with the team and their role. Typically, the coach would work with the leader of the team and its members to explore, negotiate and agree these conditions. Often work is necessary with the team leader to help them to think about their role in the work and how they will work with the coach. Finally, for the coach to be accepted and trusted, they need to form a working alliance with the team. This requires the team to experience the coach as credible, understanding and able to contain what it is struggling to resolve. The working alliance starts to develop from the earliest interactions and thoughts the team has about the coach. How a team comes to seek coaching and the initial encounter is therefore of relevance to the work; considering how the idea came about, who has bought in to it, and how the team coaching is introduced, can give important data about how the team is working together.

4.3.2 Working with the team

The coach helps the team to make sense of how it works together by:

(i)   Observing the team's process and dynamics (i.e. relational patterns),
(ii) Listening for the underlying emotional content and its meaning
(iii) Attending to the coach–team relationship
(iv) Seeing links to how the team engages in its work, and
(v)   Making interventions that help the team to become aware of and explore the above.

4.3.3 Observing the team's process and dynamics

A core skill of a team coach is to observe how the team members interact with each other and the outside world. They need to attend to:

- *Discourse*: such as what is being spoken about, who is talking when, what is not being spoken about as well as contradictions in what is being spoken about and what is done.
- *Behaviour*: including roles taken up within the team (both formal and informal), patterns of behaviour, body language and decision making.
- *Relationships*: who interacts with who, how is leadership taken up and exercised, and tensions and conflicts between different individuals, relations with other groups and teams.

At points, if the coach does not get too involved, then they can start to see how the team is governed by more unconscious and irrational motives rather than thoughtful judgements about a situation. This requires that the coach is situated on the boundary of the team, observing but not including themselves in the discussion.

Case vignette. At an off-site away day for a marketing team, the coffee room before the event started was full of the buzz of conversation. One of us as the team coach noticed two or three distinct groupings with some space between each. When the work started it was evident that there were some strong affiliations between individuals in the room and the coach reflected on this with curiosity. It became clear that the affiliations represented two distinct historic groupings going back to when two different teams were amalgamated, together with a smaller group of "newbies" who had been appointed since the merger. This proved a significant schism in the work that followed.

4.3.4   Listening for the underlying emotional content and its meaning

Harold Bridger (1976) speaks of 'listening to the music behind the words' when working with groups. This involves tuning into the mood of the team and its unconscious emotional world. To listen in this way, coaches have to stand back from the immediate content of a session and trust their intuition or own associations to what they are hearing. They may find themselves wondering about the fantasies, hopes or fears that are being expressed or the irrational wishes or desires.

One way a coach can access unconscious process is to listen to themselves and what is stirred up inside of them. What we hear inside ourselves is often (but not always) linked in some way to the emotional life of the team. A team in basic assumption dependency may pressurise the coach to take charge, to offer advice and to give them the answer. Alternatively, a desire to placate or protect oneself may suggest the team is in basic assumption fight-flight. We are talking here about the transference and counter transference between the coach and the team.

Transference was originally described by Freud (1905) who experienced his patients behaving towards him as though he were a significant figure from their past – a parent or authority figure for example. The feelings from those early relationships were unconsciously 'transferred' onto the therapist. He coined the term countertransference to refer to the opposite phenomenon, the unconscious transfer of feelings from the therapist onto the client. This term has however been completely revised in the intervening years and has now come to refer to the feelings that the therapist/coach experiences in the presence of the client or team. Countertransference is thus considered to contain elements of both the therapist/coach's own internal world and that of the team, who may be projecting unwanted or uncomfortable feelings into those around them including the coach. As such it is potentially a useful source of information about what might be going on for the team at an unconscious level. To disentangle these phenomena requires that the coach has a degree of self-awareness about their own emotional experience. We talk therefore of listening to our 'countertransference' to help make sense of our experience in a team at any given moment.

Case vignette. A university academic department asked for some help in resolving a leadership difficulty. Tradition required that the position of head of department was filled from within the senior staff members on a rotating basis for a three-year term. The previous two incumbents had left before the end of their tenure with some acrimony, and no-one could be persuaded to take it on. As a coach I tried to work with this group to understand the role and its challenges, one of which was to represent the department within the university, and why it should be so difficult. However, I felt stymied and blocked, there was a lot of expressed anger as long-standing differences surfaced but we seemed to be going nowhere. I was anxious and a bit afraid that we may never reach a resolution, but my strongest feeling – my countertransference, was one of sadness. I shared this feeling tentatively, wondering if others may feel similarly. One member then spoke of the death by suicide, three years before, of a colleague who had previously been a respected head of department. It became clear that they had not been able to mourn this loss, and this became a focus of our work.

4.3.5   Attending to the coach–team relationship

The team almost inevitably feels ambivalent about the work and therefore the presence of the coach. On the one hand, developmental forces within the team create a desire to learn about its dynamics and to develop itself (Armstrong, 2005). Yet on the other hand, the team also has a desire not to know or acknowledge the presence of more disturbing aspects of itself. The coach will therefore encounter resistance to the work. This can be informative of the unconscious life of the team. The coach might, for instance, be expected to solve the issues the team is experiencing without the team having to acknowledge and talk about them. Alternatively, they may find themselves idealised, attacked, criticised, undermined or ignored.

> **Case vignette.** One of us worked with a newly formed leadership team that was expected to integrate several functional departments of a large governmental system. All were judged to be failing and their staff were perceived to be incompetent. After the first session, I felt criticised for not exercising leadership or seemingly not knowing what to do. The feelings of incompetence that were directed towards the coach more appropriately belonged to the leadership team. Their attack on me appeared to represent their resistance to exploring such feelings and acknowledging their doubts, frustrations and fears about their role and objectives.

Such pressures and invitations are part of the relationship between the team and the coach. It is a challenge to stay in role and not to get pulled into collusion with the team's defensive processes. The coach needs to notice what is happening and help the team think about this and become aware of their unconscious dynamics. For example, a team might suggest a change to the agreed schedule of team consultation. Rather than going along with this, however sensible it may seem to be, the coach needs to be able to think about what it means in terms of who holds influence and whether it avoids the task in hand. The coach may get pulled out of role and collude with the team's defensive processes. If, however, the coach can notice and help the team to think about these ideas, then they can provide insights into the team's dynamics, which can be worked with in the group with positive effects.

4.3.6   Seeing a link to how the team engages in its work

In any team, more is going on that can be explored and made sense of at that moment. The coach needs therefore to ask themselves:

- How is what I am observing influencing the work of the team in this moment?
- Is the team on task or off task?
- If it is off task, then what is the (apparent) task that the team is currently engaged in?
- Why might this be happening?

The coach can begin to make links, in the form of hypotheses, between their felt experience and the information that they have gathered. As Dorothee Stoffels describes in Chapter 3, hypothesising in this way derives from the Milan school of systemic family therapy (Selvini et al., 1980). It has been further developed by systemic and psychodynamic organisational consultants (e.g., Campbell, Draper and Huffington, 1991) as a tool to open up thinking, based on observation and in-the-moment experience, linking experience to context.[4] It allows coaches to exercise their curiosity, whilst remaining open to whatever may arise. A hypothesis is therefore a useful device for making sense of what might be going on below the surface, linking experience to context. It is a tool to progress the coach's understanding, not a definitive idea, and it needs to be held lightly and amended when necessary. Asking questions directly to test hypotheses can sometimes be counter-productive. Framing interventions tentatively with, for example, 'I'm curious about…' I wonder if…', can allow the team more easily to take on board and reflect on the coach's ideas.

Case vignette. A small but successful design company sought some coaching for their leadership team. The three members were the founders of the company, they met at art school and had quickly established a niche market for their product designs. Demand was growing but newly appointed designers and business support staff tended not to stay, and the company had begun to have to turn work down. The three leaders described themselves as a triumvirate, a gang of three, and emphasised their likemindedness. However, my experience as their coach was that to articulate a different position, e.g., that the members of this group may have different views, felt risky. I became aware of my own difference and a sense that bringing a new perspective would not be welcome. It became clear in the work that followed that for the designers, one of them taking up a different role within the company would challenge their sense of sameness and togetherness. They did not feel ready for this. They were not able to manage difference and what this might mean.

The work gradually progressed through observation and reflection. There were many arguments without resolution and a preoccupation between the founders about who was the best designer. As their team coach I reflected on the tension in the room and the feeling that there was a great deal that was not being said. I 'wondered if' the value placed on design skills prevented any of them taking a leadership role as though leadership was a lesser, unskilled task. No-one wanted to employ a managing director because they felt unable to trust that an external manager could have the company's best interests at heart. I too felt that I was not entirely trusted. My inability to manage difference made life intolerable for incomers and impossible for the one team member who had some leadership aspiration. Reflecting this idea as a (lightly held) hypothesis allowed the team to think about their historical patterns of relating that may have been impeding the development of the company. Working through these issues of trust and difference meant revisiting their history as a friendship group, including their competitiveness academically and socially.

4.3.7 Intervening

As the coach formulates hypotheses about what might be happening, they need to judge what they can do that can influence the team. A helpful intervention transforms an experience that cannot be tolerated or expressed into something that is more manageable for the team (Bion, 1962). Interventions might include:

- Exploring the extent to which members of the group agree on its primary task.
- Helping the team to see or make links between its difficulties and external events and wider system dynamics.
- Noticing and commenting when the team appears to be off task.
- Encouraging the team to suspend its agenda and review how it is working together (Bridger, 1990).
- Encouraging the group to identify and clarify its goals.
- Noticing and describing the implicit and explicit roles that individuals take up in the team.
- Offering an observation of what is happening or not happening within the team, such as a repetitive pattern, who is taking up psychological roles on behalf of the team, etc.
- Drawing attention to underlying feelings, emotions or anxieties within the team.
- Offering hypotheses that link what is happening on the surface to deeper feelings and anxieties within the team.

When intervening they should try and use as far as possible straightforward and everyday language. They also need to judge what the team might be able to hear at a particular point in time. The depth of the work needs to progress at the pace that the team is willing to move, not at the speed and depth that the coach would like to go. In a work context, small encouragements to open sensitive issues up are usually more helpful than deep interpretations of anxieties. Proceeding too quickly or being too confronting tends to amplify a team's defensive processes.

Case vignette. One of us supervised colleagues coaching the staff team of a unit for pupils excluded from mainstream school, which had a reputation for violence and a high turnover of staff. The coaching was contracted to help the staff team feel more unified as a group and manage the difficult feelings that the work engendered. The staff team included admin and support staff, teachers and the leadership group. It was racially and culturally diverse, as were the young people who attended the unit.

The coaches felt full of admiration and respect for the team but found it difficult to hold the group to time boundaries – often the sessions started late, members would leave early or go out to take calls. The coaches had a sense of their voices not being loud enough. This mirrored the class teachers' experience – and as in the classroom it made focus difficult. One of the two coaches felt that the group was fragile and that individuals felt easily criticised and bruised. The other had a sense of a more challenging group that may "rubbish" the coaching interventions. Of course, both were true; the coaches were holding different aspects of the team dynamic that represented the different challenges with which the young people presented.

The coaches hypothesised that all of the staff in the unit experienced the emotional toll of work with such difficult and often traumatised young people. Although there was a recognition of this, there were few opportunities as a whole staff team to acknowledge and address this. Coaching interventions were gentle, pointing out how much they were dealing with, considering the toxicity in the work and the impact of this, facilitating the group to acknowledge the strength in their differences, work across their boundaries and discuss together what they might need to do to support each other – and what got in the way of them doing so.

4.4 Supporting the work: learning to listen to oneself

Teams can be emotionally intense and complicated. Feelings may be amplified in a group and the strongest of defences employed. As we have discussed, a psychodynamically informed team coach needs to be able to the use themselves as an instrument to understand and intervene in the dynamics of the team. As with individual coaching, a practice that makes time for reflection and supervision is essential for the maintenance and calibration of the 'instrument'. We need to spend time to understand our own feelings and thoughts and how they relate to the team we're working with. Supervision is essential in helping a team coach to see that their experience may be as a result of projection of unbearable feelings from the team.

This may help identify a 'parallel process' where the coach may unconsciously enact a dynamic originating in the team they are coaching. For example, in working with a team from a government department that was preoccupied with security a coach found herself in supervision paralysed by the idea that she couldn't share enough details for her supervisor to make sense of the work. This was not the case (she had contracted to bring the work to supervision) but the concern itself and subsequent paralysis exactly mirrored the way in which the team was unable to move forward because of their inhibitions over making certain things public – only through the supervisor's reflections in the here and now did that become apparent.

Table 4.1 Recognising and addressing basic assumption activity in teams

ba Fight-Flight What to look out for	What to consider
Group members blame external factors (managers, lack of time, no money) for all that feels wrong/ uncomfortable.	Acknowledge that by focusing on external factors the group is avoiding some of the angry and fearful feelings within the group.
Group members talk of confronting others.	Remind members that the task is 'in here' not 'out there'. Encourage the group to express and value different points of view.
Group members talk of giving up.	Suggest constructive roles related to the task and find strategies to provide focus on the task in hand.
Groups become distracted by peripheral tasks to avoid more contentious or anxiety-provoking issues.	Explore what might be being avoided, and why, and how it might be addressed more safely.
ba Dependency What to look out for	What to consider
Group members act as if they have no ideas of their own.	Encourage and invite all group members to take and offer ideas.
Members ask for information they already have.	Resist being seduced by the invitation to be the fount of all knowledge.
Members ask for guidance about how to do the task, denying their own capabilities.	Acknowledge the difficulties in taking responsibility but encourage people to rise to the challenge.
Difficult decisions are avoided or postponed.	Resist the pressure to do or answer for others when they have the capacity to do it for themselves.
There seems to be no initiative for action other than a reliance on the 'leader' of the group.	Acknowledge the difficulties in being a leader or being led. Suggest distributed leadership roles.

Table 4.1 (Continued)

ba Pairing What to look out for	What to consider
Group members express the hope that someone (or something) will help them 'get going' on the task.	Seek to involve all group members in discussing ideas.
There are lots of statements about new approaches or ideas being possible but nothing happens.	Acknowledge that too much talk about what 'could' happen might be a signal that what is happening is not being discussed.
Trainers/leaders are given unrealistic powers or knowledge.	Suggest individuals might lead on specific aspects of the task.
Decisions are not taken, agendas not completed.	Ask group members how their ideas could be acted upon.
The group is passively observing two people conducting an apparently lively discussion.	Ask how others may be involved in this topic/task.

ba Oneness What to look out for	What to consider
There is no expressed disagreement, even though individually there may be dissent.	Acknowledge that difference may be difficult to work with but is important to understand and value. Work to create an environment in which differences can be tolerated and the fear of difference can be understood.
The group has difficulty in identifying exactly what the consensus is.	Individually ask for opinions.

ba Me-ness What to look out for	What to consider
There is no consensus and members don't seem interested or inclined to pursue one.	Acknowledge that collaboration might be difficult but is essential for the effectiveness of the team as a whole.
There is a difficulty in staying on task, agendas may be ignored.	Individuals work in pairs or smaller groups with the task of understanding the perspective of the other.

Source: First published in Bell (2020). Reproduced with permission from the editors.

Working with colleagues

If two or more coaches are working together with a team it is essential that time is taken to debrief and explore individual experiences of the coaching and consider what aspects of the team dynamic each may be holding. In the example of coaching the team in the pupil referral unit, one of the coaches experienced a strong maternal transference, while the other felt more identified with the sense of needing to reinforce boundaries, which helped to understand the complexity of the dynamic around care in the unit.

4.5   Conclusions

We have attempted to illustrate how teams have an unconscious life that influences its members' work together and their performance. At times, aspects of this unconscious life, in the form of assumptions, beliefs and feelings about itself and the wider system, distort a team's perception of its 'reality' or hold it back from taking necessary action. We have tried to illustrate how teams try to evade such unconscious thoughts and feelings because they are threatening or uncomfortable to their members. For this very reason, a team coach can be helpful if their presence and interventions enable the team to feel more confident to talk to what is not being or has not been spoken to. It is this simple act of talking that makes the unconscious conscious and in doing so means a difficulty can be faced.

Notes

1   Many of the theoretical concepts presented in this chapter constitute what has become known as the Tavistock Paradigm, which has its origins in the work of the Tavistock Institute and Tavistock Clinic.
2   Vega Roberts has written an informative chapter titled 'The Self-Assigned Impossible Task' in the *Unconscious at Work* (Obholzer & Roberts, 1994).
3   Table 4.1 at the end of this chapter offers suggestions for recognising and addressing basic assumption activity in teams.
4   It is similar to the 'working hypothesis' or 'working note' developed in the group relations tradition (see Miller, 1995). A 'working hypothesis' is designed to capture a perspective (sometimes fleeting) on the dynamics of a group engaged in work together.

Part B

Ways of working as a relational team coach

Introduction to Part B

In this part of the book, we look at how relational coaches can work with time inside their team coaching sessions. As team coaches our main area of interest is the present moment. After all, the present moment is the only moment where we can really make a difference by means of coaching. During moment-by-moment work, however, we meet challenges that have come out of the past history of the team, organisation and individuals – and we set ourselves goals for the future of this team and their context. So, it can be helpful to be able to gather the 'patterns' that are present in the team dynamics and help the here-and-now to shed a new light on those existing or historical dynamics, 'stuckness' or routines. This is what Chapter 5 will address, making use of the theory of scripts, games and repetition through transference. Chapter 6 is a more practical chapter that helps to appreciate the richness in the present moment, and the many ways we can work with the present to make it more visible, to understand it better or to experiment with something new. Finally, Chapter 7 looks at the future and the paradoxical way that the future is wrapped up in the present, and at the same time 'neither here nor there' in the present, and therefore absent or unreachable for relational work. How can we then bring in the future into our team coaching in a meaningful way?

DOI: 10.4324/9781003325789-7

Chapter 5

Working with the past in team coaching

Charlotte Sills

In this chapter, I start from the premise that teams and organisations – like individuals – develop patterns and ways of being and behaving that become habitual, 'for good, for ill or for interesting'. In other words, habits develop that are repeated over and over: the past is repeated in the present. Commonly this sort of patterning in an organisation is called culture. Some of the behaviour and relational dynamics are a result of conscious choice – habits developed intentionally as team members learn from experience. Some, however, are unconscious – either simply unaware patterning, or actually unhelpful and dysfunctional behaviour (colleague Anne de Graaf, personal communication, defines dysfunction as 'success-sabotaging'). It can be part of the team coach's role to help a team address these patterns. In order to explore this idea, I use the concept of 'script' from transactional analysis (Berne, 1961, 1963, 1972) and show how it can apply to a team or organisation. I look at the role of the individual in furthering a team's script – and vice versa. Further I argue that teams also have the constant task of negotiating some important existential issues such as conflict and harmony, power and submission, inclusion and marginalisation; this contributes to its repeating patterns.

In 2016, I wrote an article called 'How do I know who I am?'. In it I attempted to address the conflicting ideas of human being as separate consciousness and responsible agent versus human being as a product of society, or group or team. I referred to 'the almost unbearable challenge of managing that paradoxical existential tension' (p. 109). Taking a relational lens to understanding a team, as we do in this book, inevitably steers us towards the idea of co-created dynamics and therefore the 'team as a whole' – the attitude that the individuals in the team are largely irrelevant and that it is the quality of the interactions as well as the team's relationship to the primary task that makes the difference between a high functioning team and a low functioning one. And yet it is not possible – nor humanly satisfying – to discount that a team is a collection of individuals – each with their own feelings and thoughts, preferences and proclivities.

DOI: 10.4324/9781003325789-8

5.1   Introduction: the script system

'Each of us creates our own continuous explanatory narrative that gives meaning to the past, provides a problem-solving blueprint for the present and predicts the future' (Newton, 2006, p. 186).

The script system (Sills & Salters, 1991; Sills & Mazzetti, 2009; Lapworth & Sills, 2011) describes how people make meaning of the world and use that meaning to act. It is used in coaching, therapy and supervision to help clients understand and change problematic patterns that might have developed in the past and are still manifested in the here and now.

The script system describes how, as a result of their experiences and meaning-making in childhood, people develop habitual ways of organizing their relationships and their life such that they react with feelings, thoughts, and behaviours that reflect and also reinforce and maintain those earlier patterns of meaning making. The patterns are not impervious to change, but they may be resistant. The script system maps this process as a cycle divided into four sectors, shown schematically in Figure 5.1. In the figure, sectors A and B belong to the past; sectors C and D describe the here and now. Sectors A and D concern external, largely observable processes; sectors B and C concern experiential processes that are not directly observable.

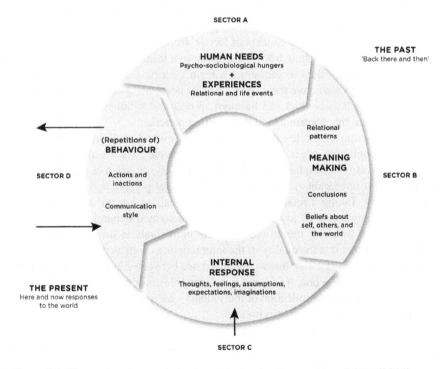

Figure 5.1 The script system in its formulation by Lapworth and Sills (2011).

(A)   The sequence begins with the early developmental experience – a combination of the random circumstances of life and the interplay between the needs of the child and the response of the environment. These are the events of the original script protocol and the subsequent partial repetitions and re-enactments shaped by culture, family, and chance that create an echo of the original scene.

(B)   The internal counterpart is the meaning-making that emerges from the experiences described in A and the largely unconscious decisions about how to live in order to get needs met enough to survive physically and emotionally. The power and resilience – or rigidity – of the life script reflect the frequency and intensity of the experiences.

As an individual grows through life, he filters his responses to the world around him through the lens of his meaning-making. Once a life script has been formulated (in B), it can be reactivated by events bearing a similarity to those in (A). It is manifested in the form of internal processes of feeling, thinking, sensing and imagining, that can limit the individual's choices (C).

(D)   The consequent external manifestation of the script, represents the individual's observable behaviour based on the reactivated script.

Case vignette: Sylvia was the oldest of three children, with two younger brothers. Her father was affectionate but often absent. Her mother – a hard-working and somewhat bitter, working mother was often angry with the children and Sylvia learned early on that it was not safe to oppose her. She also learned that a smiling, helpful demeanour calmed her mother and helped family life be more pleasant. These conclusions became part of her core script narrative and she went through life, well liked and appreciated for her friendly and helpful way of being in the world. Threat of conflict made her feel very anxious, and she avoided it assiduously. She was intelligent and hard-working, succeeding at school and university. (See Figure 5.2.)

In her twenties, she first joined a firm of Belfair, where she started as administrative assistant and fairly soon was promoted to office manager. However, those skills of spreading harmony and appeasing everyone which had been part of her likeability as a team member, were unhelpful as a team leader. She found it impossible to impose any unwelcome decisions on her team; she placated them when they complained about their working conditions but then placated management when they told her that her team was lazy and unhelpful. Team members felt betrayed by her and began to complain about her to her own manager … and so on.

Sylvia left and trained as a nurse where she thought her care-taking skills could be put to good use. She specialized in mental health and earned herself a reputation for skilful crisis management and warm supportive relationships with both colleagues and patients. She was promoted to branch manager of a mental health trust.

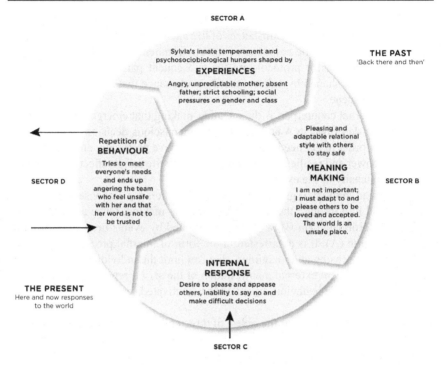

Figure 5.2 A visualisation of how we may understand Sylvia's script system.

Joanna, the team coach, was brought in because the team was full of conflict and strife. Complaints of bullying by one or two members were trickling through to HR and the team was underperforming. The team was a large one – 15 people. Joanna started by speaking to the individual members of the team and asked them about their experience. It was clear from what they said – and from a moving conversation with the team leader herself that Sylvia's reluctance – even inability – to set boundaries or say 'no' had begun to take its familiar toll. Joanna arranged for Sylvia to have some individual coaching to explore and address her script patterns. (to be continued...)

It is important to reiterate that every human being has a script. Our scripts are the way we navigate our journey through life; Gestaltists call this a 'creative adjustment'. Human beings are meaning-making creatures and we also prefer to make things predictable and familiar, even if they are uncomfortable. So we do have a natural tendency to repeat our relational patterns, and of course, every time we repeat, we are deepening the neural pathways that carry this way of being. However, a life script is not a closed system. The individual can assimilate new information and thereby update his or her beliefs and attitudes and their associated embodied experience (Sector B). Coaches and consultants often need to focus on the problematic elements when a script system of thinking, feeling and behaving has become a closed one, limiting new learning and options; and they will constantly be holding the door open to invite new perspectives and if possible corrective or reparative experiences. The script system model was designed for reflection and intervention in such instances.

However, in a team or organisation, the issues are never – or rarely – just the effect of one person's script. They result from the interplay of each person's script with the prevailing habits and behaviours of the organisation. Each shapes the other and the result is the organisational script.

5.2   The organisational script

The script system model can also be used to track the development of the culture of an organisation and/or team. This can be understood in the same way as an individual script – starting with the circumstances and context of the organisation's formation. Relevant factors include the nature of the business, the resources, the world or market context and so on, and also the personality and preferences of the founder or founders of the company. Power – be it role power or personal/psychological power – shapes the development of the script immeasurably, as those with the power can amplify or silence behaviour and processes very quickly and often almost non-consciously. Ways of being and patterns can, if not brought to awareness for question, shape the culture of the organisation, sometimes for generations – long after the original founders or directors have gone (see Figure 5.3).

A good example of this was told to me by Billy Desmond (personal communication), a respected colleague. He describes working with the top team of a company where he realised that it was customary for the CFO not to attend strategy meetings. Decisions were made, which later had to be overturned because of financial constraints. When the coach inquired into this, the team was at first surprised … 'But we have always done it like this'. It was discovered that this tradition dated back to the first years of the company's existence as a start-up, when the then Finance Director, who hitherto had been a book-keeper and accountant, would attend strategy meetings – places where creative thinking is essential – and would interrupt proceedings every few minutes to ask for a detailed analysis of how any idea was to be funded, down to the last pound. The rest of the team got into the habit of having their discussions separately and then the CEO would sit down with the FD to discuss the plans. The company was now a multi-national with an extremely competent CFO who had a fine ability for taking a wide perspective. Including her in the strategy meetings immediately changed not only the team's effectiveness but also the positive motivation of the team members, who had begun to lose their enthusiasm for the discussions (using my imagination, I hypothesise that several of the team members, including the CEO, had grown up with fathers who undermined their initiative and they had had to leave home in order to be their creative selves!).

Normally, the coach will start by looking at what is happening now (Sector D of the script system) and then explore to see where and how the meaning-making (the script narrative in Sector B) is sabotaging success.

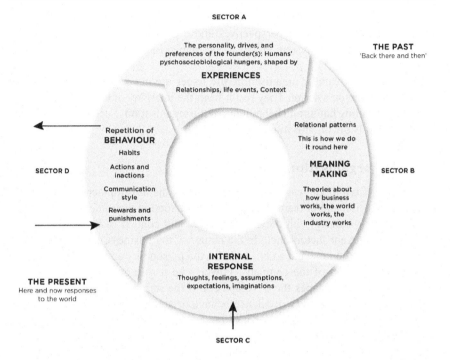

SECTOR A

The personality, drives, and preferences of the founder(s): Humans' pyschosociobiological hungers, shaped by

EXPERIENCES

Relationships, life events, Context

THE PAST
'Back there and then'

Relational patterns

This is how we do it round here

Repetition of
BEHAVIOUR

Habits

SECTOR D

Actions and inactions

Communication style

Rewards and punishments

**MEANING
MAKING**

Theories about how business works, the world works, the industry works

SECTOR B

**INTERNAL
RESPONSE**

Thoughts, feelings, assumptions, expectations, imaginations

THE PRESENT
Here and now responses to the world

SECTOR C

Figure 5.3 A visualisation of how we may think of team and organisational script patterns: the organisational script system.

Case vignette continued: Sylvia's first job was in a company whose CEO had 'rescued' it from bankruptcy by investing a considerable about of money into the failing charity. He saw himself as something of a saviour and he was, understandably perhaps, outraged when members of the previous leadership team resisted his efforts to introduce more 'business-like methods'. He flew into rages – he was particularly angry at the team for 'making me get angry' – and everyone tiptoed around him. Only one team member, herself something of a martinet, was able to manage him and she did so skilfully, while running the business with, as it turned out, a rod of iron. She too brooked no argument or disagreement.

It was easy to see how the culture of that organisation was inevitably going to trigger Sylvia's script. Her policy of please and appease was almost guaranteed here. But what about the mental health trust? Joanna's inquiry began to reveal a long history of conflict, which pre-dated the arrival of this new, rather timid and underconfident team leader, the last in a series of seemingly ineffectual leaders. Two of the team – John and Ellen – were named by several members as being bullies, fighting with each other and silencing anyone else who had a view. People generally were miserable in their work; gossiping and tale-telling were rife. Sylvia's complete inability to take the reins in any real way meant that things were getting rapidly worse. Joanna realised that this was the culture: one or two people had a voice and the rest were silenced and bitter. Because of the size of the team, she started by working with them in small groups to do the contracting about how people would like things to be different, and to teach some skills and models for effective relating. In these small groups of five she invited members to create a story by taking it in turns to add one sentence in turn, starting with the sentence 'There was once a team member of WM Trust'. The story unfolded as it went round the group five times. She asked individuals to notice how they shaped the story and how it shaped them. She invited the team to come up with a possible title, a possible next chapter. Then she facilitated a discussion where individuals discussed the themes of the story and the issues that emerged and began to voice how they related to the issues that emerged. Joanna asked everyone to take the sentence that they had contributed and write them down using the present tense and the first person; for example instead of 'She spoke to the manager and told him ...' they might put 'I speak to the manager and tell him etc ...'. In this way Joanna invited them all to recognize how their scripts might be contributing to what was happening in the team. They also began to take the risk of giving each other feedback about how they were experienced.

Joanna then met with the whole group for a full half day on several occasions. She shared the themes she had picked up in the inquiry and facilitated some semi-structured discussions and exercises. One of those was for the stories that had been created to be shared. Participants took risks in owning their own behaviour patterns. Joanna also encouraged some open and honest feedback for Sylvia. Soon after the work had started, Joanna had recommended a coach to Sylvia for her to explore her own script and understand how much it was interfering with her present life. Now she supported her to engage with her team in some strong and resilient conversations.

The power of context

There is another aspect of how the past can co-create pattern repetition and this is the history, culture and politics surrounding the creation of an organisation. I mention 'the creation' of the organisation because I believe that to be particularly significant. Of course, it is not exclusive – the current climate, political trends and market stability will be a constant influence in shaping the emotional tone and feel of a company. For example, organisations known as 'quangos' – which are assigned to carry out government-funded work and whose existence therefore relies on the government that directs them – and social care or voluntary bodies whose work can be seen as dispensable, and so on, can develop a sort of paranoid survival anxiety that can affect the feel (or 'climate' as De Haan, 2017, calls it) of the organisation and the teams within it.

However, the wider geo-socio-political context of the organisation's early years can be particularly powerful in developing organisation script. Both my colleague Erik de Haan and I have experienced working with a team whose functioning was shaped by political history. My own experience was very moving. I alter the details to preserve the anonymity of the organisation.

I was working as a team coach with my co-coach, Bill. We had been asked to coach a team who were facing an important shift in the organisation's business. There were many opportunities ahead, but the team leader was finding himself and his team feeling stuck, leaden and lacklustre. Bill and I are both white and British. The organisation was a multinational, but this team was exclusively made up of locals in the country of Karlandia (invented name) where we met them.

At the first session, Bill and I decided to divide the coach's tasks between us. Bill would work with the team on roles and tasks, ways forward and so on. I would sit slightly apart and simply 'listen' from the ears down, noticing whatever I was picking up at the more embodied level. We started the session and I noticed that Bill was working skilfully and effectively as the team started to engage with its task. I felt slightly isolated but reasonably comfortable in my role.

Suddenly, out of the blue, I experienced a wave of grief and loss flow over me. I began to think fondly about my father, who had died some ten years earlier. As this bereavement was not a current one, I was somewhat intrigued by my father 'visiting' me at that moment. When the team's work came to a pause, Bill turned to me and asked me whether I had anything to add; had I noticed anything as I had been listening? Despite the illogicality of it, I decided to share my experience of grief and that I had been thinking of my father. There was a long pause after I had finished speaking. Then the team leader said 'We have lost our father'. They then began to tell us how the founder of the organisation – a well-liked Karlandic man – had died ten years previously. The handover to his successor had been well managed and the organisation had moved forward well with their new CEO. However, this team had not. They felt as if they had lost their father – and this included the several members who had joined the team since his death. What was more, the new CEO was Norbonian. As the team talked and owned their sadness, they also began to admit that they felt outraged and betrayed that they leader had been replaced by a Norbonian. Although the two countries had been at peace with each other and the world for more than a century, their history of war and competitive empire building was deeply known and held by all the team members.

Bill and I said little after that. The team did the work of raising awareness, of grieving and of supporting each other. Those who had known the previous CEO spoke of him with affection. The team leader was impeccable in allowing space and voice to all the members. By the time the session finished they had begun to smile with relief and talk about facing the future in a realistic manner.

De Haan's example (2017 pp. 47–8) is similarly moving and also a little start-ling. He describes working with the senior management team of an organisation in the Netherlands which had collaborated with the occupiers in the Second World War. Needless to say, none of the current staff of the organisation was involved in the organisation at that time. Most were not even born. And yet, the team described being limited, restricted and oppressed by a rigid domineering CEO. Individuals felt frightened and harassed but didn't express this. Working with De Haan helped them see the ongoing dynamic of 'occupier/occupied' within the organisation. Careful inquiry into the experience of their own teams and reports revealed – much to their consternation – that the experience was felt at every level. Bringing it to their awareness allowed people to 'unhook' from this historic dynamic and engage with the CEO in more effective ways.

5.3   Role lock: focal conflict in teams

So far, I have been discussing individual and group script as the result of people making meaning of their experiences in the world. Team culture is the result of the interplay of individuals' scripts and the organisational script. In other words, even in the most dysfunctional team, people are not acting in some sort of cruel and thoughtless acting out of pathology. They are responding to the fundamental challenges of life. They are employing their creativity to find a way of getting through. It is thus a co-creative process which has the possibility of novelty and change or the possibility of repeating old habits and 'sabotaging success'.

However, there are two other dimensions to the situation of stuck patterns in teams. The first is the way a team can attempt to avoid addressing what Lieberman and Whittaker (1964) call 'the disturbing focal issues' – in other words those exist-ential issues that arise whenever a group of people exist together (which is all the time from birth onwards!). These issues include concerns about life and death, power and control, inclusion, fairness, competition, conflict, safety, love, violence – and so on. They tend to be uncomfortable to face and a group frequently avoids them (see Chapter 4 for a systems psychodynamic discussion of these issues). The theory of healthy productive groups is that groups need, either tacitly or overtly, to find a way to acknowledge these issues and include them in their group life. It they do not, then what might at first have seemed like a creative adjustment to avoid unpleasantness – a way of keeping a group together – actually causes stag-nation and dysfunction as it attempts to exclude the focal issue. What is more, the focal issue inevitably presses for attention and frequently one of the team members begins repeatedly to raise the issue in one way or another. Margaret Keyes (1983) says that script is 'an inner flirtation with a core life question'. It emerges there-fore, that the person whose script is an engagement with the same issue is likely to keep raising it (Sills, 2015). The group, in its attempt to avoid the unwelcome issue, often collaborates to resist the person – who is now in what is called 'role lock' (Bogdanoff & Elbaum, 1978). Role lock is first noticed by the team leader, consultant or coach when they become aware that one of the team members seems to be interfering with the task of the group (be that the project team, the department or the boardroom) by repeatedly raising the same issues or demonstrating the same behaviour. The group tries to manage the member – either by being quietly compliant or by trying to silence them – and the group is stuck.

Not all the focal issues will have as much valency in all teams or organisations. In some, issues of competition will be particularly relevant as, for example, partners compete for promotion and bonuses. In other organisations, a key issue might be honesty and transparency, in others, issues concerning life and death (such as the military or the hospital) and so on. What is more, team leaders and CEO's can be very influential in co-creating an avoidance of a particular issue. In the example, Sylvia's pleasing manner and clear discomfort with disagreement was a strong invitation to the team to continue their practice of keeping their discontent 'underground'. It also allowed the two 'bullies' to step into the role vacuum and then continue their aggression without check.

> **Case vignette continued:** In her own supervision, Joanna realised that she resonated with Sylvia in relation to this team. In particular, she was aware that she was somewhat afraid of the two 'bullies' and secretly agreed with the rest of the team in thinking that harmony could be restored if they – or at least one of them – were to leave. Her supervisor reminded her of the phenomenon of role lock and invited her to think that these two were raising an important issue on behalf of the team. What were they so critical of? Why were they so angry? It turned out that both these two were completely dedicated professionals and their abrasive interventions were almost exclusively speaking out for the patients, their rights and their need for appropriate care. They were confronting sloppy practices amongst their peers and woefully inadequate resources for their department, but they were doing so in such a hostile way that their message could not be heard. At the next team meeting, Joanna suggested to the group that perhaps Ellen and John were voicing something that no-one wanted to hear but was probably at the heart of much of the team's distress: how impossible a task they had as a team, to care for the overwhelming needs of a group that society had largely forgotten and excluded. How painful it was. And perhaps how courageous it was to keep naming it. The room went very quiet. And then one by one, the team members began to share their own stories of despair and hopelessness. Many of them had relatives with mental health problems and resonated with their distress. John and Ellen had previously acknowledged that they were both experienced as aggressive and critical but had always defended themselves self-righteously. As they heard the distress of the group, they began to feel 'met' in their despair about the situation and they began to soften.

Some weeks later the CEO of the trust approached Joanna. It seemed that he had received some very good feedback from and about the team with which Joanna was working and hoped she would be willing to work with other teams in the trust. Joanna took the opportunity of having a serious conversation with the CEO, who privately owned his own despair at the situation in the Trust and his own personal commitment to mental health as a result of growing up with a very disturbed mother. He asked Joanna to do some work with his own top team so they could think together about changing the culture of the organisation. Later, he chose to go into psychotherapy to work through some of the trauma he was carrying. As a result of this, a different sort of vibe began to trickle down from the top of the organisation. The CEO and his team instigated an ethos where despite the challenges, people were committed to being the best they could be within their role. They created a much more supportive structure – all the employees were offered action learning sets and support groups that were facilitated by external team coaches. The CEO astutely realised that in the current economic climate, cuts in funding and staff shortages were creating extra pressure on everyone. There was not the money for staff development. He approached a consultancy that was running a team and group coaching programme, guessing that some of the participants might be needing teams to practise on. In that way he secured a steady stream of volunteer group facilitators who were keen and committed.

5.4   The primary task

Another dimension of team culture that affects the organisational script is the subtle influence of the team's primary task – their client group or their product (see for example Obholzer & Zagier Roberts, 1994). It is always interesting, and often worthwhile and also fun, when faced by an unexpected dynamic in a team to step back and reflect a little on the nature of the work that the organisation does. Thus, doing team coaching with the staff team of a children's home felt to the coach like sitting with a room-full of bolshy teenagers. One team coach worked in a global household products company which started life as a maker of baby products. She found to her amazement that the team members definitely expected 'molly coddling'. Another team coach found that the intelligence service team were suspicious and unwilling to speak – and so on. This influence of the primary task can extend to buildings and the history they have. The company whose premises was a stately home treated its employees like tenants of the manor, both indulging them and disrespecting them in equal measure.

Often the simple raising of awareness can make the important difference. Team members are intrigued to recognise how the ubiquitous dynamics of the primary task can interfere with creativity or agility.

Sometimes, the dynamics are more embedded, even pernicious. An example of that is the NHS – the national healthcare system of the UK – an extraordinary achievement in social care, a source of pride to the country, and – at the time of writing, the tenth biggest employer in the world. Despite its excellent raison d'être, and the dedication and passion of its staff (see *Love in the NHS – Stories of Care, Kindness and Compassion* by Robin Shohet, 2018) a painful organisational dynamic developed over the decades which is only in recent years beginning to loosen. The organisation was formed to provide free medical care of every kind to everyone in the country. It thus attracted employees whose script was to care for people. However, it is also an organisation whose daily work involves life and death, which inevitably provokes anxiety. The organisation appeared to cope with this anxiety by introducing almost military-style discipline and procedures. This meant that staff could be seen and see themselves as their roles rather than as individual people with fears hopes and anxieties (for more on this see the famous research studies by psychoanalyst Isabel Menzies Lyth, 1960). These processes helped to contain the anxiety in a way, but at the cost of a more relational culture. Also, as the NHS got bigger, the benefits of belonging to a small tight-knit team run by a matron, have been overcome by the new extended structures, staff shortages and other pressures. Many team coaches have found Karpman's (1968) drama triangle to be useful in understanding how dynamics of burn out and bullying have developed amongst such good-hearted and skilled people.

The drama triangle was devised by Karpman (1968) as a means of analysing those repetitive patterns of relating that both manifest and perpetuate script for individuals and groups. Figure 5.4 shows the three roles that two or more people can play (here I use the word roles to describe the personal social and psychological

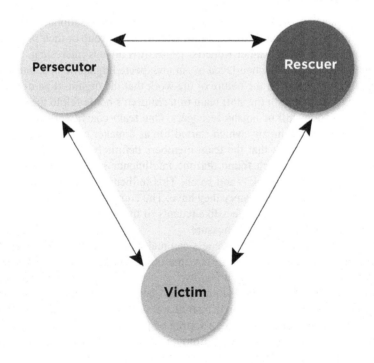

Figure 5.4 The drama triangle according to Stephen Karpman (1968).

roles we take, not the professional or organisational roles). They are rather bluntly called Victim, Persecutor and Rescuer and are given capital letters to differentiate them from real victims – for example, of abuse or of injury, real perpetrators of ill-doing and real rescuers, such as a person saving a drowning man. The Victim discounts their own power and perceives themselves to be powerless in situations where this really is not so. They believe others should make decisions for them, take care of them and tell them what to think and do. The Rescuer is one who, in order to gain recognition or from a script belief that they must always look after others, uses their 'one- up' position to benefit others but simultaneously keeps them powerless. The Persecutor, like the Rescuer, comes from a 'one- up' position, seeing themselves as powerful and competent and others as lesser. However, in order to maintain their 'safe' position, instead of 'Rescuing' others, they need to control and even belittle them. For example, a person may order another about, treat them more like an object than a person and criticize them in order to avoid facing their own feelings of inadequacy.

Karpman describes the drama that ensues as the dynamic interaction of these roles causes us to switch roles again and again, frequently reinforcing our most negative beliefs about ourselves and others. Human beings take on these roles when they are not bringing their full authentic selves to a situation. Karpman saw how these roles and dramatic switches can be seen not only throughout ordinary human communication but in all forms of dramatization of the human condition, such as fairy tales, plays, myths, legends and so on.

We have already touched on how NHS staff are often driven (by taking on their professional role, including uniform and strict codes of practise) to leave their personal selves at home. Add to this, in the current covid and post-covid world, the pressures of a system that is enormously stretched financially and economically, as well as pushed to the limits emotionally and psychologically, it is little wonder that people and teams revert to old familiar script ways of being.

It is easy to see how the roles might play out in the organisation. The patients are, of course, the Victims. Already, they are genuine victims in a sense, because of having ill health of one kind or another. Their anxiety about their health and being 'done to' by the system increases their sense of powerlessness and especially when hospitalised, they quickly become dependent and let go of their own autonomy. The nurses, doctors and therapists, whose script impels them to care for others, become Rescuers, ignoring their own needs and dedicating themselves to the patients, whom they sometimes forget to treat like human beings, seeing them instead as the melanoma in bed 23 or the broken toe in triage. However, Karpman would argue, there is a need for a Persecutor. As the stresses build up, and as many experienced staff get burned out and leave, it is not unusual for those in managerial positions to step in the Persecutor role, imposing the worst of the militaristic dehumanising culture in their attempt to 'train' new staff. This perpetuates the script reinforcing dynamics, as those who were rescuers become the Victims of the bullying Persecutors (team leaders, doctors and so on) and then, because they feel they do not have the power to stand up to their superiors, unconsciously enact their resentment onto the patients whose demands begin to feel like persecutions as well. This leads to nurses deliberately ignoring the plaintive calls of the patients in their beds, consultants feeling guilty – or self-righteously defensive about their bullying behaviour and so on. (See also Chapter 1.)

Recently, perhaps accelerated by the evidently stressful circumstances of coping with the pandemic, some NHS Trusts have become much more attentive to offering support to their staff. Team coaching has become common and team members are finding it hugely supportive to take the time for mutual support and sharing. Some team coaches have found that offering the drama triangle model to people has shone a light on some of the enduring dynamics associated with the setting. Individuals begin to recognise how they might manage their extreme anxiety with anger towards colleagues, or how they cope with the despair of not being able to save patients by sinking into incapacitated Victim position. Many realise how hard it is for them to ask for help, but experience the tender relief of sharing vulnerable feelings with each other. This experience, combined with some psychoeducation about important self-care strategies, has provided major shifts in team morale and cohesion.

5.5   Conclusion

In this chapter I have looked at some of the ways of thinking about 'the presenting past' (Jacobs, 2012) as it creates stuck patterns in teams and contributes to their dysfunction.

I suggest that stale patterns are a blend – an interplay – of individuals' personal script patterns, organisational habits and behaviour, the particular influence of those in power and a team's ability or otherwise to address the disturbing existential issues of life. Ideally, the team coach will address all these dimensions – inviting personal reflection in individuals, more effective ways of relating between team members and also awareness and engagement with unconscious focal issues that might be underlying dysfunctional behaviour in the group as a whole.

Chapter 6

In the present

Working with the team in the here and now

Simon Cavicchia and Erik de Haan

6.1 Introduction: the importance of working with the present moment

Paying attention to, and working with, the present moment in teams is not generally recognised as useful. Client teams often want to move away from their present situation into a desired end state, where they can unite, make decisions, have influence, turn losses into profits, become motivated, etc. Likewise, team coaches do not necessarily appreciate the use or importance of 'standing still' and working with what is arising in the present moment.

Traditionally, team coaching has emerged from sports coaching, leadership coaching, team building and process or organisation-development consultation. As described more extensively in Chapter 1, the different outlooks from these professions have influenced team coaches to such an extent that one can now broadly identify two approaches. One has a team coach fairly central or in charge, who plans the sessions and outcomes in a linear way towards objectives and assumes a basic causality where new learning or training will automatically lead to corresponding outcomes. The other is much less directive, has the team coach much less central as a witness, convener, even court jester, and places much less emphasis on linearity and causality, whilst multicausality, emergence and relationality come to the fore. The two broad approaches not only define different roles for the team coach but also differ in their definitions and values.

The first, 'linear approach' gives rise to a future focus in coaching, which is undoubtedly useful. It can, however, overly shape how individuals and teams relate to what is happening moment by moment in their interactions. It also places less emphasis on current team dynamics and developing relationships. A typical approach from within the 'linear' frame would identify desirable behaviours, likely to be based on a range of theories about team effectiveness and seek to amplify those that make logical sense in relation to the goals the team has articulated. The coach and team focus on the end state and interpret their present-moment behaviour in light of desired future goals and the actions required to achieve them (see also Chapter 8 for a focus on the future). This means that the team coach attends to the occasions when behaviour deviates from what is considered desirable and

DOI: 10.4324/9781003325789-9

then suggests making course corrections. Providing all team members are in align-ment as to what this should be and are equally committed to making the indi-vidual and collective changes deemed necessary for team health and effectiveness, this approach can work very well. The coach will design a series of interventions informed by sound team theory and principle to guide the team in the direction it has identified as part of the initial contract.

As organisational contexts increase in complexity and volatility, step-by-step, linear, future-directed approaches and protocolised stage models can also be lim-ited in what they have to offer teams and team coaches, appearing mechanistic and imposed rather than responsive to actual experiences occurring in a team. They are often based on a series of assumptions about human nature that gloss over the moment-by-moment complexity and unpredictability of human relationships, pro-cesses of 'teaming' and what these patterns may reveal about the less visible team dynamics that nonetheless exert a powerful influence on how teams operate.

The second, more 'emergent' team coaching model, which we denote by 'rela-tional' in this book, pays attention to how individuals interact moment by moment. By focusing on how team members relate, talk and work together (or not), the team coach can access a rich source of information about a team's habitual patterns and the extent to which these patterns and responses might be supportive of effective team functioning, goal attainment and performance, or sub-optimal in some way.

Relational perspectives see teams not as predictable, static entities or objects, but as a continuous process of 'teaming' enacted through the interactions of team members. These interactions are also influenced by the preferences and personal-ities of team members, organisational systemic issues and wider organisational, industry, social, political and global forces. Attending to these factors is a central component in enabling teams to understand the ways in which emotions, anxiety and uncertainty might impact team functioning and develop the capacity to adjust creatively to dynamic and fast changing circumstances.

Instead of conceiving of an effective team as a series of predetermined behav-iours that need to be repeated for effectiveness to be realised, the team coach work-ing with an 'emergent', present-moment orientation focuses on team members' dynamic human relationship processes and behaviours. The uniqueness of such relational patterns offers up rich information about a particular team's unique responses to their current situation moment by moment. These responses in turn elucidate the individual mind sets and frames of reference of different team mem-bers, the quality of relationships between them, their capacity for dialogue and meaning-making together, how they work with differences in perception and meaning, how they are being shaped by the pressures of the task, by forces at work within the team, and by wider organisational and societal contexts.

We are not proposing that working with protocols is bad and working in the present moment is good. Protocols do have their place, yet it can also be useful for coaches to have access to a present-moment orientation for inquiring with their team clients into the unique human processes at work in their current situation. From this perspective, this current situation is always unique, like the flowing of a river. It is possible to jump multiple times into a river from the same spot on a riverbank, but the river we are jumping into will always be different. This creates opportunities for teams to discover more about their team processes and gain new insight into not just what they are attempting to do, but how they are going about it. Often, problems related to task achievement are located in the relatively unexplored dynamics of the team as set out in Chapter 5 on psychoanalytic perspectives on teams. Relational team coaches will often work along a continuum with structure, protocol and future focus at one end, where the coach guides the team in a particular direction informed by theory and models of effective team coaching. At the other end the coach would work with attention to the present-moment dynamics of the team and what they might reveal that is of relevance to the team's task and aims. It can be very useful for the coach to be able to range along this continuum. The coach does not lurch between poles but keeps both in mind, holding the two poles in a creative tension, foregrounding structure and linear protocol when this might be optimal and supportive of team progress and foregrounding a present-moment focus when this might be what is required to move the team forward.

Case Vignette 1

When I (Erik) start my work as an external consultant or a team coach with an existing team of leaders[1] I have a favourite way of opening the session. I first allow the team to arrive, chat and be seated in their own way, and to begin the conversation as they like, as this start of sessions can afford rich observations (de Haan, 2019b).

Then when I have a chance to offer something of my own there tend to be two questions that I try out. They are both highly focused on the current moment, on the actual meeting. Before the session a team-coaching contract with (future) goals may have been formulated and we will have that in mind when we meet. However, the moment we are in a room together and are physically (or virtually) meeting, the present moment takes precedence for me. It certainly takes all my attention and is probably very 'figural' for the team members as well. Thoughts in the team will be charged and focused on the present moment: "This is an important day. We have scheduled it very much in advance. We have goals and an agenda. We are meeting in an unusual place. We have more time than is usual in our meetings, we have an outsider helping us – how will this go, what will I dare to say, what will others say, how will I come through?"

The two questions I (nearly) always ask at the start of team coaching are:

- Can you give a sense of how you are right now in this team? A metaphor for you in the team?
- Would you like to hear my first impression of you as a team?

An open and a closed question. The open question leads to a round of creativity and very often meaningful and highly relevant statements, such as the team leader who says, "I feel like Atlas carrying the world on my shoulders", or the divisional director who feels she is a 'goalie'. The metaphor always evokes a stark and felt sense of the person in the team, and of the quality of the team as a whole. A scenic understanding: a picture – or range of pictures – encapsulating the team in the here and now and the felt experience of participation. Often, the metaphors contain much relevant information pointing to ways in which the team needs to become more effective, but which has never been shared so explicitly within the team (similar to how dreams are used in psychoanalysis to determine the direction in which an individual's unconscious is guiding their development and growth).

This single question usually prepares the ground for potentially impactful interventions to follow in the rest of the sessions I have with a team. Associations and opportunities to intervene arise every time something happens that reminds me of the metaphors the team has opened with – a 'parallel process' playing out in the here and now of the team.

The second, closed question is very different. The answer does not have to be affirmative certainly not when this is a first meeting and the team feels cautious or protective. Much more frequently the question prompts a loud and nearly universal: "Yes!" From that moment on the team tends to be eagerly awaiting my observation or my 'metaphor' of how the team comes across to me. Often as we approach the ending of the session, several team members remind me of my promise in the morning – "You said you were going to tell us your first impressions of us. What are they? How are we different from other teams that you work with?" etc. At that point I know that the ground is prepared for my personal feedback, even if some feedback may be challenging. I then describe the team quite openly, based on the impressions that I have, such as "there seem to be only 2 or 3 people who do all the work here", or "have you noticed that most questions that are raised, are answered first by your leader, and then by your oldest team member, and then by the director of your largest division. And look, you are all sitting in a line as well". As long as I can phrase my observations in such a way that they can be heard they have a deep impact on the team and they become 'critical moments' in our collaboration. The next session some in the team will ask me, are we still doing this? Or: what are your impressions of the team now? From that stage in the work, the mutual here-and-now reflection on how the team and I come across to one another can really strengthen the results of team coaching.

6.2   The implicit and explicit dimensions of relating and interacting

Current developmental and neurobiological research has brought into focus an interface between what is termed the explicit verbal level of relating, the domain of the 'narrative', and the implicit, non-verbal, somatic embodied level of relating – how it feels to be with another person or persons moment by moment. These two dimensions of interaction are important processes to be attending to for working with the present moment.

For a team, the explicit verbal level includes the language that is used, the topics, themes, content and intentional focus of the team's conversations. The implicit embodied level of relating includes levels of energy, the feeling tone of the team dynamic moment by moment, and the felt sense of safety, relaxation or anxiety and nervous system activation at the levels of the whole team and in interactions between different team members and the coach moment by moment.

The Boston Change Process Study Group research into how change comes about in psychotherapeutic relationships (2010) demonstrates that implicit relational knowing underscores all relational interactions as a constantly present factor between practitioner and client. We see similar processes between coach and team members, informing our experience and construction of whatever overt narrative we are engaged in.

They describe "forms of relational meaning" (Boston Change Process Study Group, 2008) which point to how individuals make meaning about their experience through the interaction of explicit conscious thoughts and the implicit unconscious feelings being experienced moment by moment.

The domain of implicit relational experience is not experienced in conscious awareness, as individual responses arise experientially and are not yet translated into language. Although they are out of conscious awareness they have been demonstrated (Lyons Ruth, 1999) to exert a powerful influence on how individuals make meaning from experience and interact with one another. The reflective verbal domain of experience, however, involves the creation of the narratives that give meaning to our direct lived experience, the labels we attach to felt experiences. These two domains develop, co-exist and interact with one another throughout our lives. Cozolino (2006, 2013) has amply demonstrated that our brain is not a static organ. It continually changes in response to environmental stimuli and different challenges, and as coaches we can support teams to address such challenges in the context of an empathic, collaborative and accepting relationship that pays attention to the crucial interface between the implicit and the explicit.

As meaning emerges from the interaction of these two levels of communication, if there is a disjunction between them, those participating in the relationship will sense this incongruence without necessarily being able to articulate the reasons for their discomfort.

Case Vignette 2

When coaching a team facing a number of performance and commercial challenges, I (Simon) experienced team members talking in an animated and vivacious manner about how all was going very well in their plan to address difficulties, whereas at the same time I was aware of a slightly manic, brittle quality to the energy and a startled quality in the faces of certain team members. I noticed that the quality of interaction had a rather performative quality to it with a lot of talking at one another and not a lot of listening, pausing, receiving and building on one another's ideas. I registered a subtle sense of boredom and disconnection in the quality of my relationship to the team. By sensitively drawing attention to these bodily processes the team was able to recognise aspects of their felt experience they had been denying for the sake of 'putting on a brave face' as they tried to align with the active, action-oriented leadership style they imagined was expected in the team and their organisation.

Surfacing this particular pattern and the beliefs that underlied it was a vital step in team members being able to begin to accurately assess their personal and professional challenges as they experienced them and find the specific support and strategies they needed to face them squarely and creatively.

6.3   Use of self: four related ways of working with the present moment

The term 'use of self' emerged in the context of relational perspectives in the world of psychotherapy (Jacobs & Rowan, 2002; Wosket, 1999) and entered the fields of organisational development and coaching (Rainey et al., 2006). It refers to how the person as well as the moment-by-moment experience of the practitioner are considered to be a central element in the change process. In simple terms the coach brings to his or her work life experience, personality, professional development, particular training and orientations to coaching. In addition to this, the moment by moment experience the coach has in interactions with the team and their context also provides a rich source of information about the coach, the client, the quality of relationship between them, the context in which they are working and how this is permeating the field of the coaching relationship and interventions.

A core principle in relational coaching is that human beings, including coach and coachee, are always in a process of influencing one another's feelings and thoughts, which in turn give rise to behaviour. As the team coach experiences moment by moment interactions with a team, he will be accessing information about aspects of the team's dynamics, relational patterns, expressed and hidden preoccupations and concerns. This may also point to more general ways in which the team impacts others be they individuals or other teams in its organisational context.

This orientation requires that coaches be willing to sense more into their subtle bodily experience and track the physical sensations, emotions, thoughts, associations and images that arise when being with a specific client in their context. It requires a capacity to hold both a sense of the direction of the work and a present moment focus, where what is emerging in the here and now is seen to always have potential bearing on the team's development of awareness and meaning-making. In this way, the team coach and team are seen to be part of an "embodied relational field" (Clemmens, 2012) where individual felt experience is seen as profoundly connected to the relationships, conversations and wider context in which the work is taking place. Cavanagh (2006) points to the importance of the body in the context of coaching when he says "All conversations are embodied. All human communication is initiated in bodies and is interpreted through bodies. Our emotional states are the physical reaction we have to the communication in which we are involved" (p. 333).

Clemmens (2012) sets out four core skills and practices that are required to attend to the embodied relational field. In all four team coaches make use of their own here-and-now experience in service of the client. They are embodiment, attunement, resonance and articulation. Used together, these practices enable coaches to track in themselves and their clients the ways in which meaning arises from direct experience. It supports inquiry and meaning-making to be grounded more in direct experience rather than abstract conceptualisation alone. It connects the visceral to the symbolic, the implicit to the explicit.

Embodiment

This is the experiential quality of the team coach experiencing herself as a 'full self' as opposed to a 'role self' ('pretending' in order to be seen as he/she would like to be seen; Yontef, 2007, p. 21) . We can achieve this by becoming present to the breadth of our experience in the moment. Clemmens (2012) suggests we might notice our breath, feel our feet on the ground, notice the quality of our muscle tone in our bodies and faces, paying close attention to how we are orienting ourselves in relation to the client. These will be different in different contexts and with different clients moment by moment. He stresses that "all of this process needs to be an ongoing discipline and as figural as my thoughts or theories about the client and our process" (p. 42).

Central to the practice of embodiment is presence, the coach's state and orientation to the coachee. Silsbee (2008) stresses "your way of being is fundamental to your ability to produce genuine new shifts, insights and behaviours with those you coach. The coach is an instrument for the client's development" (p. 27). Nancy Kline (1999) points to the relationship between coach presence and the capacity for thought in the coachee – "the quality of a person's attention determines the quality of other people's thinking" (p. 17). Fogel (2009) continues in this vein by discussing the value of "slowing down and being in the subjective emotional present" (p. 23). Sills, Lapworth and Desmond (2012) describe presence as "being in the here and now, ready to be alive to every facet of the moment" (p. 103). It is characterised by an aware sensing into oneself, being authentic, maintaining non-attachment to specific outcomes and attuning to the coachee and their context (Denham, 2006). It involves holding a tension between simply noticing experience and also being oriented towards a team's development and the relevance of what is arising for this objective. Chidiac and Denham-Vaughan (2007) describe this as "fully being while doing" (p. 11). In this process the coach moves between 'grace' as a quality of receptivity to what is experienced and 'will' in the form of directed action or taking initiative in service of the coachee's learning and growth (Denham-Vaughan, 2005). It requires holding the tension of the polarities of receptivity and activity.

Case Vignette 3

I (Simon) am about to spend a day with the HR leadership team of a national charity in the UK. As I sit in a quiet corner of a café near to the venue I gather my attention and direct it inwards. I sense my feet on the ground and bring the focus of my attention to the movement of my breath. As I focus in this way I notice a settling feeling and experience a quality of stillness and space in my core. Whilst remaining present to this stillness I expand the focus of my attention and bring the team I shall be working with into my inner perceptual field. I experience a sense of warmth and an opening in my heart. I recall a number of challenges the team has been experiencing as a result of the Covid pandemic and changes to ways of working. I sense the arising of compassion for the individuals who make up the team who are deeply values oriented. I am reminded of what I have been told by the Chief Executive, that team members are exhausted from two years of intense activity and that in addition to the business of the day which is to prepare for a new period of strategy implementation, she hopes they have a chance to pause and connect more fully with each other as human beings. I maintain this quality of inner attention as I enter the building, make my way to the meeting room and team members begin to arrive.

Attunement

Against the background of embodiment and the presence this gives rise to, attunement involves the opening of or reaching out with our senses to what is presently resonating or shifting within us and our clients. This requires the coach to be at least in part rooted in sensing into his or her felt experience whilst also including the experience of the other in his or her awareness. We often practice sensing our bodies via a body scan before the team arrives or in breaks, and during the team coaching as well. We believe it is good practice to shuttle back and forth between our external sense impressions, our internal bodily impressions and our meaning making in the moment. Even as we listen or speak, we try to stay connected with the feeling in our bodies by shuttling back and forth. Though initially challenging, such body scans where, for example, we may attend to parts of our bodies from crown to feet, support coaches to become focused on their body sensations as they are impacted by the team, and they cut across the tendency in many coaches to leave their connection with their bodies and focus their attention and energy in thinking. Attunement supports coaches to enter into a receptive mode, open to noticing what subtle and not so subtle shifts are occurring in team members, the team dynamic and in themselves. Clemmens (2012) stresses that in "order to do this we must empty our task-oriented mind and allow our bodily experience to be part of the foreground" (p.42). With attunement the goal is awareness of how the coach is being impacted by the team and also inviting the team to become curious about their sensory experience in relationship with the practitioner and context.

Case Vignette 3 (continued)

All the team are now present and sitting in a circle. I welcome them and invite them to orient to the team and take in the faces and the group. There is a gentle falling away of social interaction and I notice a quality of stillness and antici-pation arise in the external group field as team members look to one another and then to me. In response I notice a flutter in my solar plexus and a sense of responsibility which I imagine is being evoked by the way the team is relating to me as the team coach, projecting their needs and desires for support and con-tainment onto me. This leads to a curiosity about how much internal support is available to them in their interactions with one another. It is early days in our work together and in the meeting, so I simply allow my sensations, feelings and thoughts to arise and hold them lightly. It feels too premature to share them, and I also catch a thought that if I were to share this it might play into the co-creation of me as the provider of wisdom, whereas I believe team coaching needs to focus, among other things, on developing confidence and capability in the team itself. Moreover, at this stage I have not explicitly contracted with the team to share my in-the-moment impression of the team, as in the way described in Case Vignette 1 of this chapter.

Resonance

Building on attunement, resonance is where we as team coaches notice our own movements, breathing and posture in relation to the team, and stay present and open to what we notice as we are impacted at a bodily level. This 'staying with' allows what is emerging in us to become more developed and unfold. Clemmens and Bursztyn (2003) compare this to being a bowl or resonant instrument. This is an embodied form of empathy (Kepner, 2003) where we experience being touched and impacted by the coachee and where our own experience is shaped in this process.

Case Vignette 3 (continued)

The work continues and the team arrives at the part of the meeting that was designed following the diagnostic phase of the engagement to make room to celebrate the successes of the last two years. To foster greater intimacy, I have contracted with the team that this take the form of a story-telling process with individuals sharing their experiences rather than a more transactional flip-chart exercise to capture a list of achievements. As the team turn their attention to this part of the meeting, conversation falls away and, although quiet descends, there is much looking askance and slight shifting of body posture among a number of members. I sense a subtle anxiety arise and tightness in my solar plexus. I feel a pull into action and the thought occurs to me to move into a more authorita-tive mode of facilitation and ask, "who would like to begin?". I notice how this thought feels like a flight from the present moment and I choose to wait and bring my attention fully back to the feelings of discomfort that are increasing in me. One of the team members says in a rather matter of fact and perfunctory tone, "I suppose I can start". I notice how her tone jangles me a little and resonates with my own inner impulse to flee from emotion that might be uncomfortable. As she goes about the task and gives an example of something she is proud of the team having achieved, I find myself becoming more interested in the sense of disjunction between the words, the intention of the task – to 'celebrate' – the hesitation in the group and increasing sense of emotional disconnection I am feeling.

Articulation

Articulation is the process whereby we as team coaches allow that which is resonating to form into thought, language or gesture. Aspects of our sensory experience might unfold and amplify, they may then give rise to an image, thought or association, to a memory or theoretical perspective. It is the process whereby we put our experience into meaning through our own thought processes and then articulate this to the team in gestures, words and statements. Embodiment, attunement and resonance are closer to implicit modes of relating, whereas articulation moves into the explicit domain where felt experience is connected to language and thought.

The four practices of embodiment, attunement, resonance and articulation allow team coaches to move between implicit and explicit relating, whilst inviting their clients also to do so. This process corresponds also to John Heron's (2001) hierarchical model of the human mind where sensation and affect (feelings) give rise to the imaginal realm of experience which includes the somewhat more explicit creativity of imagination, memory and perception. The next more explicit dimension is the conceptual domain of thought and language. Here, our experience is translated into beliefs, assumptions and propositions about ourselves and the world. This domain is also mediated through the team coach's existing guiding principles, assumptions, beliefs and theories. How these guiding principles arise or not is important to consider. Cavanagh (2006) points to how new insight is an emergent property of dialogue and relationships as opposed to something finite which is either acquired or lost, for example in forgetfulness. Access to insight moment by moment is shaped by our relationship to self and other. A relational, intersubjective orientation sees insight as arising where the subjectivities of team members meet and interact with one another and with the team coach and where differences can be explored and negotiated. In this way the coaching conversation is "an organisation that emerges from the complex interaction of the coach and client(s) – it is a co-created conversation" (Cavanagh, 2006, p. 337).

When practising articulation, we listen deeply to the richness of data entering into the shared space between team members and the coach and team. We cannot help but notice and select certain aspects that capture our attention based on the filtering of our own experience, emotional responses and energetic attention. We pay attention to the feeling tone of what the client is saying and the feeling tone it elicits in us. Cavanagh (2006) describes how "the client's communication enters into the coach's personal reflection space. Here it continues to interact with the coach's experience, mental models, emotions, personality, history and so on, and we begin to see patterns as the client data elicits ideas, images, metaphors and theories. Meaning or insight begins to emerge for us in this process. This processing often continues post-session and during the coach's supervision" (p. 339).

"Articulation is the process of making known either to our self or the client the embodied shifts current in the field as we sense them" (Clemmens, 2012, p.43). The form, manner and timing of our articulation has to take into consideration the team's levels of resilience, maturity, cultural and linguistic register, patterns of interaction, functioning, stage of the relationship and field conditions. The Gestalt principle of possible relevance (Parlett, 1991) is important here. All experience in the team coaching relationship can be considered potentially relevant. This allows coaches and coachees alike to support an attitude of open curiosity, exploration and experimentation. We track closely how implicit bodily experience and explicit cognitive processes are intertwined.

Case Vignette 3 (continued)
I continue to listen to team members whilst tracking the inner impact for me of their words and the feeling tone of their interactions. As I experience a tentativeness and flatness in their storytelling, I have an association to another client system I worked with in a similar field of health and social care and I remember a similar quality of response to the invitation to make room for celebrating success. On a number of occasions one team member appreciates another colleague for their contribution and the recipient of the positive feedback very quickly hands the compliment back. My Gestalt training inclines me to view this as an example of deflection, a way of deflecting attention away and dissipating anxiety when the relational experience feels too intense or exposing. As I watch and feel the effect of these interactions, I notice they are accompanied in me by a feeling of flatness and emptiness. As I stay with this feeling, I have the association to all the health workers I have worked with who have difficulty with taking in the nourishment of feedback. I remember a team member telling me at the start of the meeting how exhausted and 'wrung out' he was feeling after a long period of frenetic activity. Informed by this inner processing, the next time I noticed a team member give positive feedback to a colleague, only to have it pushed back, I interrupted the group process and said in an empathic tone, "Would it be OK if I shared an observation?" As I had contracted earlier with the group for the possibility of my intervening in this way from time to time they all nodded. To the person who had deflected the positive feedback, I said, "I noticed that when Mary was appreciating the hard work and commitment you demonstrated, you very quickly turned it back to Mary and commented on her

hard work too". This was followed by what I call a 'tumbleweed' moment of silence and an interruption to the previous behaviour pattern.

I was able to make this intervention because the team and I now had established enough trust and psychological safety and the team members with one another. In addition, we had contracted together for me to point out patterns as I saw them. I describe these as tumble weed moments, as in the familiar scene in western movies where a desolate landscape is pictured with only the sound of the wind blowing and tumble weed moving across the empty space, because the felt sense of them is often of an empty space opening up in the team's habitual pattern or process. It can feel to team coaches, especially if we are inclined to strive for perfection and/or tend to be critical of our performance, as if we have done something wrong. We can feel anxiety, which is often a countertransference (see Chapter 4) echo of the team's anxiety and disorientation in the face of having a familiar pattern named which leaves them facing the unknown space between an old pattern and new, as yet undiscovered, possibilities. As often happens, after a little while a team member began to speak of his difficulty in taking in positive feedback and others joined in with their own stories. The quality of intimacy and contact increased, and the conversation unfolded into an exploration of what was difficult in receiving feedback. The team explored cultural factors, a tendency towards a negativity bias and deficit model of assessing their progress where they quickly skirted over achievements in order to focus on the next stretch, challenge or what was not yet going well. They were able to see that unless they could slow down to work through their resistances to taking in the nourishment of positive feedback and feel satisfaction in the face of their achievements, it wouldn't matter how much they achieved, they would continue to feel 'wrung out' and as if they were running on empty. The team recognised that in order to stay the course of a never ending and ongoing process of change in the organisation, it was vital that they made time to really feel and celebrate their achievements, however apparently small in relation to their strategic objectives, in order to maintain motivation and a sense of their agency. Far from being an abstract conversation (another form of deflection) the team seemed energised by their acknowledgements of shared difficulties and were able to acknowledge discomfort whilst also taking in more positive feedback. Team members appeared visibly moved by the experience.

Team coaches working with the present moment need to develop a capacity to tolerate 'tumbleweed' moments in such a way that they do not take them personally and keep tuning in to the team and their own felt bodily sense of the present moment. Only then can they hold up a mirror to a pattern of behaviour that brings something potentially new into the team's awareness.

6.4 Final part of sessions: making use of the closing present moments

Working in the present moment can be particularly important near the beginning and end of sessions, where pressure can be somewhat higher as there are the dual tasks of beginning or ending well combined with the ongoing needs of team coaching. At the beginning of sessions, we can experience a particular richness of phenomena where oftentimes a lot of information is revealed because nobody is in control and self-censorship has not kicked in yet (see De Haan, 2019b, and Gaudart, 2021). The end of the session is similarly meaningful as people in the team start to realise what has been achieved and what not, including what hopes have been dashed and what understanding remains elusive. The team coach can make very good use of time elapsing and the approaching ending just by paying attention and perhaps drawing attention to it. If a new strategy needs to be agreed on one can agree a short amount of time to provide a first agreement, and the clock ticking away will focus the minds (sometimes it can help in such cases to state the correct time every ten minutes or to make it more into a team challenge by turning seats around or switching cameras off on Zoom. Equally powerful, in a more reflective team coaching context, can be just to ask everyone to describe the feelings that they have right now, as they are preparing to move out of the session.

Case Vignette 4

I (Erik) worked with a team recently where I experimented with a kind of intervention that often comes to me when tough decisions need to be made or a new strategy has to be set. This was the board of a consulting firm and they had been talking about some highly sensitive issues such as the composition of their own team and expected changes because of retirements, as well as about changes in their rather complex systems of remuneration, where some of them felt they needed to reward management better in their organisation, which would come at the price of rewarding sales less. They all felt that despite their differences they had come to a rather good place as a team. At the same time, I noticed how several board members were keeping their commitments and their agreements to what had been achieved a little bit vague. There was agreement on some new directions of travel and at the same time an avoidance of mentioning specific terms and numbers. They seemed to be mostly 'on their best behaviour'. At the start of the final hour, I suggested to them that this was a very unique moment, they would not get any further team coaching on this issue and so this was the moment to speak up. "If anything is not right with what we have decided, or there are any other niggles – speak now, otherwise the moment of this important strategy day will be gone". I immediately sensed a deepening, a pregnant silence after which some of the previously more reluctant members spoke out, naming their pain of letting go and their doubts about the future. This included quite a few tears and an opening up of some areas for more personal development for individuals. One of the partners stated that he wanted to start personal therapy in the near future. In this way the team was able to experience and acknowledge the deeper reality of the choices they faced and the impacts of their decisions. I felt that in the last hour they contributed a lot to reducing the tendency of unexpressed needs and experience to form into resistance and a lack of follow through on the decisions made, which had been a pattern in this team.

In conclusion, we hope we have shared some of our own favourite ways of paying attention to the 'present' in team coaching, varying from sensitising ourselves to the present moment, to making what is present more explicit so that questions can be asked, implicit patterns can be converted into (more or less) explicit insight, and development can take place within the team that is grounded in common (here and now) experiences and challenges. We started out by highlighting ways to bring the present into the start of team coaching. Then we had a longer section on how the present is current and relevant throughout the whole journey of team coaching, as illustrated by case vignettes 2 and 3. Finally, we ended with an example about the final stretch of a team coaching session and how paying attention to the ending and the loss of opportunity and relationship at the cusp of a session, can make the team more aware of the passing of time and more willing to take a risk at the very end of a session. We have all heard about the door-knob effect... it is our firmly held view that team coaches can help inviting door-knob revelations and bringing them forward in time, so that there is still time during a session to reap the learning that is contained in them.

6.5 Conclusion

We hope you have enjoyed the chapter and have found ways to bring together the 'linear', programmatic part of team coaching with the 'emergent', relational alternative, by paying more explicit attention to present-moment process.

Note

1   Whether the team coaching work is focused on enhancing understanding of one another, growing alignment between team members, or any work around taking decisions, whether preparing for decision by understanding context and challenges or arriving at a decision that makes use of a variety of views and is well supported by the team; or any other of a myriad of applications of team coaching.

Chapter 7

For the future

Working with the team's objectives

Tammy Tawadros and Erik de Haan

7.1 Introduction

Teams are often confronted with the possibility or urgency that their future conditions need to be different to how they are at present. Perhaps current structures are unsustainable. Or market conditions, resources, or legislation cum regulation change so rapidly or profoundly, that continuing as before becomes no longer possible. The threat to continuity throws the future into sharp relief for the team. This threat may eclipse the team's capacity to reflect. We see the ability for a team to be reflective and to reflect regularly, as a necessary, if not essential condition for being effective in fulfilling the team's task and role. Team coaching provides a space in which teams can develop this reflective ability to understand themselves in terms of their feelings, behaviours, motivations, relationships, and ways of functioning as a team within the wider organisation and context. Team coaching can also serve to provide the opportunity for teams to reflect together to broaden their awareness and deepen their insights in service of their current objectives, as well as for the future. This chapter explores how team coaches can work in these circumstances.

7.2 The presence of the future in team coaching

A lot of team coaching has the future as its main focus. Team coaching is often used to impact a team's future in some way, e.g., to increase motivation and agility in the face of impending changes, to further alignment for decisions or to simulate and prepare for new ways of working. While these may be important questions to consider, they also present something of a conundrum for team coaching, in that the future is essentially unknowable and beyond our grasp in the here-and-now of the work. In many instances, talking about the future may turn team coaching into a vehicle for wishful thinking, empty promises, and a focus on irrelevant or unrealistic outcomes. To an extent, focusing on the future *distracts* from the important reflective work that the team can do in the present, to bring greater awareness and understanding of the team itself and the current pressures it faces. From a relational perspective we would argue that what is not here now, is both a distraction and a pretend form of coaching, one which involves speculative dialogue rather than

DOI: 10.4324/9781003325789-10

conversation about what is relevant in the present moment. This gives rise to a paradox between the power of team coaching to impact the future, and the vulnerability of team coaching to be annihilated by attempts to bring the future into the room. Although the future is yet to come, it is both not present here and at the same time highly present symbolically, as the ultimate 'client' of team coaching. It is as if we are saying, "Don't look ahead, pay attention to where you are now": being sufficiently grounded in the present will give us a good enough basis for looking ahead. We will explore how team coaches can navigate this paradox, as well as other perplexing tensions that we encounter when considering the future together with the team.

Nevertheless, team coaching is often directed at the future and therefore enters this problematic field of reflecting-on-what-is-by-definition-not-here. A coach is asked to support an important strategy formulation process, or a top team struggles to take certain decisions that they must now take together as a team. These are obvious occasions where team coaches get involved, and for good reason. The team may be hoping that reflection deepens, so that different and more relevant options are found, or the commissioner of team coaching thinks that with the presence of an outsider the team will be on their best behaviour and will muster the courage to take the really difficult decisions.

Despite attempts at prediction, certainty remains elusive, and the future is always therefore largely an 'unknown', which can only be represented or thought about in the present. As a result, the future, whether conceived as a looming monolithic existential question, or bite-size proximal goals (Grant, 2020), poses considerable psychological challenges for teams, as it does for individuals, whole organisations, and beyond. As in the representation of a ticking clock going backwards in *Alice in Wonderland,* a future focus and future-oriented conversations can fall prey to all sorts of illusions, fantasies, and delusions. When so much in the wider sociopolitical global system is unknown and unbounded, fear and anxiety about the future's precariousness are inevitably present for the team and evident in the team coaching room, even if the future itself is not.

Case vignette 1: "Turkeys voting for Christmas": the top team of the largest faculty of a traditional university had received a request to make considerable cost savings over the next five years. The reasons behind this were lower predicted student numbers in the longer term, and a reduction in national research grants. Internal and external strategy consultants had developed several options including 'salami slicing' every department, merging several departments, and making savings in a few departments where student numbers were particularly low. The team consisted of the Dean, a company secretary, and the heads of all six departments.

As this was an experiment with a new form of decision-making in a very difficult situation, the Dean selected one of us as a team coach and planned five biweekly sessions over three months. Everyone in the team was told that they needed to reach agreement on the way forward by a certain deadline. And if not, the Dean would make a final decision with the University Board. I undertook interviews with all professors and prepared for each session in advance, with both the Dean and the board secretary. Sessions were held in a quiet and comfortable location at the university, and the atmosphere during the team coaching was pleasant. The department leaders used the time to describe the departmental work to their colleagues, and to think through options for the future, which they did in a friendly and rather non-committal way.

As the sessions progressed the organising committee of Dean, secretary and coach felt more urgency, however they could not find a way to share this with the team. I as the team coach decided on an intervention that offered a number of different interpretations of the current situation for the team members. For example, interpretations of the team as loyalties that were balanced towards departments rather than the faculty as a whole, well masked anxiety for the future, a possible competitive game where no-one wanted to lose (as in the well-known prisoner's dilemma), and even as turkeys voting against Christmas. The team was always interested in these interpretations and sometimes slightly amused, though they never forcefully argued against even highly critical perspectives I gave them.

The Dean and I collaborated more and, working against the clock, we took the opportunity to narrow down options, forcing the team's hand to make a decision. Whenever the options came close to threatening the size or independence of a particular department, conversations slowed down and became more hesitant. Unable to reach a decision in time, the Dean was left to choose. In the event, he did not get to make the final decision, which was taken by his superiors who had lost patience by that time.

In this case it is hard to see how team coaching was beneficial. It certainly brought a team of university professors much closer in their stubborn refusal to move anywhere near a collective decision. They enjoyed the process and the interpretations that I offered them during sessions, and as one might expect in the circumstances, there was full attendance for all the sessions – but in the end team coaching could not bring in joint decision making despite a heroic effort by all concerned.

Protecting what we have and 'resisting' loss and change may be a wholly understandable response in teams. Our collective instinct for survival, and the need to maintain our sense of integrity, of remaining intact, and staying as we are, may be as strong for departmental teams, as it is for the individuals who lead them. The thought of being dispensed with, disposed of, or got rid of when cuts in 'headcount' are a probability, poses a real threat, but it may also play into deeper primal concerns about death and survival (Marris, 1993). These can set in motion great hidden anxiety, but also competition between team members. One might even speculate that such high levels of psychological defensiveness are proportionately related to the high existential anxiety the university team experienced. Anxiety which may have led the professors to operate in a basic assumption mentality (see Chapter 4), behaving 'as if' the task was an intellectual exercise rather than a practical one leading to a decision with real life consequences. There may be a conscious or unconscious game that is set in motion, whereby benign amusement and pleasant civilities possibly provide 'cover' for more unpleasant and 'primitive' feelings of rivalry with peers, and perhaps, of resentment towards the Dean and University Board who may be experienced as malign figures with larger-than-life powers to magic away the need for, or impact of, the proposed research funding reductions. Moreover, the team were perhaps caught in a bind between a covert wish to survive as a department or departmental leader, and the desire to show loyalty to the wider team. In this situation the process was further compounded not only by the impossibility of turkeys voting for their own demise, but also by a double generational jeopardy: professional demise of the older generation professors and the slowing birth replacement rate of the next younger generation of students.

One way a relational team coach might work more productively with this kind of situation, could be to surface and name the dynamics playing out, though it would ultimately be for the team to respond as they saw fit.

7.3   Team coaching in the presence of pressures on targets

Leadership teams shoulder considerable responsibility for the future and the seemingly impossible tasks of forecasting and delivering future targets of various kinds. The pressure and strain of leading into uncertainty, into a state of 'not knowing', while simultaneously being responsible or accountable for predetermined outcomes, can stir up all sorts of powerful and often conflicting emotions. Finding themselves in such a bind of responsibility and vulnerability may lead teams into different defensive responses. They may retreat into a collective fantasy of guaranteed success or indeed failure, rather than tempering their certainty or factoring in the wild cards of the unpredictable, or the prevailing uncertainties in the wider context. In this kind of situation, team coaching may provide something of an oasis for teams: a valuable space for dialogue and holding, for finding a balanced approach, as the team grapples with the paradoxical problems and perplexing emotions of holding the future in mind, whilst continuing to develop in the present.

To formulate its future objectives, the team needs to have both an outward and inward-looking focus (see also Chapter 9). On the one hand, involving alignment and agreement with the wider organisation and on the other, between team members, on how these objectives are to be achieved. There is also likely to be a requirement for further, possibly multiple agreements that take account of the interfacing boundary with other functions and teams, depending on the size of the organisation. These processes can give rise to all kinds of proto-familial dynamics and internecine sibling rivalries (Wilke, 2014), which in turn can divert the efforts and energy of a team away from their core task and their key objectives. Instead of looking ahead and remaining connected to a perspective of the future, they may get caught up in a basic assumption mentality (Chapter 4). This may appear to be a kind of *folie à plusieurs,* in which team members respond to an alternative set of unconscious forces, quite separate from the performance of their formal organisational task.

In such circumstances, the team's patterns of relating and behaving become manifestations of largely indistinct and interconnected, unseen dynamics. First, those that reflect each individual team member's unique psychological 'signature'. Second, the manifestation of shared common ground and below-the-surface assumptions that give rise to the dynamics of team life. And third, as reflections of the wider organisational and environmental context. In this, the team may come to express something of the wider systems within which it is operating. Just as the individual 'emerges' in social interaction, the team, by the same token, emerges in and through the complex interplay between individual, team and wider systemic needs and patterns, which often remain hidden and unconscious.

Case vignette 2: Part A: One of us was engaged to coach a new sales team securing high-value cross-sales contracts to airlines and travel companies, thereby increasing the client's revenue from travelling customers purchasing pre-paid currency cards and travel insurance products. Tom, the CEO, had previously been a peer of Neil, director of corporate sales, a newly created specialist directorate and team. During an individual contracting meeting, Tom spoke about coming from a large sibship and that he relished competitive endeavours. At other 'discovery' meetings with individuals in preparation for the team coaching work, he rubbed his hands with glee at the prospect of Neil's team's 'wins' and spoke about wanting to see "the fire in Neil and the team's belly". Neil was an only child, who had been brought up by his single-parent mother. His first career had been as a professional musician, and his diffident, gentle manner, always struck me as being slightly out of place in the world of cut-throat sales and financial services. All members of the team had been recruited internally: 'handpicked' by Neil. They struck me as rather similar to him in demeanour and temperament. Several of them had held 'techie' and tech trouble-shooting roles within the company, prior to gaining experience in sales and being recruited to the team. As a team, they came across as thoughtful, curious, socially and professionally at ease with each other.

During our first sessions, they characterised themselves as a well-networked and emotionally intelligent team, who underlined the importance of empathy and relational sales techniques. They saw themselves as rather noble 'ambiverts' (without a strong preference for either extraversion or introversion), who cultivated long-term relationships with influential corporate figures in the industry, contrasting their approach with the uber-extravert telesales teams elsewhere in the organisation, whom they considered brash and given to morally questionable practices. As a team, they seemed to be energised and confident about their overall purpose and goal.

Midway through our contracted sessions, the team seemed to become rather agitated, losing their previous composure and 'form'. They had received an ultimatum from Tom along the lines of: "deliver (your objectives) or die". They felt Tom was discouraging their reliance on feelings and empathy, inviting them to pursue more aggressive sales pressure methods. They seemed to be caught in a vicious cycle whereby the team was drawing away, as if creating a boundary around themselves to protect and sustain a separate and more nurturing climate. This seemed to make Tom and the top team suspicious, leading them to demand more 'accountability' from the sales team, in turn driving the team to withdraw further. The organisation as symbolised and personified by Tom, became the team's wicked withholding parent, and the telesales teams became the bad relatives in an extended family where only Neil and his team could represent a virtuous family with a 'good enough' parent.

On the face of it the senior team and the CEO had made their expectations clear, in setting ambitious sales targets for them. For their part the team had done the work of 'teaming'; forging the positive relationships and constructive climate that they regarded as essential for them to collaborate. As with any quest for growth, there are inevitably risks and uncertainties, and the future course cannot be fully predicted or known. Under the surface of this ordinary organisational reality, however, what we saw play out was a war for the future identity of the organisation. Would the future company be one that takes care of its employees, offers customers the security of insurance and assured travel, at the same time as growing value for the company? Or would the future company grow sales at speed, enabling the business to survive, even at the cost of sacrificing the team's health and well-being? Nobody knew what the definitive picture would be, but increasingly people were taking sides. How was I as a team coach to respond? Would staying with the team and nurturing their reflections mean taking sides with the team, and moving against Tom? Or was there a way to keep the opposing perspectives on the future – and additionally, remain open to reflections on the apparent 'struggle for the future'? In any case, this became a real struggle for me as the team coach, and I found it increasingly difficult to preserve my neutrality, and to hold the space for fresh ideas about the current and future situation.

We often find, when the focus of the work is a future objective, goal, target, or is oriented towards a new strategy for the future, direct and open questions can elicit an atmosphere of 'silent dread', and sometimes the expression of existential fears about fragmentation, conflict and dissolution ("We're a broken team"; "It's the end of an era"). Or a dread about stagnating or being stuck ("It's like walking through treacle"; "We're mired in the politics"; "We're tangled in the weeds"). When the dread is silent, we find that simply sitting in that silence, albeit attentively, can sometimes be unhelpful. What we believe can be even more helpful in engaging teams with future themes that elicit dread or indeed other strong emotions and views, is to tap into a more associative mode of co-inquiry. This might involve using the images, language, metaphors, and symbols that the team uses and reflecting on what we are noticing. We might also invite the team to share their fantasies and dreams, whether of a 'future perfect' or of a dystopic or nightmarish future. This associative, indirect exploration of the future, and using it to inform hunches and hypotheses with the team, can be a rich and important source of insight and meaning in team coaching.

Case vignette 2: Part B: what happened next in this assignment. I found myself going from joining with, to becoming quite identified with Neil and the team. I had gradually got drawn into the organisation's and into the team's either/or thinking and seduced by their defensive 'self-protective' manoeuvres. They seemed to be coping according to some familiar internal model of the world, which seemed to align, cohere, and resonate with Neil's family experience (Schwartz, 1989). The team's experience had resonated strongly with my own experience of migrating to a different culture and finding solace and security in family life, making it hard for me to help the team to connect with their broader purpose and wider business context.

The team came to feel increasingly driven and under considerable pressure, with no regard for their own well-being. As they continued to withdraw further from the rest of the organisation, Tom interpreted Neil's apparent passivity and the team's quiet self-sufficiency as lack of commitment and even as harbingers of failure. As a result, the team was disbanded and the entire company was re-structured, following a merger with another travel insurance firm. Neither Tom nor Neil, and by extension his team, were in the end, able to let go of their established familial patterns and expectations. The team held fast to the ideal view of themselves as a caring and morally courageous band of like-minded siblings, autonomous and largely accountable only to their immediate boss, Neil. Tom, for his part, also seemed to be holding on to and acting on an internal model of teams as energised by ambition and competition, quite at odds with the team's image of themselves. An image which perhaps denied something of the realities of competition and rivalry in the business marketplace. This made it difficult for them to grasp the objective circumstances they were in, or respond more constructively, for example by inquiring into the attendant sense of pressure for them to deliver their targets, seeking more support or re-negotiating target delivery.

This sequence of deeply felt emotional exchanges struck me as being powerful expressions of the personal and interpersonal realm of experience. Perhaps, they can also be understood as an expression of the issues facing the wider system; of the risks, uncertainties and feelings of anxiety that come with any quest for future change. Teams can often become a focal point for the organisation's hopes for the future. In the case of this sales team, there seemed to be an implicit expectation that they carry both the responsibility for assuring the future of the company (by meeting the ambitious sales targets set) *and* for the management of risk and uncertainty at the same time. Risk and uncertainty which is inherent in the future endeavour for the whole organisational system, and which remained apparently hidden from view and undiscussable. Yet it was implicitly understood to be the preserve of the sales team alone. Despite mixed feelings and the theme of being stuck, the sense of an impending future, whatever it held, felt palpable in these later team coaching sessions. In the event, the die had already been cast, and the fate of the team and the organisation had been sealed by the decision taken by the top team. As often happens, the moving, unstoppable future was felt within the team-coaching room, long before the future plans had come into view. For the coaching work, this offered a valuable opportunity to reflect honestly about feelings and to make sense together of the experience of being part of the team, and part of a wider organisational system, operating within a still wider contextual system.

7.4   Experimenting with the future: deep listening and scenario planning

As we have suggested already, we believe that the core stance of the team coach when working with the future, is one which is paradoxically mostly directed at the here and now. Relational coaching involves exploring and making explicit what is going on right here and right now in relationship, whether in the relationships within the team or in our own relationship with the 'team-in-mind' as felt and experienced in the moment. In those relationships we can notice the relative presence or absence of the future. We can detect to what extent the future is figural, present to the team – and when it is not very present despite a clear task around future strategy or future planning. We tend to ask ourselves, where is the future? Is the future somehow integrated into present experiencing? Or is the future actively kept away from the present, is the future suppressed? One can often see when the conversation is brought to the future, how the team quickly glosses over it and moves the conversation on to another topic. In this way we can form hypotheses as a team coach:

- the future challenge is present and in awareness;
- the future challenge is present and out of awareness;
- the future challenge is absent and kept out of awareness;
- the future challenge is possibly tinged with anxiety and fear;
- the future challenge is associated with excitement and possibility;
- the future challenge is overlaid with brittle optimism or exaggerated confidence.

(just to name a few possibilities).

Case vignette 3: A Clinical Team on the threshold of change. One of us worked with a multi-disciplinary clinical team that had taken on expanded responsibility for community services, in addition to hospital-based specialist care. The team coaching work was divided into three phases. The first involved working with the joint service and clinical leads; the second one-to-one interviews with the wider senior leadership team; and the final phase was to be a series of six team coaching sessions with the wider leadership team.

During the first phase, the joint leads described the overwhelming demands and strains of taking a new strategic direction which involved shifting the focus away from hospital-based services, to community services and extended provision. All of which was to take place within the existing financial constraints, and the requirement to adopt a system of payment by results, based on specialist services. Over three sessions, the leads reflected on what a tall order this service re-design had proved to be. I noticed that the conversation would often skirt around the here-and-now realities of being a new joint top team tasked with leading a complex strategic change. The conversation kept returning to the wider team members' misdemeanours, whom they often described as inexplicably naughty children. Sharing this observation with them had initially met with little response, until the second session when Maria, the clinical lead, made an angry retort, saying that she and her colleagues felt hounded by my persistence on the topic.

At the third and final session, I decided to share that I had felt a bit 'crushed and deflated' at the end of the previous meeting, but that I also wanted to leave them feeling hopeful after this, the last session. I was surprised by their response. The service leads spoke about the intense loneliness they felt, about how little 'face time' they had with each other, and how little contact or support of any kind they received from the Trust. Their days were consistently filled to the brim with interminable clinics and ward rounds, with intense meetings to consider, review patients with critical and complex needs, often involving life and death decisions, eking out meagre resources. There was little hope to be had, they concluded, in what they sardonically came to call "the Russian roulette routine". This was a powerful metaphor, given that Russian roulette involved the player risking their own death in an arbitrary manner. This was a theme that emerged in subsequent phases of the wider team coaching work. I suggested using some time in the last session to inquire into what they needed and what the 'smallest' manageable steps available to them to feel less alone and isolated might be. They reported feeling immensely buoyed by being asked that question. It paralleled the way I had felt moved by the support they described offering their patients, and the lengths they went to make sure that they and their families didn't feel alone. It struck me as rather sad that no one ever asked them what practical; let alone emotional support they needed.

In the session that followed, with the wider team, I suggested creating a timeline. This seemed to engender an atmosphere of energetic collaboration and apparent relief as people recalled events, wrote things down and chatted quietly as they did so. The team seemed to tense considerably as they reflected on the timeline. When I prompted the team to describe their sensations right now, only the three joint and clinical team leaders spoke. They felt battered and exhausted, in a constant state of rushing and doing, desperately fixing on the patient front and trying to make the new service transformation design 'work', in time for the new financial year. Their account was met with awkward silence, which left me at a bit of a loss. After a break, I invited the team to describe how they experienced the silence. Rather strangely, at that moment, I had a vivid fleeting image of the parting of the Red Sea, which I decided not to share. Members of the wider team began talking quite spontaneously about their misgivings about the new style of decision-making, questioning why the three joint clinical leads no longer involved them in funding decisions, sparking a fast and furious exchange between the clinical leads and the rest of the leadership team.

At the next session, I opened by sharing the vivid image of the Red Sea that had come to me during the previous session. Initially, team members were distracted by news of the pandemic, leaving the room at various points to answer their bleeps. This left me feeling a bit annoyed and disrespected, and I felt my confidence slipping away. One team member jokingly remarked that they 'wouldn't like to be Moses leading this lot', and I noticed that both the physiotherapist and consultant had remained very still and quiet. They then reflected that it felt as though "there's been a very painful parting which has been hard on everyone, making it difficult for team members to do their jobs, whether in overall charge of the team or not". After this, the consultant, in tears, described her feelings of inexorable loss of the team as it was, of the close support from the clinical lead, and the risks and demands involved in working with patients with complex life limiting conditions when there was so little resource and support to draw on. It was a profound moment which enabled several others in the team to acknowledge their own feelings of anger, loss and overwhelm. The acknowledgment of powerful feelings associated with change, loss and transition had proved to be very liberating.

In this case, the team had been congested with strong feelings they had not had an opportunity to work through. Using the timeline activity to revisit past events for the team, helped them to express and to bear witness to one another's feelings. It also helped them to make sense of their experience in the context of the systemic changes that were taking place, rather than focus on a particular individual or set of individuals in the team (Krantz, 1998). This was a team who also seemed to feel emotionally and professionally depleted by the demands of the work; their own psychological resources were overstretched, mirroring or paralleling the stretched and meagre resources within their services. This is what Cardona (2020) characterises as the 'sponge effect': when the nature of the team's work gets soaked up by them, affecting the social and psychological realm of the team's experience, and their behaviour. Distracted by 'undigested' emotions and events of the past (Day, 2020), they were not able to invest energy and attention in collaborating and planning for the future, particularly as the previously established relationships that had hitherto been sources of professional and psychological support had become disrupted (King et al., 2018). The loss of the familiar, with the containing functions of known routines, and dependable support from colleagues, in combination with a more uncertain future, requiring new ways to adapt, can pose great psychological challenge for the team (Miller, 1979). These, together with the unrelenting demands of the day-to-day work, made it difficult for them to think about their patients very much, let alone the changes to the service for those patients that they needed to orientate themselves to.

Having described in brief the key 'approach' of the relational coach to working with the future in team coaching, it is worth thinking about methodologies we can use when the team is actively working on future strategy and/or planning. Several methodologies have been proposed in the literature, such as futuring (Cornish, 2004), scenario planning (Schoemaker, 1995), simulations (Boin et al., 2004) and phenomenology (Chidiac, 2018). Out of these four we think the phenomenological method is closest to relational team coaching but all of the others can be integrated well too. Here is an example of the use of a combination of phenomenology and scenario planning in relational coaching:

Case vignette 4: Scenario Planning with an Arts-based Charity. The senior leadership team had reached a point of stagnation following many rounds of ever decreasing public funding and shrinking opportunities for generating alternative funds. Robert had joined as a CEO following the previous CEO's retirement, after 25 years in the role. Much younger in age than the established team members, he recruited two younger directors, and younger trustees. Robert also set the organisation on a new strategic trajectory. The charity had hitherto provided education and work opportunities to young people who were vulnerable or excluded, often using tried and tested drama projects and theatre placements. Their new strategy would extend these opportunities to a wider range of performing arts to engage and support young people.

Robert commissioned ten sessions of team coaching from one of us. At our first 'scoping' meeting he came across as a considerate and thoughtful person, at the same time as being conscientious and ambitious for his organisation and its beneficiaries. The goal for team coaching was to help the team integrate its newer members, and to explore new ideas and possibilities for their future direction.

In the first session, everyone seemed nervous. I also felt decidedly jumpy and jittery as their team coach. Making a joke at the start in an effort to diffuse the nervousness did not seem to work. I changed tack and offered a more serious way to begin, which involved rounds of introduction first by name and role, then by naming a simple pleasure, a positive memory about Dramaworks, noticing the room, each other, and finally characterising how each felt about the team at this moment, using any image, analogy or metaphor that came to mind. I was struck by the powerful images and metaphors that team members used to describe themselves and their situation. These included: "rooted to the spot", "fixed in our ways", "watching the slicer edging ever closer", "a noose around our necks", "in the cold light of day", and "nature red in tooth and claw", among others. Although I had contracted with them to feedback what I noticed about them and the ways they communicated, they were a bit nonplussed when I commented about the vivid language they had used, which seemed to invoke fear and horror. The team insisted that these were "just typically colourful, Northern turns of phrase".

In subsequent sessions, several team members reflected that they had experienced prolonged periods of feeling helpless and fearful, paralysed in the constant face of actual or anticipated scarcity. They had grown used to "keeping the wolf at the door", and long fallen into a habit of meeting for business, confining themselves to rounds of dry factual updates. This was a routine which they still maintained with the newer team members. As our work progressed, they gradually tried out different ways of sharing what they were concerned about and working on.

Over time they developed a regular routine of checking in and discussing shared endeavours as part of their periodic leadership meetings.

As the financial year drew to a close, with several sources of major funding coming to a close, the team was feeling understandably worried. Some team members expressed their anxieties about the future of the organisation and others began to express frustration with my style as a team coach, and with the 'unstructured' team coaching process. After all, they reasoned, "all this talk was not work"- what they really wanted was "concrete contract, not conjecture". For some members of the team, and in particular the finance, business development and IT directors, team coaching was not working. They seemed to be increasingly on the margins, arriving late for the sessions and leaving early, on the edge of what they experienced and characterised as fruitless speculation and unhelpful big picture thinking. At session 5, their manner towards me and to some extent towards Robert, the CEO, came across as terse and sarcastic. I began to feel very uncomfortable, sensing that the team was forming two camps, poised for a clash of perception and styles, with me being clearly associated with an unproductive, insubstantial, big ideas, big picture approach, and the three other directors firmly in operating within the realm of the tangible, planned, detailed and the more immediately attainable. Neither was better or worse, neither was mutually exclusive. For me, the task of team coaching at this point, appeared to be largely about re-thinking the organisation's identity and direction of travel, where some continuity was assured through a small number of continuing funding streams, but where discontinuity was almost certain. The whole leadership team was on the threshold of taking several risks, in trying out a new strategy and a new business model. I recall feeling rather frightened, and torn between wanting to 'stand up' for my big picture preference, which felt familiar and potentially more generative, although I knew that this felt alien and nebulous for some members of the team.

I had a hunch that working online, and occasionally in hybrid settings, when one or two team members would be co-located in the office, might also have been adding to a sense of 'intangibility' about our conversations. I decided on an experiment: to invite those who were in the office to use the whiteboard to begin to record some of the ideas and specific details they had talked about. This seemed to animate and bring the team a little bit closer during the session. Together they resolved to use the next two sessions for 'scenario planning' (Schoemaker, 1995). Using the whiteboard work as a basis, they spent the remainder of our contracted sessions constructing 'flexible' possible scenarios for the future. This landed well with the whole team, who, without prompting, took up roles that seemed to suit their preferred styles. The Financial Director and Business Director 'held the pen' and joined the meetings together in-person, from the office, recording the detail of the conversations, as well as pressing their colleagues joining online, to provide supporting arguments for the alternate future scenarios they proposed. The team members online offered up some eight scenarios to begin with, and the team worked through each potential future scenario together, discussing and debating the likely risks associated with each, the likelihood of success or failure of each option given what they already knew or based on the best possible predictions. In the final scenario-planning session, I encouraged the team to throw in 'wild card' suggestions for barriers and unexpected events that might impact the outcome of the particular scenario being considered. And in the spirit of scenario-planning methodology, I suggested they whittle the number of scenarios down to four or five, rather than the original unwieldy eight. This technique proved to be very productive at a practical level. The team could grasp their future strategy by grounding it in what they already knew from their experience, at both a big picture level and a more granular level of detail. It helped the team co-operate on a tangible task, where the differing preferences, styles and knowledge of team members were of value. This seemed to strengthen their endeavour, enabling their diverse approaches to become an asset rather than a hinderance. At a psychological level, it enabled the team to meet their unknown future with some degree of agency, if not certainty, in a way that allowed them to operate with flexibility depending on the future contingencies at play.

Having offered case examples of relational work to keep the future figural in the present and with the art of scenario planning, we would like to elaborate on what we mean by a phenomenological approach. Since Husserl (1935) a phenomenological inquiry has been understood as a method of reflective attentiveness focusing on the individual's lived experience, i.e., a mindful attempt at full immersion into the phenomenon at hand. This could be attempted by means of, e.g., a silent reflection on a possible future and how this future can be achieved; or in the form of a walk through the organisation's premises soaking up observations and asking oneself how this sense-awareness might change in the future; or a 'transposing' exercise: imagine yourself five years from now, imagine your organisation as a menu in a restaurant, a prize winner on TV in five years, etc. Other examples of *phenomenological* practices that can help teams feel and embody future possibilities would be:

First, one notices together with the team what is figural here in this moment (this can be done by an open 'check in', just allowing everyone to associate on where they are right now and where the team is). Second, one notices where the primary task (assuming this is somehow to do with the future) is in the associations of the team: has it been mentioned, has it been given importance, how is it being experienced right now? Third, after taking enough time to explore the future in the here and now, one can move the team into a phenomenological inquiry.

7.5   Conclusion

As we have seen in this chapter, team coaching for the future can be extremely challenging. Both when the future is a topic of conversation in a rather cognitive or escapist way, or when the future of the team is not a topic when it should be. As we have shown, team coaches can help in a variety of ways. We believe it is important to help revealing the *future within the present*, the way the unknown future plays a role right now in the team, and then to work towards an *experienced future in the session*, either with the help of scenarios, simulations, or phenomenology. A good way to check the quality of the work for the future is by asking the team itself how successful we have been to (1) stay in contact with our realistic future challenges in the session itself; (2) make a difference to our sense of preparedness for the future; and (3) strengthen our own confidence and robustness in moving into the unknown future. In our view, preparing in this way will prepare the way for a more successful team.

Part C

Ways of stepping up as a relational team coach

Introduction to Part C

In this final part of the book, we introduce six different highly practical models that we ourselves will not do without in our own practice, as they guide us and inform the decisions we make with teams:

Chapter 8 covers Sills' contracting model with six different dimensions of contracting, which helps us to firm up and contain our work as team coaches. We bring future goals (the material of the previous chapter) into the here-and-now of team coaching, and show how we can achieve dynamic agreement around outcomes and ways of working with our team clients.

Chapter 9 introduces the Talik model for team effectiveness, with five areas that teams need to manage in their everyday existence. Contracting with the team on these areas can help to make explicit where team coaching needs to help, whether the area to focus on is e.g. mainly inside the team or directed towards the interface with its external environment.

Chapter 10 contains our model of team coaching interventions with an emphasis on being relationally present and observant before developing hypotheses and finally, and occasionally, guidance as a team coach. After developing presence and attunement, five core skills or interventions for team coaches are introduced.

Chapter 11 contains a model for working with top teams or teams under stress, where team coaches may feel that they are under additional pressure. The chapter introduces four key contributions to top teams that help a team coach to both balance and contain herself as she begins to make a positive impact on top leadership teams.

Chapter 12 provides help with the challenges and opportunities of diversity that every team faces. The chapter helps to grow awareness of the current, increasing tensions and to grow courage in speaking openly about issues of identity and exclusion.

Chapter 13 provides particular help with endings, an often overlooked or avoided part of team coaching. Endings provide specific challenges for team coaches which lead to a dual task and invite the skill of simultaneously attending to the impact of the ending and remaining fully present as a team coach.

DOI: 10.4324/9781003325789-11

Chapter 8

Contracting as a container for relational team coaching

Charlotte Sills and Ann Knights

8.1 Introduction

In earlier chapters colleagues have described in detail what we mean by relational team coaching. In brief, we hold that development, change and growth happen in relationship – with ourselves, with other humans, with our current situation and with the world. People in teams, trying to get something done, are involved in a complex web of relationships. When we, as team coaches, work with them, we are interested in drawing their attention to patterns of relating at multiple levels – including with us in our role as team coaches. We are dedicated to fostering connection and good quality relating within teams and between teams and their environment in the service of their purposeful effectiveness.

In team coaching work, contracting is essential to creating the dynamic container for all that juicy work to take place. By juicy we mean lively, real, emergent work, which responds to the relational complexity which is inevitably present in teams. The dynamic container for this kind of work must provide enough clarity (for example about intent, desired outcomes, ways of working) to make it safe and purposeful enough for those involved (whether as stakeholders, participants or coaches). It must also allow enough flexibility to respond to what emerges in the work to "let the main thing be the main thing" as Angus Igwe puts it (Sills, 2006). Contracting allows us to surface and make explicit expectations and roles in the work with the different stakeholders in the process. In the absence of appropriate contracting we are likely to encounter a great deal more uncertainty, confusion and potentially frustration, which can act as a severe distraction from the work.

What then can we draw on for insight to help us to form a 'good enough' contract for relational team coaching? As one-to-one coaches, we may well have drawn on good practice from the more developed and mature field of psychotherapy, or as organisational development consultants, from a sound understanding of the client "system". We are used as OD practitioners to discovering and relating to the system as part of contracting and working with the complex question, "who is the client?"

DOI: 10.4324/9781003325789-12

In this chapter we intend to offer a model or framework which draws together insights from the fields of psychotherapy, organisation development and social theory to support team coaches in shaping contracts that will provide clarity, containment and responsiveness for relational team coaching work.

8.2   Levels of contracting in team coaching

The model shown in 8.1 presents a number of levels or foci of contract along with a number of dimensions. Our colleague Brigid Proctor (2008) describes this idea through the metaphor of Russian frogs, conveying the idea that each of the levels of contract is a container for the next.

We offer a diagram of the model (Figure 8.1) as a map – necessarily simplified, but attempting to capture the nature of the team coach's task as they address the different aspects of the situation by shuttling between them as the landscape changes.

Figure 8.1 Levels of contracting in team coaching.

Source: Adapted from Sills, 2006.

Level 1: Our contract with the wider world

This refers to the contract that the team coach makes – privately and sometimes overtly – with their conscience, their values, their priorities in terms of the world, the planet and society. How often have coaches got deeply into working with an organisation, only to find that there is something about its nature or practices that makes them deeply uncomfortable and reluctant to be there? Taking the time to reflect on their purpose in life, the sort of work they are willing to do, any industries they would avoid, and practices that they would not condone can be an enriching activity. One of our colleagues, for example, speaks of "wearing my green heart on my sleeve", by which she means that her care for the environment is ever present in her practice and her choices about where to work. See Chapter 12 for an exploration by the authors of the contracts that they make about their intent around equity, diversity and inclusion in their work.

Reflecting on your own 'contract with the world'

Take a moment to reflect on what your values are – what work would you seek, what turn down? You may wish to use these prompts to articulate and refresh your proposition:

• What is your intent and purpose in working as a team coach?
• What are your underpinning philosophy and informing principles?
• How would you describe your approach, style and skillset?

When we have these conversations with team coaches, some name certain industries that they wouldn't work in. Others declare a commitment to social impact. Others refuse to work internally or virtually only in certain circumstances, and so on. And occasionally there is somebody who says they would never refuse any team coaching engagement because they believe that the client team would benefit from coaching and be a better influence in their context and the world.

One internal team coach speaks simply of "being in the service of the growth and development of teams and the individuals in them".

There is no right or wrong, simply a growing awareness for the coach of who they are as a practitioner and a person – an essential part of working relationally, as this forms the relational ground on which genuine presence can be founded.

Vignette – A reflection: In March 2020, the UK experienced the beginning of the first of four major lockdowns aimed at reducing the impact of the emerging Covid-19 pandemic. We, like many team coaches, received requests from organisations (directly or via umbrella organisations such as Ashridge) to support teams seeking to navigate the unprecedented turmoil engendered by the spread of the disease and responses to it.

We were faced with the requirement to make clear choices about how to use our time, what boundaries we might hold about how we would work (for example what work we would take on in a virtual format), what to say yes to and what we might argue was less important and could wait until later. We felt the need to be as clear as we could be about how we worked as team coaches and what teams could reasonably expect of us given our orientation and experience – for example would we and could we shift to facilitation or a more content based expert role if needed. We needed to consider what work we would be prepared to take on at a reduced rate or even pro-bono to support those in the so-called frontline, in health and social care, for example. All of these considerations, which might always be present somewhere in the field, became figural in a rather urgent way and we found ourselves becoming clear about what matters to us in our practice and in particular what is our intent in our team coaching work, and how can we help.

As lockdowns became less severe, even more choices (such as when will we work face to face) emerged. We notice that we offered to travel to some teams (for example those in hospital trusts who were in any case working face to face) and not to others (for example a government agency). After the last lockdown ended, I (Ann) found myself, like some of the teams I was working with, asking myself, what has become clear to me about what matters over the last two years, and how might I hold on to that clarity? For example, I had travelled extensively overseas with my work in the past, and post lock-downs a new focus on supporting teams in my locality emerged.

Level 2: Contracting in the organisation

Level 2 contracting is essentially concerned with establishing the broad parameters and the commercial/administrative agreement for the team coaching work. It is at this level that we are likely to incorporate the organisation into the contracting process. Later the organisation may fade more into the background as commercial considerations and agreements give way to team developmental ones. Often, the significant challenge for the team coach is to determine who, in the constellation that surrounds the work, represents the organisation and to manage/understand their expectations, including around their involvement.

Essentially, a request is made from one organisation (the one with the team in it) to another (the one with the team coach in it) for the delivery of a service (team coaching). This request can be highly formal initially, for example via a request for proposal to an organisation which hosts a number of team coaches to provide a team coach. Alternatively, it could be highly informal and personal, such as from a personal contact to an individual team coach that one knows well. The request can be highly complex with multiple stakeholders – for example a whole organisation intervention with 30 new teams following a restructure, offered via an RFP to a large consulting organisation – or it could be relatively simple with a single key stakeholder, where the team leader is commissioning the work.

The important point is that, one way or another, the team coach will have to make some agreements about the broad purpose of and the administrative/commercial arrangements for the work. Now the question comes, with whom? And the answer: it depends.

The "What"

We might think of these agreements as 'terms of reference' (to draw on the project management terminology). As such, this aspect of contracting typically includes the scope of the intervention: who will be involved directly and who in support of it and what their roles will be; how it might be evaluated and the shape of the intervention in terms of timing, place (including considerations about the possibilities and limitations of virtual work, for example), duration, frequency. It is also likely to include commercial factors such as payment and cancellation. The team coach may also need to make an explicit agreement about confidentiality, particularly if there is an organisational commissioner outside the team who has expectations about what the team coach will share with them about the content and progress of the work.

In one assignment for example, my (Ann) work with a leadership team was commissioned by the People Team and administered by a very knowledgeable L&D lead (Jane). Jane and I agreed commercial arrangements, carefully negotiated how Jane would hold appropriate responsibility for the quality of the intervention, whilst maintaining confidentiality around the actual content of the work.

The 'who and the how'

We would advocate some early 'constellating' of the players in the work. By constellating, we mean a map which represents the people involved and their relationship to each other. Drawing on the well-known three-cornered contract (English, 1975) we tend to experience three key perspectives at play at this level of contracting (and indeed beyond), constellations surrounding the coach, the team and the organisation respectively (see Figure 8.2).

English's work can be elaborated to capture some of the complexity in the potential multiplicity of stakeholders at any time in the process. Micholt (1992) developed the model further to constellate the different possible allegiances and loyalties, and to show relative distance in negotiations (see Figures 8.3 and 8.4)

Figure 8.5 shows a systemic way of mapping the key players in the contracting process. It includes the constellation of the **team coach** – which at a simple level might just be the team coach themselves – but might include an organisation which they are part of, or in some cases involve a co-coach. Then there is *the team* itself, which is likely to be represented by the team leader – but in some cases at the early stage of contracting is represented by the senior specialist – such as the HR lead,

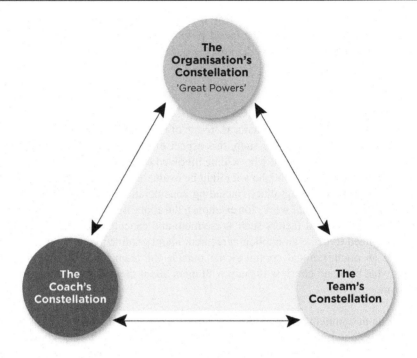

Figure 8.2 The three-cornered contract, based on English (1975).

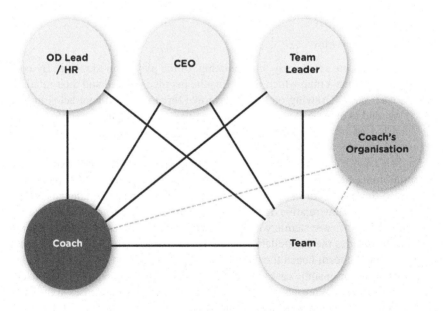

Figure 8.3 Stakeholder map, based on Micholt (1992).

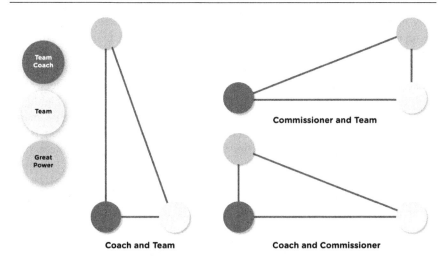

Figure 8.4 Relative psychological distance in contract negotiations.
Source: After Micholt, 1992.

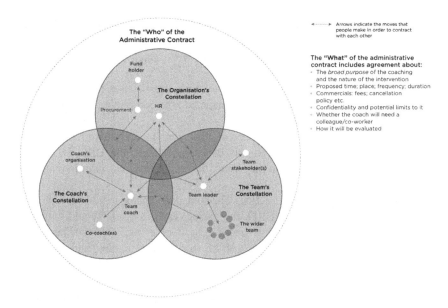

Figure 8.5 The contracting constellation.

who may or may not be a member of the team. In the background, stakeholders such as a Chair of the Board might also be present. Finally, there is the constellation of *the organisation*. These representatives might take a back seat role (leaving the team leader to take a lead so that the coach never has any contact with them) or may be at the forefront, acting as gatekeepers to the actual team until early commercial or administrative terms have been agreed. The arrows in the diagram show how different players connect with each other to contract. For example, we see that in this case the team coach will move into the intersection with the organisation to make agreements with an HR sponsor and procurement lead, into the intersection with the team to agree some broad scope with the team. The map also highlights some areas outside the coach's influence where players may be making agreements about the work. The team coach might construct their own map of the system based on their experience of early contracting work to bring some form to their contracting work.

Case vignette – Level 2 Contracting: Charlotte was contacted by the HRD of an FMCG business. A new CEO (Phil) and ops manager (Herah) had recently been appointed, and the HRD, who had a longstanding relationship with Charlotte, had persuaded the CEO to consider inviting in a team coach, principally to support the team in forming with its new members – and boss. A powerful sub text was some poor results for the business which had resulted in the departure of the previous CEO.

The HRD (Chris) knew Charlotte was very committed to working with underlying relational dynamics, and he hoped her style of direct, but 'care-full' challenge would work well with what he suspected was some underlying vulnerability in the team. Charlotte was aware from the outset that she would want to work with a co-coach, as was her usual preference, and particularly in this multidimensional case.

Already in these first few sentences, the three perspectives (or constellations) of the contract are beginning to take shape and the complexity of working with teams is becoming apparent.

Clearly the organisation is present. But who in particular represents the organisational commissioner in this case? Is it Chris, the HRD or Phil, the CEO – or both? And how do they enact their dual roles as commissioners and team members?

In the early stages of contracting, Charlotte participated in a series of increasingly formal calls with the HRD, the initial very informal "Would you be up for it?" call, a second "This is what it might involve" and a third "This is what I (Chris) see as the broad purpose of the work" conversation (with the caveat that Phil as CEO and team leader would ultimately shape the work). As the HRD, with his expertise in OD and Leadership Development, Chris also had a role as subject matter expert, and had some views on a potential broad shape for the intervention: a six-month intervention, with four team coaching sessions roughly every six weeks, at their offices. In this way Charlotte and Chris began to shape the broad scope of the work.

Charlotte was explicit about the dual role that Chris was playing as commissioner and client team member; engaging her as team coach on behalf of the organisation and at the same time being a member of the senior team – with his own experiences, his part in the dynamics and his concerns. In the more substantial conversation, Charlotte asked "How will we hold the boundary between your role as HRD – and organisational sponsor for the work – and your role as team member?". They talked about what conflicts might come up – and addressed them as they arose. For example, when Chris started to share his feelings about the new CEO and about the role he took up in the team, Charlotte was explicit about this falling into the team member role and asked how this impacted the "commissioner" one. Later, when Charlotte and her co-coach had short one to one relationship building conversations with each of the team members, Chris was included, and interestingly, a very different conversation emerged when Chris was speaking for himself (rather than representing the organisation) about what mattered for him personally in the working relationship with the coach. In English's 1975 original work about the three-cornered contract, she refers to the 'great power' in the apex of the triangle. In this case, there was a great deal of ambiguity in terms of Chris's power as commissioner. As a direct report of the team leader, he held much less positional power than the CEO, and he drew much more on informal sources of power such as his expertise, longevity in the business and network power (Raven & French, 1958).

Following the organisation-level conversation with Chris, Charlotte prepared a short proposal including estimated costs for the framework they had discussed and her usual terms of business. She also included her bio and that of her co-coach for Chris to share with Phil.

This was followed by an interesting 'parallel process' (which they reflected on later), with Charlotte going off to engage and brief her co-coach (Ann), and Chris briefing Phil. Chris contracted with Phil around an agreed framework (timings, location, format) and purpose for the work, "To form the new team and develop our effectiveness as a leadership team". Chris also helped Phil to explore the options for engaging the team in the contracting process.

In this case the administrative contract between coach and team was incorporated into the next level of contracting – contracting about the Development Contract with the team – perhaps because the administrative work had been covered with Chris in his dual role.

Level 3: The development contract with the team

This level involves the contracting with the team itself, where the process of emergent renegotiation becomes even more significant. One begins to name what, within the constraints of the previous two levels, the team wants to achieve through the coaching. Here we refer the reader to the Chapter 9 which describes engaging with the team, co-inquiring and identifying what needs to be the focus of the coaching. While this important work is going on, it can be helpful to make use of the Contracting Matrix (Sills, 2006, 2012) as a way of lightly holding the process and the focus as it unfolds and of helping the team to become aware of the different possibilities for development available to them. The contracting matrix (Figure 8.6) describes the coaching territory. There are two axes – the vertical indicates the range of possible goals, from the measurable and observable (what Berne (1966) called a 'hard' contract) to the intangible and subjective (what Berne called 'soft'). The horizontal axis refers to the degree of self-awareness and insight that the team and its members have about the issues facing them. This opens up four types of work that the coaching might involve.

The team might have:

- High degree of understanding and a clear articulation of desired outcome – "We know what we want and what we need to do" (For example: "We need to become much faster moving, collective in our decision making and commercial in our outlook") – a **Behavioural change** contract.
- Clarity about the desired goal, but no idea what is needed to achieve it – or indeed why they haven't already achieved it (For example, "We need much faster- moving, collaborative and commercial in our outlook but we seem constantly to be drawn to discussing operational issues in our silos. We don't know why that keeps happening or how two make the shift.?) – a **Clarifying** contract.
- No measurable goal in view but an awareness that all is not right and a desire to 'function better' in some way. (For example: "We are extremely stretched and want to be effective as a team – but are not sure what that looks like or what is stopping us being at our best. We like each other and get on fine ... but

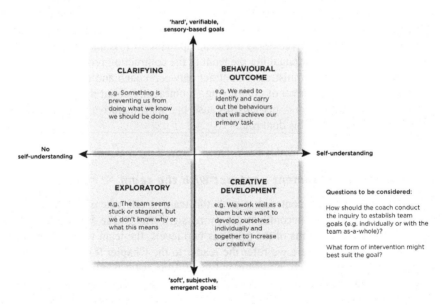

Figure 8.6 The contracting matrix as originated by Sills (2006).

something isn't working") – an **Exploratory** contract – exploring 'what is'. Here the words of C.S. Lewis – "How can we come face to face with the gods until we have faces" – seem to sum up that existential importance of knowing 'what is' or 'who the team is' before deciding exactly where they want to go.

- A clear understanding by the team of what they want, but it is not a tangible outcome. It is described for example as a sense of purpose or a need to 'pause on the landing and take in the view'. (For example: Post Brexit and post pandemic we want to take stock of what we have learned about our leadership and incorporate our learning into the way we operate as a leadership team) – a **Creative Development** contract. This type of contract is summed up in the words of a team who said, "What are we capable of?"

Case vignette continued. With our FMCG leadership team, Charlotte had initial conversations about the development contract in the terms of reference conversations with Chris (the HRD). But it was in the three-way conversation with Chris, Charlotte and Phil (the CEO) that she really started to explore what was the developmental purpose of the work. Phil was deeply concerned about the capability of his team to lead the organisation in an increasingly competitive market, with demanding shareholders and shifting requirements from customers. He recognised that this was a new team, split between the long serving members and the three newer members (him, the HRD and Ops Director). He felt that the first priority was to develop relationships in the team, so that the team could pull together to think about some of the options and difficult choices they needed to make about the strategic direction of the business. This had the feel of a clarifying contract, in that there were some tangible desired outcomes (forming connections in the newly formed team and between the subgroups – old hands and new people, becoming clear how they would work together on the pressing issues), but neither Phil, nor others in the team, were aware of how these relationships were currently working or what good would look like. This would be the work, to start with at least. There was also a tricky undertow; Phil's doubts about the capability of some of the team members. Charlotte (and her co-coach, Ann, who joined subsequent contracting conversations) explicitly asked Phil to reflect on how transparent he wanted to be about his doubts. Charlotte and Ann encouraged him not to share his thoughts with them (the coaches) – but rather to consider how he might share them with the team as part of the work. Phil agreed that he would speak to the team at their next meeting about the team coaching and his view on the focus for the work, and that conversations about his expectations of the team would form part of the team coaching work. Charlotte and Ann agreed that they would speak to each of the team members after that meeting to hear their perspectives on what needed attention in the team and to build their relationship with each of them in advance of the work with the team as whole. Charlotte and Ann were keen to avoid taking up a role of presenting back or summarising the contents of their calls with individual team members. Instead, they positioned the calls as relationship building and priming. Priming in this case meant helping each team member to surface their own thinking – so that they could bring it to the team in the first whole-team coaching session.

Level 4: Terms of Engagement with the team

Often running concurrently with Level 3 – sometimes preceding it – is the important agreement which we call 'Terms of Engagement'. The team makes an agreement about how they want to work together with each other and the team coach. Not everything can be decided at the start of course. Much will be tacitly agreed as the norms emerge during the work. However, it can be enormously useful to articulate the commitment to work together in a way that is likely to promote trust and openness, support honesty and build psychological safety. A key, and often challenging aspect of this level of contract is around confidentiality. How will the team coach treat what is shared with them "in confidence" both by the team leader and team members? What *will* the coach share with the team leader or sponsors outside the team and what not? It is helpful to carefully head off expectations about what will be shared and not shared, very explicitly, very early – and very frequently. For example, if the coach is having one to one conversations with team members, they might check out what they intend to share from the conversation and in what form.

We have found in recent years that our conversations with teams about virtual delivery of team coaching have become increasingly sophisticated. Teams have become more used to working in that format in their day-to-day work – and perversely, this has led to our needing to be firmer about what needs to be in place for relational virtual work in teams. Each coach will have their own way of holding the virtual space, in our case we emphasise the difference between the regular team meetings they might be used to having virtually – and team coaching work. Important considerations are; where possible participating on the same basis (i.e. one virtual – all virtual), allowing more – not less – time for the work and agreements about cameras, mute, virtual nods and listening.

Depending on the nature of the work, the individuals in the team might make a personal commitment to self-disclosure, offering and receiving feedback, using rules of 'emotional literacy' in their statements and so on. Having these good intentions put into words is not, of course, a guarantee of ideal communication in practice. However, it does provide both permission and encouragement to bring goodwill to their interactions.

Case vignette continued. Ann and Charlotte had resolved to treat all the team members the same, by including the CEO and HRD in the one-to-one conversations so that all had a chance to reflect on their own personal perspective, needs, preferences and even doubts. Following an upbeat email from the CEO to the whole team introducing them and the intended team coaching work, Ann and

Charlotte divided the eight-person team between them and personally invited them to a 40-minute call.

Charlotte and Ann each have their own style – and so they agreed a broad approach for the calls. They would include; A brief reiteration of the intent of the team coaching (which had already been shared in the CEO's email and in his conversation with them in their team meeting), followed by an invitation to the team member to explore; "What you would like us to know about you and your part of the business?"

"What are your hopes from this work?", and "What do you need from us and from your colleagues to do that work together?"

Ann and Charlotte were curious to hear the individual team members' perspectives on the team, the business and the situation, but they explicitly encouraged team members to bring these perspectives to the team coaching session themselves. In this way they modelled one of their core ways of working as coaches, which is to avoid being 'carriers of content'.

In her conversation with the Ops Director, Ann found it difficult to stem the flow of detailed, analytical information about the business and its problems. Charlotte had a similar experience with the Commercial Director. Whilst as coaches they expected, and appreciated, some insight into the business context for the work, they noted that both team members located their attention entirely outside themselves and the team. Both Ann and Charlotte found themselves reframing expectations of the coaching in those conversations. When Ann asked, "Do you need me to know all of this?", the Ops Director expressed his surprise as he had held some expectations of advisory work. Ann described the team coach role as helping the team to reflect on and improve their effectiveness and working relationship rather than providing advice on how to resolve their issues. He became rather enthusiastic about this and reflected "That is what we need. Actually, we are constantly running at breakneck speed. We need this process to slow us down".

This theme of a change of pace emerged in many of the conversations, as did wanting to speak candidly with each other, to be supportive but to be able to raise concerns and challenges and to be practical. There were also some differences. Some members of the team were feeling more vulnerable than others, and so there were different wants and needs around support and challenge. As these came up in the conversations, Ann and Charlotte encouraged the team members to bring their emerging sense of what they wanted from the coaches and from each other to the first session where they would contract in the team as a whole.

In the first session, following an introduction from the CEO, Charlotte held a space for the team to talk about their hopes for the work, and to firm up the development contract. Whilst the sense of urgency still remained, as did a focus on shoring up the business, gone was much of the manic energy which she had picked up in some of the one-to-ones. With the 'what' aspect of the work clarified and agreed. Charlotte invited each team member to express what was important to them about 'how' they (the team and the team coaches) might work together in the service of this intent. Unsurprisingly, in working out how they wanted to be in the coaching work, the team revealed a lot about how they wanted to be together as a leadership team. Charlotte and Ann helped the team to navigate the conversation by noting tensions and staying with differences (when they were tempted to gloss over them). This led to some interesting developments on the themes raised in the one-to-ones – such as the reality that they wanted to be candid with each other – but that this was an ideal – and that they would at least try to be open and notice when they felt they could not. They also somehow reconnected with their shared love of and belief in the organisation, and so said that they wanted this care to be part of their way of being together, but without letting go of the need to make some tough decisions within the team and in the wider business.

Level 5: The contract for the session

Here the contracting matrix can be particularly useful as it frames what the team might need in any particular session, depending on what is emerging. Relational team coaches develop their own style regarding sessional contracts. Some choose a structured start to the session, beginning with reporting and reflecting on any agreements made in the previous session and getting a clear outcome articulated for the day's session. This can help to build the psychological safety that a team needs. Other coaches have a more emergent and unstructured style, especially when the team is functioning well together, starting the session with "What is uppermost today" or "What do you want to think about today" or indeed simply "What is important today?" Any agreement can be a contract. We simply need to remember that this is what we agreed and be ready to revisit the agreement when the time is right. For example, a member of the team might say "I think we should start with looking at the disagreement that came up last time – it feels very important to clarify our team policy on that issue". The team coach checks that others seem in agreement. Then they hold that contract in mind and at a certain point is ready to return to it "You agreed that you wanted to visit the team decision about sales. Where are you with that? Do you have a sense of where you would like to go now?". Still other coaches may be in touch with the team, or the team leader, in advance about what needs attention in the upcoming session and make an offer of a process or approach for the session at the outset, which the team can shape.

The fundamental thing is that coaches don't make contracts simply because the rules say they should. We make contracts when *they are needed* – to help us focus, to clarify the direction, to contain the complexity.

Case vignette continued. With the FMCG team, the process for sessional contracting was a little different for each of the four sessions. In the first session,

Ann and Charlotte felt they needed to have a containing structure – including high-level design for the session, with estimated timings, which they shared in advance with the CEO and the HRD, who commented on and shaped it with them. They then offered this to the team on the day, who broadly accepted it. Ann and Charlotte had, in their "back pockets" ideas about some models (such as some of Charlotte's work (see e.g. 2021) on window of tolerance[1] in teams) that might be helpful and they contracted in the moment to bring to the group if it seemed they might be relevant. As the work progressed, Ann and Charlotte's conversations with the CEO shifted away from seeking his approval for a pre-determined structure for the session, to helping him to think through how he wanted to be in the session. As the team became used to the coaching environment, the coaches felt less requirement to provide the reassurance of structure in advance. However, regardless of the amount of planning or design they had done in advance, Ann and Charlotte always held it relatively lightly and asked the question "What needs attention in this session?" at the beginning of the session.

Level 6: Present moment

Present moment contracts are those small but important negotiations in an inter-action – such as "This sounds important – do you want to explore that as a team?" "I have some feedback – may I give it to you?" Permission is asked for a change of direction in the contract or for the introduction of something new. Both Ann and Charlotte are strong proponents of the Gestalt approach (see Chapter 2) and value working 'in the moment'. Therefore, they pay attention to what is emerging in the present, take an interest in the unexpected gesture, word or expression, invite experiments to explore something. All these may require a brief negotiation for a change of direction. We believe that it is useful not only to secure agreement for something different, but also it serves as a sort of signal that 'something new is coming' and an invitation to a person to engage their Adult ego state (as Berne (1961) would put it) to face the potentially disconcerting or, on the contrary, an invitation to play and experiment.

In our case vignette, there were countless instances of present moment contract-ing. There were relatively simple ones such as, "may we offer our reflections on what we're noticing at this point?" There were also many moments of checking whether the team wanted to explore something further; such as when they were skirting round power differentials in the team, and Charlotte asked "Would it be helpful to stay with and explore the issue of power in a different way?", before inviting the team into a power line up. Ann and Charlotte also modelled contracting in the present moment with each other, "Would it be ok if I stepped in here?", a practice which the team copied and brought into their own work together.

8.3   A special mention for contracting with the co-coach

This is an important, but often neglected, part of contracting. It is helpful to bear in mind that the same levels of contract that we hold for the team coaching work as a whole, are relevant to our working relationship with our co-coach. For example, we might choose to work with someone because we assume some alignment in our worldviews or sense of what matters. It might be helpful to check out those assumptions (Level 1). We will need to make explicit something about the broad purpose of the work – and expectations about time commitment, timing, how dates, etc. will be agreed – even how responsive we will be to communications (Level 2). We might want to be explicit about how we view the development contract – and indeed, whether both co-coaches feel able to support the development contract that is emerging (Level 3). An important aspect of contracting with a co-coach is around role expectations, both in terms of preparation, reflection and ongoing review as well as contact with the client, and also in the team coaching sessions themselves. With this in mind, it is often at the level of "Terms of Engagement" (Level 4) that much of the contracting work with a co-coach is needed. How will you support and complement each other in the sessions? What specific roles might you take up? How will you relate to each other in front of the team? How will you review your work together? This all comes to life in the moment-to-moment work with the team (Level 5), when co-coaches engage in live mini-contracting, "May I share an idea?", "Do you think a break would be a good idea?" or as our colleague Simon often says "I'm just going to check in with my colleague". The psychological contract between co-coaches can be particularly laden and is worthy of attention. It is easy, for example, to fall unknowingly into comfortable patterns in pairs that work together often, such as where one always takes a lead and the other defers. What is important is that co-coaches allow adequate time to attend to their own contracting at each level.

8.4   The psychological contract

No matter how assiduous the team coach is about bringing clarity to the aims and processes of the work, there will still be 'glitches' – and so should there be! It is in the glitches that the psychological contract and the underlying dynamics are revealed. As the unconscious processes reveal themselves, the coach and the team are able to begin to recognise and name whatever disturbing issues (see Chapters 5 and 6) might be derailing the team.

The term psychological contract was first used by Eric Berne (1966) to describe that unspoken and largely unconscious agreement that exists between people 'underneath' their overt contract. It is the implicit level of communication rather than explicit. It is considered a problem when it is at odds with the spoken agreement and undermines its intent. A simple, though not unusual example is that of the CEO who urges the team coach "Just treat me like one of the team. We are here to work and I want you to challenge me. I can't be doing with some namby-pamby coach who doesn't speak his mind". The coach agrees and shortly after the work starts delivers a straightforward challenge to the CEO about the way he is interrupting his team members. Too late he realises that the psychological contract was to treat the CEO with unfailing deference. The CEO's fragile sense of self required him to act tough but he was actually a very sensitive soul. Shortly thereafter the coach was dismissed.

As Michael Carroll puts it "Our psychological contracts often end up in us blaming others for things they do not see, and did not sign up to" (Carroll, 2015, p. 25). Since psychological contracts are essentially our internal agreements with others in our world, our role as coaches in working with the psychological contract is to be alive to their existence, and bring the unspoken terms of those contracts into the light.

> This was evident in a rather sticky moment in the early relationship with the FMCG client. In Ann's first meeting with the CEO, during which he had been quite critical of his team and she had offered some challenges which she felt had not landed well, he asked her "Do you think you are the right person to work with us?" Ann responded, honestly, "I am not sure. I have my doubts about it". This led to quite an initially difficult – but eventually very fruitful conversation. The unspoken expectation of the CEO was that both Ann and Charlotte should be at all times supremely competent and confident, to contain the anxiety he and his team felt. Whereas Ann had (perhaps rather naively) assumed that her honesty would be valued above all else. Luckily Ann survived this moment and this led to a very helpful conversation later about how feelings of doubt and incompetence in the face of the organisation's challenges were hidden in the team.

8.5   Conclusion: the process of contracting

The Levels of Contracting framework helps to answer the question, what do I need to address and be aware of in contracting as a team coach? The implication is that there are both enduring, relatively stable elements of the contract which provide the boundaries and containment for the work, *and* highly fluid, emergent aspects which are the subject of ongoing "negotiation". Our work as team coach is to hold this sense of emergence within a containing (but not rigid) frame. We may find ourselves returning to different levels throughout the whole engagement, as we meet and start to work together. With this in mind a key aspect of our work in contracting is to help the client team to be aware of what is emerging in their context and within and between us, and to explore how this impacts our work and our contract.

In this chapter we have attempted to elaborate the notion of contract as container and frame for relational work. We describe different levels of attention in the process of formal mutual agreement for the work, from the broadest philosophy down to the moment of human meeting. We describe how thoughtful attention to the nuances of agreement at each level of contracting not only helps to reveal the potentially derailing unspoken expectations and fantasies of participants but also creates a sort of safe container in which the unexpected, the unsettling and the dynamically evolving can emerge.

Note

1   Dan Siegal originally coined the term "Window of Tolerance" to refer to the optimum state of arousal or stimulation in which we are able to best function in everyday life. When we move out of this "zone", we can move into flight/flight or freeze responses – among others. The idea was developed further by Pat Ogden, particularly in the context of working with trauma.

Chapter 9

Discovering what needs attention

The inner and outer world of the team

Ann Knights and Alexandra Stubbings

One of the central challenges of leadership team coaching work, and of coaching and OD work in general, is determining what the work is. It is not uncommon, at the early contracting phase, for team members to articulate a problem or concern (or indeed many competing concerns!), framed as if 'the problem' is already clearly understood and the coaching work is about resolving it. Yet for the coach, the discovery of what is happening and what needs attention is an *on-going process*, at once part of the contracting, part of the inquiry and part of the core work. It demands that we maintain an open curiosity at all times to what is emerging through the dialogic interactions with and within the team, constantly discovering and refreshing our sense together of what *now* needs attention. As Gregory Bateson put it, we're asking: "what is the difference that will make the difference?" (Bateson, 1978).

In this chapter we intend to offer some orientation for the team coach working with this challenge. We set out a model based on Alexandra's (one of the authors) research, which has helped us to give some shape to the inquiry which we undertake with teams, as we contract and engage with them. We introduce the model and its underpinning theory and use our work with clients to show how we draw on it fluidly in our practice.

9.1 Introduction: a relational orientation

We situate the role of the coach in the 'relational turn' described in Chapter 1, with its attention to the mutable nature of meaning-making and the influence of context on group sense-making. This is a subjective, systemic space, distinguished from the more linear and objectivist view that assumes a singular reality out there to be discovered. It reflects most closely our own phenomenological experience as coaches, as we, alongside our clients, tussle with confusion, messiness and uncertainty. In practice it is the difference, as Gervase Bushe and Bob Marshak put it, between a diagnostic approach that assumes an objective truth to be diagnosed by the coach, and a dialogic approach, which holds that context-based, shifting, multiple realities exist which can only be discovered in dialogue

DOI: 10.4324/9781003325789-13

(Bushe and Marshak, 2015). The former lends itself to analytical instruments often including quantitative assessments, implemented by the team coach, with data collated by or for the coach to present back in some way to the team. These instruments, particularly those which have a 360-degree element involving the team's stakeholders, can be time efficient and illuminating, but they are like all diagnostic instruments, partial in nature, with their focus on a limited set of pre-determined qualities, and a shortcut, cutting out the time-consuming, challenging and relational aspects of the team's discovering these things for themselves in relationship with each other, their colleagues and their stakeholders. In some instances, diagnostics can even be a form of defence, a guard against the dis-comfort of ambiguity perhaps, against confrontation with peers, or even just of entering the unfamiliar territory of affect and emotional ground. At the very least a request for 'objective' data may signify a belief in an a priori universal standard of 'good' team effectiveness, a set of criteria against which team members can compare themselves in order to 'start the work'. From our dialogic and subjective orientation however, we hold that no such common standard is possible and gen-erally find that such requests arise from a team being concerned too early with 'how well are we doing?' If possible, we would rather encourage a team, in the early stages of contracting, not to dive into using diagnostics too soon, but to stay with noticing, as they work in a constantly shifting and emerging relationship with each other, their wider organisation and environment, how they are continu-ally reshaping what 'good' looks like for them, and how 'the work' – what needs attention – is likewise constantly in flux.

9.2   How then do we determine what or where the work is in team coaching?

So, in such a dynamic and co-created environment, how can team coaches deter-mine where the work is? Posing the question "What is the focus of the team coach-ing work?" will, in itself, unearth an abundance of material for a team to reflect on. The various responses from individual team members can quickly reveal prefer-ences for more or less tangibility, action orientation, reflexivity, intuition and so on. But perhaps more importantly, the question points to the likelihood that the most substantive, consequential work is not what is first presented. This realisation can be quite uncomfortable for team members, especially for those who believe they've already done the hard graft of deciding what their problem is before the coach arrives and perhaps only submitted to coaching to 'fix the problem'!

The sense of making a retrograde step can present the first notable challenge for the coach, maybe the first significant moment of *re*contracting, when in concert with the team, we start to loosen the ground upon which 'the work' is located. We may find we are disrupting an entrenched mental model, moving from the familiar 'problem to fix' (possibly through some quick behavioural or governance adjust-ments), to 'collaborative exploration', a richer co-inquiry into 'what is' that lets go of easy answers and simple solutions.

Not only might this feel more laborious and challenging, not every team is confident or prepared to make a rapid switch into this less structured way of working. Understandably so. It might be the water we swim in as coaches, but for executives or board members used to tight task-oriented agendas, it can be disorienting, anxiety-provoking even. We notice this particularly in organisations and cultures where linear delivery models and cultures dominate. The need for certainty and a sequential, predictable plan, even for a social process like coaching, can be very high.

Case vignette: Team coaching in an engineering environment (Part 1)
This was very much in evidence as we started work with the leadership team of one engineering business. Their meetings had become rigid, tightly controlled events, a series of updates and governance procedures that felt more at home in a courtroom than a boardroom. The need to predict outcomes in the room led to increasing politicking outside and careful choreographing of the meetings themselves. Ironically, trust between team members was high at a personal level and they would participate in frank debate in informal settings, but the moment the team entered the boardroom and took up their roles, their capacity for free-ranging exploration shut down. Novelty, innovation, complex problem-solving, employee engagement, were all suffering as a result of this high need for control.

In our early contracting, as we conducted a series of initial one-to-one conversations and began to organise the first 'offsite', we developed a vivid sense of how deep this ran. The team members approached us with requests for detailed agendas and pre-reading; they attempted to influence our own sense-making through 'back-channel' communications.

The first session together was awkward. We invited the group to attend to the discomfort of messiness and not knowing whilst we loosely 'held the space' for dialogue. Our reflective way of working, bringing in-the-moment curiosity to micro-moments of behaviour, encouraging noticing in the here-and-now, was initially interpreted as being unpolished and ill-prepared; beliefs about the role of 'expert' as all-knowing advisor were projected onto us. On the other hand, this was valuable material to work with. We created simple processes which helped the team to appreciate the time to be together differently – such as walking in nature and talking together in more reflective and intimate ways. They could then begin to detach from the need for us (or them) to 'know'. They could start to investigate how this team culture had emerged and how it was influencing the wider organisation.

Encounters like this, and many other less intense examples, remind us how unfamiliar the milieu of coaching can be and the importance of bringing *just enough* structure to a team so that they can situate themselves in a field of inquiry, and *just enough* predictable process to sustain a sense of direction and momentum. Getting this balance right can enable the team to focus more on being present and curious to what is arising between them.

9.3   Introducing the Talik Model

To help in providing this containing structure, we have come to draw on a theory of relational change, the 'Talik model', as a map and process. We us this mostly implicitly, sometimes explicitly to help to orient ourselves and the team, as we explore 'what matters' with them.

---

tä·lik (n.)

(i)   Geological feature. Area of perpetually unfrozen ground surrounded by permafrost.
(ii) Organisation kept relevant and resilient through purpose-led and adaptive practices.

The Talik Model originated from Alexandra's doctoral research into cultural change for sustainability in the early 2010s, an inquiry into the leadership challenges of developing sustainable enterprises and, in particular, the importance of congruence between a company's expressed pro-social and environmental values and the actions that leaders took (Stubbings & Ceasar, 2012).

Looking to create a change methodology fit for the complex nature of values-driven transformation, the research drew together a number of multi-disciplinary threads: from the ecological – how change takes place dynamically in natural systems as organisms interact with their environment (Capra, 2004; Gould, 2007) – through complexity theory, such as with Ralph Stacey's emphasis on organisations as patterns of relating in the living present (Stacey, 2003), to Social Identity Theory, asserting how identity is created and transformed in relationship (Mead, 1967; Dalal, 1998). Alexandra's inquiry with a number of large organisations highlighted just how important social identity is in transformational change. This perspective reveals how difficult it is to change behaviour if we hold onto fixed beliefs about 'who we are together here'.

Social identity theory maintains that our sense of self, whether as individual, group or organisation, is fluid, malleable and contextual. It is continually influenced by and influencing the context and the many relationships we have, making aspects of self more or less prominent in any moment. This framing of self – inherently relational, embedded in webs of relationship, influenced by context and attentive to multiple 'levels' of identity – is entirely congruent with the relational turn in coaching.

The Talik model is grounded in the belief that our sense of who we are – as individuals, teams, companies – is undergoing a continual process of negotiation as we express some aspect of ourselves to others and some version of that is reflected back. We act into that information through our internal thinking processes and micro practices (little moment by moment actions) which become embedded into our routines and habits of behaviour, over time the emerging social identity becomes encoded in our day-to-day processes and ways of organising ourselves.

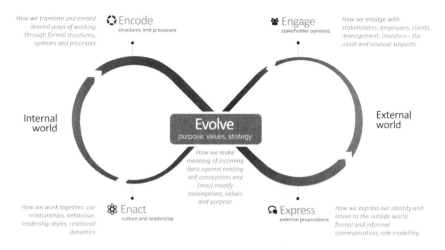

Figure 9.1 The Talik team coaching model.

On a team or organisational level, these patterns of habits and beliefs, with the structures and systems that support them, become 'the way we do things around here' (McLean, 2013), in other words, the prevailing culture. The model integrates these ideas into a simplified systemic framework for teams to explore what they currently attend to and what they do not. It enables a team to explore how change happens as a process of interaction with environment, generating fresh meaning-making and embedding new norms.

Alexandra's research, which chimed with Ann's experience of organisational change, reinforced and illuminated how change in human systems is a systemic and relational phenomenon, emergent and contested, subject to changes in external context and internal power relationships, thus pointing to the central need for inquiry, conversation and joint sense-making to inform action. Although first developed with organisational change in mind, the model has proved to be applicable across a number of scales and scenarios, so the question is only where the boundary around the group of interest is drawn.

The model is depicted simply as two interacting feedback loops, one focused on the team's interaction with its external environment, the second focused internally. Congruity across both 'worlds' can be imagined as a figure of eight flowing between the external and internal, mediated through processes of sense-making (see Figure 9.1).

9.4 Applying the Talik Model

In our coaching work we often use the model as a means to explore what needs attention in the team, both in the early stages of the work, where we are framing the focus of the team coaching and throughout as the team inquires into its effectiveness. The five 'E's in the model describe areas of focus which flow naturally from one to another, so when the team coach makes this explicit it is possible for the team to notice and make choices about what needs their attention at any one time. (We offer more detail about each of the 'E's and how they inter-relate below.) In an early inquiry session, for example, the team coach can invite the team to reflect on "Where on the model does the team currently place its energy and attention", "How are we constructing what the work is?" or "What sense do we make of the internal workings of the team in relationship to its context and stakeholders?".

In practical terms the team coach can use the model with the team, implicitly or explicitly, in contracting and throughout, as a way of thinking about:

- What is the team attending to?
- How effective are we in looking at these different areas as a team?
- What might need to shift and change?

As a systems model that incorporates both social processes of relating (e.g., Enacting leadership) as well as 'hard systems' (e.g. Encoding governance), the team can view themselves in an integrated way within their context, noticing how it both creates and is constrained by its organisational structures.

Our hypothesis is that, in order to be effective, the leadership team will need at some point to attend to all of these areas of focus and a well-functioning team will naturally shift between them. However, teams can get stuck in fixed patterns of relating internally and externally and in a set of assumptions which impede their creative responsiveness and leadership. The team coach can support the team in becoming more aware of what is, what the team is attending to and how, using the model to highlight areas of interest rather than, as we outlined above, rushing to assessment and diagnostics.

Example continued: Team coaching in an engineering environment (Part 2)
Introducing the model to the engineering leadership team in an early group session enabled us to do a number of things. First, we were able to normalise and address their experience of feeling lost by providing a framework in which they could situate themselves ("We default to 'Encode' as our place of safety, focusing on governance and policies to manage behaviour".) Second, they could identify where the urgent work was ("we need to focus on Evolve, our sense-making and reframing"). Third, we could frame their responsibilities as an executive team relationally, focusing on the intended and unintended consequences of their pronouncements, who they engage with and how. Fourth, we could visualise the systemic nature of their roles in context ("when we pull a thread here, it creates puckering over there") surfacing opportunities for new meaning-making and action options that would follow.

The team coach may choose to use the model implicitly as a mental map for their own reflection, supporting their navigation through the complex meanderings of a coaching assignment. Alternatively, the coach can introduce the model to the team early on in the client relationship as described in the engineering team example above, or later as a means to highlight stuck patterns of meaning-making, for instance how over-emphasis in one domain (e.g. Encode – governance, procedures) can be detrimental to others (e.g. Enact – congruent honest interaction).

Deciding whether, when and how to introduce a model, this one or any, is a matter of careful discernment for a team coach and we are keen to offer a "health warning" for using any model or framework, implicitly or explicitly. In our practice we aim to meet teams with open minds about what might come up. We either have the model in our 'back pockets' or offer it lightly as a potential framing if it seems relevant to what they bring. We certainly don't march in brandishing our model as *the* map which will illuminate their experience. With this in mind, we invite you to explore the Talik as one possible way of helping you and a team coaching client to discover what needs their attention.

Exploring the model: the 5 'Es' in detail

The first thing to note is that you can start anywhere on the model, and teams do. We find it interesting to notice what we hear about first and where the team places the emphasis as we begin our relationship. This is very often an early source of insight, into say, beliefs about leadership and change, cultural norms and unquestioned assumptions.

That said, we've found many teams, particularly those who come to coaching with an interest in understanding their effectiveness as a leadership team (a 'Creative Development' contract in Chapter 8), find a logical starting point in 'Engaging' then circulating through the model as a figure-of-eight to Evolve, Enact, Encode and back through Evolve to Express. This follows the change process described above and draws attention to the questions of congruity and alignment around the system.

Often just talking through the Talik itself is enough for a group to begin to generate their own questions. We have also developed a set of generic questions that can help a team shape their inquiry (see Figure 9.2).

With a systemic and relational orientation in mind, at each stage the coach can offer a 'reframe' to habitual assumptions, to help shift the team to broaden and deepen their scope of inquiry. Examples of reframes are offered in each of the five 'Es' below.

Engage

All leadership teams are in relationship with their contexts, within and outside the organisation. Information from stakeholders is often a source of disturbance and disequilibrium and a stimulus for change. In turn, employees, service users, customers, citizens, volunteers, suppliers, opinion formers and so on all have their own experience of the team, directly or via the organisation's activities.

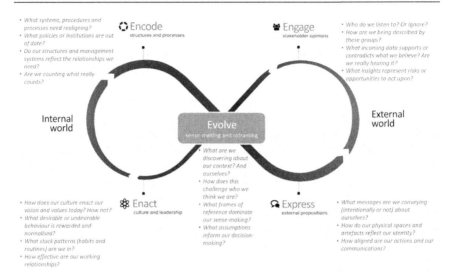

Figure 9.2 The Talik team coaching model with specific questions for the team we are working with.

With this in mind, how the team engages with these groups and how they in turn interpret those impressions can have profound consequences. For example, the team can become very inward looking and introspective, with only scant or occasional contact with stakeholders. They may, through choice or lack of awareness, habitually screen out certain groups, fail to hear what message they are trying to convey. Conversely, they may be excessively 'porous', giving disproportionate weight to external sources and getting caught up in reacting to conflicting opinions and demands.

The coach might ask: "As a team how do you engage with people outside your team? With stakeholders, with employees, the non-executive Board, investors, regulators, with customers, patients, volunteers, campaigners, lobby groups and so on? Who are the usual and unusual suspects? What moves are you making to engage those people and what sources do you, and could you, listen to more? What do you, or could you, learn from those sources? Who and what do you ignore or overlook?"

Here the coach can offer the reframe: *and who are we to these people?* Who do they need us or want us to be? This can be a significant 'empathetic turn' for a team, shifting perspective from the habitual 'inside-out, us-them' perspective to an 'outside-in, them-us' point of view. It can help the team and coach to deepen their inquiry into what the work is by giving the team insight into the quality of relationships and vital sources of information and influence from outside the team boundary, encouraging them to go exploring, asking new questions of others, as well as surfacing uncontested assumptions about existing relationships and sources.

Evolve

The increased awareness of how the team engages with their external environment leads naturally towards a process of reflection as they respond to new incoming information, moving into deeper inquiry into their own values, beliefs, biases and habitual framings. This is where self-conceptions, unquestioned beliefs about the team's identity, come to the fore and can be examined. At the heart of the Talik model, Evolve is where reflection on novel sources of information, 'news of difference' (McLean, 2013) takes place; where the creation of new meaning, new symbols, has both the capacity to generate new behaviour internally in the team as well as new expressions outward of what matters now. The focus here is not purely meaning-making within the existing paradigm but challenging the paradigm, breaking the construct such that new meaning can emerge. The role of the team coach here is to support the reflective process, drawing attention to values and beliefs that are out of awareness, asking questions that help the team scrutinise their frames, 'holding' the team with encouragement to stay with any discomfort that arises from the uncertainty, messiness and personal challenge of exploring deeply held beliefs.

This space became known as 'Evolve' for a couple of reasons. First, it reflects the original research into processes of change in nature, how evolution happens through contact with external environment and internal response, through non-linear processes of punctuated equilibrium (Gould, 2007). This theory states that rather than being an ongoing continuous process as Darwin imagined (1859), evolution happens through spurts of rapid change amidst periods of stasis in which little happens (Gould, 2007). What's more, organisms don't change purely as a reaction to their environment, but *with it*, changing their ecological systems as they themselves change. The recent discovery, for instance, that trees contribute to rainfall through 'seeding' aerosols that allow water droplets and thus clouds to form is a perfect example of this (Pöhlker et al., 2012). Using 'Evolve' here is a reminder of our embodied nature as human beings and draws attention to the 'whole person'. Secondly it is used metaphorically to describe the often subtle but substantive shifts in sense-making and reframing that lead to adaptation, and to emphasise what it is not, 'big bang', planned change.

With this in mind, the team coach can support inquiry into the team's processes of dialogue and co-inquiry: the patterns of dialogic turn-taking, quality of listening, preferences for participation, capacity to stay with ambiguity as the conversation unfolds. Questions here can include: what assumptions/beliefs/biases predominate in our meaning-making? What discursive patterns are visible? Which open up or close down dialogue? How is difference engaged with? Who holds responsibility for articulating difference?

Case vignette continued. Team coaching in an engineering environment (Part 3)

For the engineering leadership team this challenge came about with the realisation that their efforts to control their environment might be having the opposite effect. By attending to subtle signals coming from interactions with their people (Engage) and sharing these together, stories began to emerge of how they themselves were being managed by their direct reports. It became apparent that the risks arising from not being included in difficult debates about projects and investment needs were greater than the risk of losing control of the discussion. From here a new conversation about what the executives' role in the business could and should be – provocateurs, champions, coaches(!) – and a new set of self-identity labels for the team began to emerge.

As the coach notices the team's awareness of these norms of relating strengthen, they can draw the team's attention to the habitual frames that inform their sense-making. It is not uncommon for teams to default to one or two common frames like risk, finance or performance. Often individuals 'hold the frame' on behalf of the team and over-emphasis on one or two leads to partial meaning-making, closing down the field for solution finding and decision-making.

The team coach can invite the team to apply alternative frames, not unlike an ophthalmologist applying different spectacle lenses, to widen the discursive space and bring new content into focus. Reframes can be any that the team can think of, but could include culture, effectiveness, agility, social and environmental responsibility, purpose. The coach's role here is not to suggest alternatives, but to hold the team to generating their own.

The evolve space at the heart of the Talik can act like a prism, reflecting, refracting, magnifying tropes and themes, opening them up to scrutiny. This space can be revelatory for teams as they become conscious of their patterns and what is habitually out-of-awareness. As such, Evolve can feel, for the team and the coach, like this is the 'real work' – challenging, robust, attentive to the inner life of the team, messy.

Enact

Here we are moving into the internal world of the team.

In our experience, this is another potential starting point for the team coaching conversation. We are often approached by teams who are looking to improve team dynamics and relationships. When this is the case, we might invite them to take a step back into some of the Evolve work of sense making, or even further back to Engage, to understand what in their external world is influencing or impacting them. The process of sense making helps the team to become clearer about what behaviour, attitudes, norms they want to shift, and what changes to ways of working or experiments that they might want to make to try out alternatives ways of relating to each other.

The team coach might support an inquiry with the team into the behavioural patterns in their relationships. What desirable and undesirable behaviour do they have that is rewarded and normalised and what stuck patterns they are in? More broadly, what is the culture and the leadership culture that the team is creating and sustaining through their actions? Is it congruent with the espoused values and vision?

The role of the coach here is to encourage the team to stay with trying things out and to be open to emerging new norms, behaviour and relational dynamics at a time when there can be a strong pull towards quickly nailing them down and codifying them. The urge for a team charter, for instance, can reflect a reasonable desire to encode unfamiliar behaviour in tangible terms and to demonstrate group consensus. But it can also be a defence against staying with the uncertain and strange, a way of closing down real contact with each other and experimenting with uncomfortable forms of interaction. It can even be a way to delay changes in behaviour – by writing down how the team members *will* act in future meetings, they avoid making adjustments here and now.

Here the coach may maintain a deliberate focus on co-inquiry at this stage, noticing the ebb and flow of comfort with experimentation and applying mini-reflective cycles to experiments. The aim is to keep the team alive to notable shifts in their relating and to points of stuckness they may wish to address. Schön's reflection before action, reflection in action, reflection after action' provides a useful frame here (Schön, 2017).

Encode

Sooner or later, it will likely become apparent that certain systems, processes, structures no longer align with a team's (new) preferred ways of working. New or adjusted policies and management systems may be needed to reflect the new norms and maintain congruity throughout the system. Questions like: "Are we counting what really counts?" arise here, as well as conversely, "What unwanted behaviour are we sustaining by attending to the wrong indicators?"

For the team items of interest may include meeting structures and agendas, governance, processes for working with non-execs and decision-making processes. Adjustments may be supported by the coach or take place outside the coaching relationship.

Because this can be more familiar territory for teams there is the risk of reverting to old ways of operating, the very systems they are trying to adjust acting as a powerful attractor back to comfortable norms. The reframe here then is summed up in the question: "How do we undertake this change in a way that reflects our preferred norms and behaviour?" For instance, if 'taking more visible collective responsibility' is the concern, how might they author their communications about this?

The team, with support from the coach, can focus on holding themselves honest to their preferred norms and values.

Returning back through Evolve

This point in the process is concerned with turning attention outward again and asking what aspects of the team's emerging identity, value proposition, leadership story they wish to express to the outside world, what version of themselves they want to make visible. The coach can offer generic questions to understand what this moment means.

This second pass through Evolve is an opportunity to pause. It invites the team to reflect on: Where have they have come from and what matters now? Where have their efforts to adopt new relational habits and encode them into their systems been more or less successful compared to their intent? What are they learning about what is possible in their context?

The reframe at this point is simply about the pause – taking the opportunity to reflect, acknowledge progress and learning. In our coaching practice, we tend to assert a more appreciative focus here, shifting away from tendencies to pick over what could have gone better, ascribing blame and so on, to focus more positively on continuing to emphasise and embed new norms. This is somewhat dependent on the group however and, as with all coaching interventions, is highly contextual.

Case vignette (continued): Team coaching in an engineering environment (Part 4)

Having spent some months weaving back and forth between deeper inquiry with their people and stakeholders to understand the impacts of their controlling behaviour (Engage) and making sense of this whilst also paying attention to their dynamics of meaning-making (Evolve), the engineering leadership team chose to experiment in a number of small ways with how they turned up to team meetings. Allocating time for structured and non-structured discussion in advance, giving responsibility to team members to 'play back' what they noticed of group behaviour, inviting in non-team members to participate in innovation discussions, all allowed more freedom to try out different ways of being in a relatively contained environment. As new behavioural norms developed and sustained, they become codified into new styles of agenda-setting with more time allowed for 'messy' expression and creative thinking. Referring back to the model, members of the team noted how subtly their language was becoming more expressive with their people, a reflection of a desire to be seen as more human and authentic, rather than relying on what they had called robotic 'corporate speak'.

Express

In this mode, the team attend to their methods and styles of external communication, how they as a team express their identity and intent.

Questions the coach can help the team with here include: "How are we now articulating our purpose and to whom? What forms of formal and informal communication, role-modelling, presentation are consistent with the values, beliefs, norms being espoused?"

Express is not only about what is stated explicitly, but also what is inferred and unintentional. It is not only the strategy pronouncements, town halls and all staff communiques, but also the impromptu 'elevator chats', even clothes, offices and cars. What adjustments might be needed here?

For Alexandra's research with organisations' intent on building sustainable enterprises, this was their most frequent mistake and the point of greatest incongruity, as their urge to express their positive green credentials ran ahead of their capacity to enact and encode new procedures. It's what has become known in the field as 'greenwash'.

For teams of any type to avoid such accusations requires vigilance and the transparency and integrity referred to earlier. Plus, not everything that is expressed may be in the team's gift to adjust and this needs honest appraisal. Not surprisingly, such a question can set off another loop around the Talik, as the team ask themselves who now they need to engage with and how.

Talik lite

It may not always be appropriate or needed to use the model in depth. In some cases, we use it as part of early Level 3 contracting with the team (see Chapter 8) to explore the focus of the work. For example, we are often given an overarching brief in our Level 2 contracting (with the organisation) about the broad purpose of the work of attending to the team's effectiveness. In such a case we might invite the team to think about where they as a leadership team would like to start, put their energy, focus their attention in terms of developing their effectiveness. What, we ask, is going to be the difference that makes a difference? They might do a mini, in the moment assessment with the 3 questions in the early part of the chapter (What is the team attending to? How effective are we in looking at these different areas as a team? What might need to shift and change?).

At other times we have found part way through a series of team coaching sessions something comes up, which reveals a block or lack of attention to one of the foci.

For example, we noticed that a healthcare leadership team we were working with had become stuck in an internal loop of working to improve relationships within the team (which were actually pretty good) and seeking to *encode* rules about the relationships (such as what certain meetings might cover and individual's roles in them) in formal governance processes. This had its place, but what was missing was attention to the external arc, a real engagement with the people in the wider system that supported them in delivering and which they served. They instinctively felt the struggles of the wider organisation and system and felt that something different was needed from them, but without explicitly *engaging* with their external stakeholders they could only guess what that was.

Case vignette: Applying the 5 E's of the Talik in practice

We worked with a corporate function team in a public sector organisation who, in the post-lockdown era of increased virtual working, came to coaching with a desire to articulate a story about their brand or 'who we are as a team' to the wider organisation and stakeholder community. Such a presenting intent can belie any number of conscious and less conscious concerns: about shared identity (who are we together?), collective endeavour and role (what is our purpose?), organisational value added (what is our contribution?) and what it means to be a team (what can we do together that can't be achieved alone?). In this case, the team had spent little time addressing such questions virtually over the preceding two years and, with new members joining, had never met in their current configuration in person.

Over the course of two full day sessions in consecutive weeks, we offered the Talik model as a way to frame a dialogue about their relationship to their external stakeholders, which could then open up themes of identity, purpose and values within the team. As is often the case, as the dialogue progressed, it appeared that the team members had multiple interpretations of what constitutes 'team', and notably divergent values and even worldviews that were leading to conflicting opinions about what they fundamentally exist to do.

Their presenting questions were mostly inside-out focused: what do we want to say about ourselves? Who are we speaking to? What are we offering? These felt like questions self-definition typical of the Express space. We drew attention to the external feedback loop, inviting a reframe from a primarily 'inside-out' to an 'outside-in perspective': We asked "what do, and what do you want, your people, your external stakeholders, your senior leaders, to say, feel, believe about you? What stories do you hope they might tell? What is the relationship you want to have?" and "What do they think of you? And how do you know?"

The presenting 'rebrand' this team were intending was from 'service provider' to 'trusted advisor', meaning a shift from being a passive responder to incoming requests to an active, strategic partner to the organisation. Viewed through a systemic and relational lens, we asked 'how does your current way of operating serve your 'clients'?', framing this question not only in practical terms of 'what do you deliver for them?', but in psychological terms of 'what needs are you meeting?' In this case, the team believed they were meeting a current need of offering 'unquestioning support' and being 'unproblematic problem-solvers', doing precisely what was asked of them when it was asked, a paragon of service, or 'a doormat' as one team member said.

In the second team coaching session, as the dialogue progressed, the team challenged each other honestly about how much influence they could truly hope to have in framing their identity, how far they could hope to shift the narrative given the varied perceptions held across a diverse constellation of stakeholders.

Reflecting on their relationships to others, and 'treatment at their hands', not surprisingly raised the emotional temperature significantly in the room.

We feared that the team might get stuck in retelling familiar stories of demeaning experiences, recalling moments of hurt and shame. Whilst some sense-making to reframe such recollections can be healing, getting stuck in a game of 'ain't it awful' (Berne, 1964)) generally isn't. Our role as coaches here was to return to that fundamental query: is this conversation useful? Is it moving the team forward?

Throughout the process, but here particularly, our role was to hold the space for messy, ambiguous dialogue long enough for something novel to emerge in their thinking. We found, as we very often find, that judging when to intervene, when to invite the group to interrupt their conversation and reflect on their process, was a tricky and subjective process for us. And we were grateful that we were a pair so that we could check and challenge our assumptions about what the group needed from us.

Ultimately this conversation, reflecting on what stakeholders think of the team, revealed an opportunity for some useful co-inquiry with key individuals, leading to the team designing a short process of Appreciative Inquiry and planning to strengthen relationships with some less familiar but important leaders.

It also brought us to the centre of the Talik, turning attention to how the team were sense-making together and how they were now framing their own role and purpose.

For ourselves as coaches, the Talik can provide a useful map to locate where a conversation is, and we can point to this with clients as a way to normalise the process they are in and sometimes to nudge the conversation forward.

When we did intervene, we asked the team what conversation they felt they were having and what were some of the dominant frames informing it. They noted a strong risk frame – the risks of staying as they are versus the risks of changing; also, a strong control frame – who has authority to determine their objectives and moreover, how they realise them; and a power frame – the tendency to think of power in zero-sum terms.

We paused again at this point. Is this 'where the work is'? Differences of opinion in the team revealed how for some their longer tenure or more prominent role was a source of power and influence for them. Hardly uncommon in any team, but an important acknowledgement for this one – status and capacity to act are not equally distributed, and the implications are that attempts to build a 'trusted advisor' brand would thus be easier for some than others. This was another emotive conversation that some engaged in more readily than others, offering a reminder that we, Ann and Alexandra, also have different levels of comfort with conflict. One of the benefits of coaching in a pair is holding each other as well as the group when the dialogue gets heated.

After further discussion and a break, the energy shifted towards action and a more positive tone. Checking in that this was a move that all were ready to make, we turned to the Enact space in the Talik. Being acutely aware of the difference in power and influence within the team, the move to action at this point focused on how team members could support and champion each other, particularly in client interactions, to strengthen personal brands and subtly start to act into more 'consultative' ways of working – inquiring more, anticipating needs, offering strategic insight.

Too early to think about Encoding, the team decided to introduce regular action learning style sessions into their meeting calendars, to develop their individual and shared capability as internal consultants, and to use the stakeholder inquiry they had already agreed as a subtle means to start to signal their desire for a more strategic relationship.

9.5   Conclusion

In this chapter we have explored use of the Talik model for discovering what and where the work is for coaching at any time in the on-going practice of a coaching relationship. To paraphrase the statistician George Box, "all models are wrong, some are useful". In tricky circumstances, any map or framework can help alleviate anxiety, for coach as well as team. We have found the Talik model useful in providing an orientating framework to respond to the question "What needs attention?", one which considers the dynamic interaction between the inner and outer worlds of the team. The model can also help to illuminate aspects of team dynamics that might otherwise stay out of awareness. We hope that in using the Talik model as and when we do, that we are finding the right balance between the felt need for order and certainty that diagnostic approaches provide and the more emergent, systemic insights that a fully dialogic approach affords. Our intention in mindfully walking this line is to meet our clients where they are and open up a wider rich territory to explore.

Chapter 10

Working at relational depth
Skills in relational team coaching

Andrew Day and Dorothee Stoffels

10.1 Introduction: skills in team coaching

Team coaching is a craft that is honed through practice and experience. What we do in the room (and increasingly in the virtual space) with the client is a skill that reflects: our beliefs around theory (how do we think change happens), personal experience (our formal and informal knowledge and time working with groups, teams and organisations) and in-the-moment judgments (how we decide what we do when). Part A of this book has offered both an overall relational frame (Chapter 1) and three theoretical lenses through which to view and approach our work with teams (Chapters 2–4). In this chapter we describe a meta-framework of the core skills for relational team coaching, which finds its grounding in the theory offered in this book. It covers the skills needed for tuning in and making sense of moment-by-moment interactions and the choices that exist around how a coach might intervene at any given juncture. In this we consider all behaviour (or non-behaviour), not just speech or silence, as communication. It is important to highlight that interventions can only happen when we are in relationship with others. We do not consider interventions as something we do 'to' others, but 'with' others. As relational team coaches we bring our full self to the work, which means our choice of intervention and how we intervene is as much shaped by us as by the team and the work at hand.

Perhaps the most important skill for a coach is the ability to tune into and connect with a team. It is this capacity to sense what is happening and what is necessary that informs our judgements about what is needed or called for at any given moment. Knowing what to say, how to say it and when to say it is a judgement. Equally, our choice of words and timing matters. Skill is the art of finding the right words and tone in the right moment. It is equally about knowing when to sit back and give the team space to work on itself. All interventions and how they are made represent a *choice* for the coach. We choose what we feel fits and we cannot know where an intervention will take us and the team or where a different choice would have taken us. With this in mind, it is helpful to let go of the idea that there might be a 'right' choice of intervention, only a more or less useful one.

DOI: 10.4324/9781003325789-14

In any field of professional practice one can be seduced by orthodoxy, a belief that there is a right way and a wrong way of working. There is however great freedom in how we practice. Carl Rogers (1971), when describing his approach to facilitating encounter groups, encouraged each practitioner to "ultimately develop a style which is truly his own, and hence is most effective for him". Each of us bring ourselves, our past experiences, personal and professional identities and theoretical preferences to our practice. We each have our personal style of coaching which is reflected in how we take up the role of team coach and how we work with a team. When we are aware of ourselves and what we believe is helpful, we can be more authoritative in our presence and bring a sharper intentionality to our practice.

In this chapter we present one way of conceptualising the moment-by-moment practice of team coaching. We hope this offers choices and possibilities whilst not being constraining or seen as a set of 'should's' and 'ought's' or a set of 'techniques'. Rather we hope it provides a map of choice points that is grounded in the coach being fully present and tuning into the team's needs. The model should therefore also be seen as flexible and allowing the coach to improvise rather than follow it in a linear fashion.

We need to be aware that our interventions will be experienced as a communication within an existing pattern of communication. For example, if we ignore the repetitive complaints of heavy workload by one team member and not inquire into this further, we might be experienced as siding with the team leader who is no longer responding to such complaints. We need therefore to remain curious about what our interventions might evoke in different team members and work with patterns that emerge between the different team members, the team and the wider system, as well as between ourselves and the team.

10.2   Team coaching skills model

We offer a framework (Figure 10.1) that describes a typology of interventions for relational team coaching. We have used a triangle to offer a view on the frequency with which different forms of interventions are typically used. For instance, a coach needs to be constantly tuning into a team using observing, listening and sensing skills to connect with the team and understand what is going on. Coaches also use inquiry questions regularly to raise awareness and understand dynamics. As one moves further up the triangle, we propose that interventions are used more sparingly and with very clear intent. Disclosure, for instance, although helpful and illuminating for a team, would be used less frequently since the team starts privileging the coach's feelings and responses rather than focusing on their responses and feelings. Working hypotheses and interpretations can provide a reframe or an alternative view and experiments can actively encourage the team to shift patterns by doing something different. These interventions are powerful when used less frequently but well timed. Finally, at the top of the pyramid, offering guidance if overdone puts the coach into an expert role and that can close down dialogue.

Figure 10.1 The team coaching skills model.

As we move up the triangle the interventions involve stronger assumptions and become more directive. Those at the base are more descriptive, phenomenological and non-directive.

10.3   On connecting and understanding

Connecting and understanding provide the basis for any kind of intervening. Unless we connect with and relate to team members (and help them to do the same with each other) our interventions are not grounded in the team's experience. At the same time, we need to understand what is going on for the team and for us in any given moment.

Tuning in and making sense

To tune into a team, a coach draws on their senses and intuition, taking in information from the external environment and listening to themselves. To do this the coach calls upon:

* Attentive observation;
* Empathic listening; and
* Tuning into themselves and their senses.

It is human nature to look for meaning in situations, however, we risk jumping to conclusions. In doing so, we can overlook important data and alternative perspectives. Our encouragement to coaches therefore is to strive for maintaining, in Freud's words an attitude of evenly hovering or free-floating attention (Freud, 1912). This is an ideal however allowing oneself to simply notice and take in what is happening, guard against imposing one's views, preconceived ideas, prejudices or biases. Gestalt's phenomenological tradition also encourages the *bracketing* of assumptions and *horizontalization* – taking care not to impose order on what is observed (see definitions in Chapter 2 and Sills et al., 2012). The coach needs to allow their attention to shuffle between figure and ground – the forms or patterns that they perceive and the context or background from which these figures arise (see also Chapter 2). They also need to move between an outer arc of awareness – what is happening outside of themselves – and an inner arc of awareness – what is happening within themselves (Heron, 2001).

(a) Attentive observation

As teams are in their essence patterns of interactions, the main material coaches observe are patterns of gesture and response and patterns of communication (Stacey, 2003). These patterns might exist at the level of the wider system, the group-as-a-whole, or at an interpersonal level between team members. This way of observing encourages the coach to be curious about how one actor's behaviour is connected to patterns of interaction.

Potentially relevant 'data' or 'information' includes:

- Body language, facial expressions, eye contact and non-verbal behaviour;
- Physical features of the environment, such as the room or seating arrangements;
- The task and psychological roles taken up by individuals in the team, such as individuals taking up a victim position or overly dominating conversations;
- Tensions and conflicts within the team;
- Who speaks, to whom and how often;
- The quality of listening; and
- How decisions are made or not made.

These broad categories, although not exclusive, offer a framework to guide observation.

(b) Empathic listening

What a team talks about, its language and patterns of communication are self-evidently central. Listening to and hearing what is being spoken about is a critical skill. A coach needs to listen to both the explicit, content-level of a conversation and the implicit, covert or implied levels of communication. The skill is to be able to follow what is being discussed about the work (e.g. the nature of the problem, the task or decision) whilst at the same time tracking what is happening at the relational level (e.g. emotional sentiments, power relations, etc.). To do this a coach needs to listen to:

- The content of the discussion and the 'facts' of the situation.
- The spoken or unspoken feelings and emotions that are being expressed both through what is being said and through non-verbal communication.
- The assumptions and beliefs, metaphors and fantasies that underpin the communication and behaviour of the team.

Listening with compassion and understanding helps to contribute to the feeling of psychological safety during coaching sessions. Carl Rogers (1971) made the following statement of his attitude when working with a group:

> I wish very much to make the climate psychologically safe for the individual. I want him to feel from the first that if he risks saying something highly personal, or absurd, or hostile, or cynical, that there will be at least one person in the circle who respects him enough to hear him clearly, and to listen to that statement as an authentic expression of himself.

(c) Use of self

A coach's subjective and intuitive experience, emotional reactions and feelings, or embodied responses can be informative. They may be responses to or be triggered by the dynamics of the team or from projections of the team onto the coach. Alternatively, they may be signals to the coach that they are projecting onto the team or one of its members. Being aware of their process can therefore help a coach to tune into a team, sense what is happening and avoid making assumptions.

Informative responses can include:

- Physical sensations, such as a tightness in the chest or a sinking feeling in the stomach;
- Unexpected or unfamiliar emotional responses, such as a sense of dread, deep sorrow or a strong sense of excitement and elevated hope;
- Strong value judgements about the team or its members;
- Intuitions or sudden insights; or
- Images, fantasies or associations, such as an image of a car crash or memories of long forgotten memories.

Case Vignette 1:
One of us worked with an executive team of a construction business who were meeting to review several studies that different members of the team had led on possible strategic moves. When I arrived my heart sank as I saw a long, thin board table in the centre of the room. When the Chief Executive shared the agenda for the meeting, it was packed full of items to discuss, ranging from near-term operational issues and around five to six possible strategic projects. I felt my anxiety rise, a tightness in my body and a growing sense of urgency to get started. I noted that my anxiety appeared at odds with that of the executive team who were smiling and joking with each other. After about an hour of

detailed updates, I now felt bored and anxious. The team eventually got to the first strategic option. One member of the executive team, who had clearly done a great deal of work, described in detail the issues, the opportunity and the level of investment the company would need to make to deliver what would be a new service. Different team members expressed their views. I felt the evidence in favour of moving forward was compelling, although some level of risk and uncertainty was also evident. The team continued to discuss the evidence and to my surprise the Chief Executive suggested that further research was necessary and the team should revisit the decision in six months. At this point, I was struck by how cautions the team appeared and started to conclude they were procrastinating. This led me to ask the team whether it had a pattern of putting off important strategic decisions. This resonated with them and they started to speak to their doubts and concerns around risks and their fears of doing something different in the market.

In practice, we scan the team as it interacts but pick up only a fraction of what is going on. We need therefore to be circumspect in our judgements about what is happening in a team and how we attribute meaning. The coach does however need to formulate a sense of what is happening, how the team is performing and where the team needs help or support. This is a refining process which sifts and sorts – sees patterns and meanings (Casey et al., 1992). The coach draws upon her theories, personal beliefs and implicit assumptions in this process of making sense. Kurt Lewin observed, many years ago, "If you want truly to understand something, try to change it" (Tolman, 1996). In this spirit, sensemaking is best thought of as an active process that involves gathering information, intervening and learning from what happens.

Attentive observation, empathic listening and tuning into oneself and one's senses all produce some form of 'data' for the coach and the team to make sense of and provides the basis from which the team coach decides to make an intervention. Often the question is to decide which data to use and which to let go off. As team coaches we are never able to use everything we notice or hear and our task is to make some judgement as to what is most pertinent or helpful for the team. Important is often to notice the feedback we get back from different team members as we offer an intervention. By feedback we do not mean verbal feedback in the traditional sense, but rather what reaction does this evoke in the team. Does the intervention get picked up by the team or ignored? How strong is the reaction? Again observing, listening and sensing become key skills at this point as we are entering a new loop of meaning-making and intervening.

10.4   On interventions

Intervening covers everything that a coach does to help a team. This includes the following:

- Exploring
- Offering a perspective

- Hypothesising
- Experiments
- Guidance

Viewing intervening through a relational lens, we see all interventions as something co-created between us and the team. This means that as we are tuning in and making sense of the data available around us, we are impacted and this informs how we intervene. Note that not doing something, is paradoxically to do something. John Heron (2001) described an intervention as an "identifiable piece of verbal and/or non-verbal behaviour that is part of the practitioner's service to the client". The important thing following any intervention is what happens next and what this might reveal to the team about how it functions and how it might develop.

Case Vignette 2:
One of us was working with a team that wanted help with forming and becoming closer with each other. I suggested a process where each team member shared a bit about their backgrounds, what was important to them and how this related to their membership of the team. The first couple of individuals that spoke shared little of any personal significance and showed little vulnerability. The other members of the team equally showed little curiosity in what they were hearing. At one level, my intervention was unsuccessful however the team's response to the intervention revealed considerable information about the team's struggle with intimacy, vulnerability and trust. My next intervention was an observation of the degree of caution that the team was taking in the exercise and how few risks the team appeared to be taking. Several team members acknowledged their reticence about disclosing personal details and their responses were in themselves a disclosure of feelings that helped to increase the level of risk taking.

The overall aims of interventions are to support the team's development, growth and capacity. An intervention may therefore be intended to achieve a combination of the following:

- Help create the necessary conditions for growth
- Model a different form of conversation
- Facilitate learning from experience
- Raise awareness of patterns of interaction
- To value and take seriously different perspectives
- To challenge assumptions.

Exploring

(a) Inquiry

The aims of inquiry interventions are for the coach to gather information about the team and to help the team or individuals explore their experience. The coach facilitates this process by asking questions that encourage individuals to share their experience, to surface assumptions or express feelings. Team coaches can use inquiry at any point of their work with the team and system around the team, however, there is often an emphasis on spending time in inquiry in the early stages of an engagement with a team. This could involve one-to-one conversations with the team leader, team members, key stakeholders etc. and/or the whole team to explore what the work is.

Coaches use both open and closed questions. Open questions, such as Who? What? When? How?, facilitate the development of the team's own thinking, insights and meaning-making. Closed questions help to clarify specific points or different positions within a team. A coach might for instance say: "Satinder do you agree or disagree with the decision to do X?". Inquiry questions also vary on a continuum from more pure forms, such as "What was the situation?" or "Who was involved" to more diagnostic forms that direct the team's attention to specific phenomenon, such as "How did you feel about that?" or "What was the consequence of x?" (Schein, 1999).

Inquiry interventions can: bring others into a conversation ("What do others think?"); help explore different perspectives ("What alternative perspectives exist in the team?"); offer up choices to the team ("Do you need to focus on *this* or *that*?") or help clarify ambiguous statements or euphemism ("When you say this team has a problem, what specifically do you see as the problem?"). Specific types of questions such as circular and reflexive questions (see Chapter 3) can also be used to help teams and team members appreciate the interconnectedness of their behaviours and communication and allow the team coach to actively intervene in the patterns the team creates by enhancing reflexivity.

(b) Summarising and reflecting back

A coach also inquires by summarising and reflecting back to the team what they are seeing, hearing and sensing is happening in the here and now. By reflecting back their understanding of what is being communicated by the team or is being experienced the coach helps the team to 'hear' itself. Such interventions also model to the team effective listening and helps to create an atmosphere of curiosity and listening to understand.

Offering a perspective

The next level of intervention involves the coach offering selected information back to the team. This could be focused on an individual, interpersonal dyad, subgroup or team-as-a-whole. At this level the coach is more actively identifying data or observations that they believe will help the team to develop, grow or achieve its aims. As far as they can the coach should strive to be as precise, clear and direct in what they offer to the group. Often when a coach is ambiguous or long-winded in what they say, they are anxious about how their intervention will be received by others. More often than not, teams and individuals can hear a clear, accurate and non-judgemental observation or piece of feedback.

They can do this by:

(a)   Sharing an observation

This is a descriptive observation of what they are (or are not) noticing, observing or hearing either in the moment or over time. For example: "A pattern I have observed is ..."

Case Vignette 3:
One of us was working with a multi-systems leadership team, which brought several organisational leaders together to make system-wide decisions and agree budgets. The team coaching work focused on creating greater trust and intimacy in working relationships to become more effective at decision-making. During one of the sessions, it became evident that whenever someone offered a more risky thought, a new idea or disclosed something more personal, no-one would acknowledge this or follow up with a question. Becoming aware of this pattern, I shared my observation. This was met initially with stunned silence and then one of the leaders started speaking about how often they didn't feel seen or heard in this group as her contributions were not acknowledged and followed up. Others followed suit and began speaking about their experience of participating in discussions.

(b)   Disclosure

This involves the coach sharing with the group feelings, emotions, responses or associations that they have either in the moment, in response to specific events or more generally in their work with the team. For instance: "As we check in with each other, I notice a growing sense of sadness in myself". When used selectively and when attuned to the mood of the team, disclosure can help to deepen intimacy and surface deeper feelings that may not be acknowledged.

(c)   Offering feedback to the team or an individual

Feedback is an observation about behaviour or dynamics and its consequences that also implicitly or explicitly conveys an alternative way of behaving or being. Skilful feedback tends to be specific, descriptive and non-judgemental. An example of feedback might be: "I notice that when the CEO makes a proposal that some of you look down and remain quiet. In these moments, I'd encourage each of you to say something about your response to the proposal. Otherwise, the CEO and your colleagues are left wondering what you are thinking about the proposal".

Hypothesising

Under 'hypothesising' we have distinguished between 'working hypotheses' and 'interpretations'. Both are based on association and hunches and their purpose is to raise awareness and invite change. We want to acknowledge here that the difference when used in team coaching is small, however we do find it helpful to make the distinction. Working hypotheses are focused on exploring more visible patterns, whilst an interpretation usually looks more into the unconscious processes of a team.

(a)   Sharing working hypotheses

As team coaches we consciously or unconsciously develop working hypotheses about observed patterns and interactions amongst team members and in relation to their task. Hypotheses are usually seen as tentative and not a key to the absolute truth. Sharing our hypotheses explicitly with the team is an intervention that can offer a different perspective and help the team develop insight into what is going on. Alternatively, the team coach can ask different team members what their hypothesis about the current challenges of the team is. This introduces multiple perspectives into the work and can often make hidden sense-making of the team explicit. Chapter 3 gives a detailed account on how to develop systemic hypotheses.

"Let me share what I think is happening in the team right now…"; "I have been wondering whether X is going on in your team". "Can I share my hypothesis with you?" "What are your thoughts or hypotheses why this team is struggling with X?". These can all be helpful sentence stems to frame sharing a working hypothesis.

Case Vignette 4:
One of us was involved in working with a sales team that has had previously multiple interventions from different professionals with not much success. The team was underperforming, relationships between the team and team leader were strained and there had been lots of staff turnover and people were frequently going off sick with stress. The situation seemed very stuck as there was a dominant narrative in the team that the team leader was the problem and if only he left, the team would be happier and functioning better. I held the working hypothesis that there was a pattern of more complex, circular interpersonal dynamics at play rather than just the linear idea that the team leader was 'the problem'. After sharing my hypothesis with the team, I then asked every team member whether they could share a hypothesis about what they thought was going on in the team. What was holding them back? As each member started to express their hunches about what was going on, suddenly a much more complex web of different stories emerged about the team's relationships and challenges. The team began to realise that everyone had a different experience of the situation and that blaming the team leader had simplified people's experiences and denied the multiple realities people were experiencing.

(b)   Offering interpretations

An interpretation is best thought of as a working hypothesis about what is happening for the team, but goes further by delving into what might be the reasons that this is happening, at this moment in time and in this context. Interpretations tend to be directed towards unconscious or subconscious motives and influences. When accurate they can help name or put into words an implicit concern or issue. A basic form for an interpretation is:

I observe 'X' happening '*because*' of .... .

Case Vignette 5:
One of the authors was working with a newly formed team made up of the Heads of function for a government department. The team had been formed as part of a re-organisation of the department. The functions were now called 'centre' and were expected to form a new unit. After several meetings the team had struggled to make any meaningful decisions about how the new unit would function and any proposals tended to be criticised or knocked down relatively quickly. I started to wonder about what might be stopping the team from forming. I noticed an absence of enthusiasm at the meetings, a dominance of the use of "I" and statements that emphasised the difference between the functions. This led me to observe some of these patterns and wonder whether this was because the idea of forming a new team represented a threat to each of the function's identifies and autonomy that was being experienced and expressed through each of the members of the team (i.e. the heads of the functions).

This interpretation was met with some acknowledgement and a sense of being understood by the group. The central concern in the room felt like it had been named and acknowledged. This helped the members of the team to talk about their resistances to the new structure, the fears of their teams and the differences between them that they felt the new structure did not acknowledge.

Interpretations or hypotheses are most helpful when they are linked to observations, are clear and are informed by theory and / or intuition. They are best offered when a coach has tuned into to the team, has corroborating evidence and offered when the team is likely to be receptive. Skilful interpretations, as with all interventions, invite others to participate in the sense-making process.

Interpretations are high-risk interventions and are used sparingly. Plunging or deep interpretations that draw attention to material that is completely out of sight should on the whole be avoided. Even if they are accurate, they position the coach as someone who is able to see what others cannot. This can be disempowering and emotionally disturbing for some. At their best, interpretations represent moments of deep empathy and insight on the part of the coach. They can help a team become aware of deeper processes and emotional conflicts. At their worst, however, they can be the imposition of the coach's judgements, wild ideas or theoretical beliefs. In other words, wholly inaccurate and unhelpful. When this is the case, they tend to increase defensiveness and distrust of the coach. Hypotheses are therefore best offered tentatively and held lightly by the coach.

Experiments

Both 'gestalt' experiments or experiential exercises can help to interrupt patterns, raising awareness of deeper emotions or feelings, and support learning for a team. They can be used to help create movement during periods of stuckness or when energy is lacking.

(a)   Gestalt experiments

Gestalt experiments tend to be bespoke and emergent in nature. Zinker (1977) called experiments 'permission to be creative'. An experiment could be as simple as inviting a team to try something out and to review the experience. For instance, a coach might invite one team member to be more direct in the feedback they are offering to another. Then review with each party the experience.

To achieve some or all of these aims, the intervention needs to be:

- Designed to support its intention
- Clearly explained to and set up *with* the team
- Agreed and contracted with the team,
- Involve some risk for the team but not to the extent that it could be damaging or get out of hand.
- Reviewed and debriefed to help the team to identify what it has learnt.

Case Vignette 6:
Whilst working with one of the authors, an executive team of a government department had become aware of its pattern of avoiding conflicts and disagreements when making decisions. I proposed that at their next session the team would choose an important decision they needed to make with the aim of being consciously different. I agreed specific review points during the meeting when the team would suspend the meeting to review its process. This experiment gave permission to individuals to experiment, and the review points provided the opportunity for the team to notice what was different and similar. It also shifted the group from thinking about behaving differently to having an experience of behaving differently.

(b)   Experiential exercises

Experiential exercises are specific activities that are often creative, using alternative means of imagining or playing out something. They can be emergent and designed in the moment by the team coach or planned ahead of time based on a hypothesis of what the team might need. Examples of experiential interventions include:

- role-playing scenarios;
- constellations;
- changing seating arrangements;
- use of object;
- asking the team to draw;
- physical expressions of feelings; and
- body sculpts, etc.

A wide range of experiential exercises have been documented to support different learning outcomes, for example, Pfeiffer's encyclopaedia of Team Development Activities and Team Building Activities (1990). Exercises however risk being contrived or make significant assumptions or judgements about what the team needs to learn. This is particularly the case with 'off-the-shelf' exercises.

Case Vignette 7:
A team in the insurance sector that one of us was supporting, wanted to do some work around decision-making and their team dynamics. In order to help the team members who were working in a very rational, thinking-dominated environment articulate their experience of being in the team, I asked each other them to pick a metaphor or image for the team. Once they had created an image that represented the team, they shared it with each other. Apart from producing quite a lot of laughter, the exercise enabled people to speak movingly about their emotional experience of being part of the team and how at times they felt shut down or overlooked.

Guidance

(a)   Educational input

At times, a team may lack information, knowledge or expertise. A coach may helpfully offer advice or suggestions on what to do or how to do it or frameworks or theories which help the group to learn and develop. This is most effectively done when the coach has a good understanding of the needs and capability of the team, and is not making assumptions. A coach may, for instance, offer a team a framework on how to give and receive feedback because the team is anxious about doing it and is relatively unskilled. It is often useful to frame educational inputs as 'offers' that could be helpful to the team's development and hold them lightly rather than seeing them as rigid truth applied to a team.

Case Vignette 8:
One of us was commencing a piece of team coaching with a colleague with the executive team of a think tank. As we started on the first morning we offered the team a process model that addressed 3 aspects of working together: content, process and climate. Our inquiry conversations ahead of the day had highlighted

that team members found it difficult to open up with each other and agree ways of working together. We felt that this model would provide a process and frame that would offer containment and enough safety for the team to start having the difficult conversations about their relational dynamics they wanted to have. We particularly used it to open up a conversation about the climate they wanted to create with each other for the team coaching work and beyond. As we jointly made sense of the model, a 'contract' started to emerge in conversation between team members about how they wanted to behave towards each other, which became a reference point throughout the team coaching work and in their team meetings.

(b)   Sharing information

We acknowledge that as team coaches we often have a lot of experience in the world of organisations and hold information about specific aspects of organizational life, including specific sectors, organizational structure and processes etc. We might also be well-versed in theories pertaining to organizational life including, strategy, organizational change, team and group development or leadership, etc. At times and with clear intent, it can be very helpful to the team if we share a particular piece of information or experience that we have that is relevant to the team's immediate challenge, e.g. "I don't know whether this is helpful, but I just wanted to share with you that from my experience and knowledge of supporting organisations through change, staff go through a range of emotions as they adjust to new situations". One danger of sharing too much information is that we move too much into the role of an advisor or guiding facilitator and remain there. It is therefore key that we contract very carefully around any information we share.

(c)   Offering advice

On rare occasions, a team may benefit from direct advice or guidance from the coach. This might involve suggesting to the team what to do and not to do. Examples would be: "I suggest that you allow less time in your team meeting for presentations and create more space for discussion" or "I think you should not exclude your colleagues from the sales team from this project because of the effect it would have on your relationship". Team coaches sometimes will find themselves in the position of giving advice, if they feel really strongly the team would benefit from this or if there are issues around risk and well-being. It can often be helpful to lead with an intervention further down the triangle e.g. offering a perspective before giving advice as this can frame the advice and why the coach is giving it. Helpful are also follow up inquiry questions such as "what do you think about this suggestion?" or "what is your reaction to this?"

If the coach, finds themselves offering advice on a regular basis then there might be two reasons for it: they either consciously or unconsciously have stepped out of the role of a coach and have become an advisor or guiding facilitator to the team or alternatively a particular dynamic has developed between the coach and the team for example that the coach has been invited to become the quasi-leader of the team. If this is the case the team coach needs to reflect on and resolve the emerging dynamic with the team.

10.5 Conclusion

The team coaching skills model that we have explored in this chapter offers the team coach a map of choice points when working with teams. Interventions are made within an existing relationship, and we have tried to illustrate how their meaning emerges within an existing pattern of communication. The coach therefore needs to be aware of their intent, be attuned to the team and notice how team members react and respond. What they do next therefore is in response to what happened and is happening in the moment. In this sense, interventions are an emergent process that unfolds and cannot be pre-determined or planned. A skilled coach therefore is mindful of the moment-by-moment interpretations and choices they make and the unfolding process of the team.

Chapter 11

Working with power, derailment, and top teams

Erik de Haan

11.1 What is different about top teams?

Although they share many characteristics with other types of teams, it can feel very different to coach top teams. They are usually more focused on making decisions for other people and for wider systems. Whilst the feeling of being in a group and what is evoked for us may often be similar, it is still worth looking at coaching for top teams separately. Top teams embody 'leadership' for a wider organisation. They have decision-making power with end responsibility for all or most of the decisions taken. In this chapter I will look at some characteristics of top teams which trace the pressures they experience and influence how they operate. I will follow the difficulties they have to overcome in their functioning, before finally exploring how team coaches can respond to these and be of help.

Starting then with some characteristics of top teams:

First, the main job of top teams is to make decisions for the whole of the organisation, not so much to think (or strategise) about those decisions nor to implement
   them, but really to *make* them. The team regularly needs to formulate and argue
   a way forward (in the shape of a strategy, plan, approach, or measure), and then
   to formally adopt an unequivocal decision. Top teams will often describe themselves as 'decision-making machines'. This gives top teams enormous power as
   the ultimate decision-makers for the organisation. A highly visible power which
   also renders them somewhat vulnerable particularly given the fact that access
   and transparency have increased exponentially in the last few decades. Another
   source of vulnerability comes from the awareness that good decision making is
   dependent on both subject-matter experts and experts with deep experience of
   the organisation itself. To pursue this core task of decision making, the top team
   needs to be well-informed, not only about the context, general markets, and
   stakeholders around the organisation, but also about the internal capabilities of
   the organisation and the state of all relevant operations and functional special-
   isms. Key to the functioning of a top team is the flow of information into the
   decision-making arena. This information includes 'upwards feedback': information about how the top team is experienced, including motivation levels and

DOI: 10.4324/9781003325789-15

the degree of 'alignment' between the organisation and the top. There is good evidence to indicate that upwards feedback is a key determinant of effectiveness in the top team (De Haan & Kasozi, 2014, Chapter 11). After all, decisions only get implemented through an ongoing feedback loop with other organisational layers.

Second, top teams need to withstand particular pressures from within and outside the organisation, which may be explicit or implicit, and which in turn affect both conscious and unconscious decision making. In exercising their power, maintaining their decision-making abilities means that they have to integrate their own priorities with the expectations and influences from all around them. Both from inside the organisation and from important stakeholders outside, explicit and implicit pressures will be exerted on how the team should behave and what decisions should be taken. Such powerful invitations to embody views of how the leader 'should' represent the group or organisation can add to the internal pressures on the top team and constrain the team's ability to take high-quality decisions together. Petriglieri and Stein (2012) describe this aspect as leaders often having little choice but to identify with the very strong projections and expectations directed at them – a process technically known as 'projective identification'.

Third, top teams are 'authority figures' within the organisation. They are very much in view and a constant presence in the minds of not only the individuals they work with directly, but also, for everyone in the wider organisation, many of whom they may hardly know or even meet. Some of the work of top teams is performative and representational, acting in a ceremonial capacity on behalf of the organisation, both within and outside it. These seemingly easier and more enjoyable ambassadorial duties can sometimes distract top team members from other aspects of their work (see, e.g., Bandiera et al., 2011).

Case vignette: The top team of a large ministry asked for two days of team coaching because, as they said, "we do not know each other. We hardly talk with one another except about long documents that have options and decisions prepared. Recently, we had to decide about a very large expenditure over two decades into our infrastructure, which would impact several of our departments, and we could not move ahead. We stuck to our pre-existing positions, nobody was willing to give up any of their budget and the department that would have to grow to spend the new money was pressing for an 'urgent' decision ever more strongly. We went back to the minister, we involved the Ministry of Finance, but all to no avail. It was to be our decision – and we just could not do it. At the current time our Permanent Secretary, the team lead, has given the rest of the team an ultimatum. If we do not take the decision within two weeks, she will do it all by herself. But we are not even sure if we will be able to work with that either".

During the work with the coach, they learned how 'avoidant' they had become of the big decisions. They found it easier to decide for others in their organisation, or on projects that were delegated by the government's manifesto. Now that they really had to rise beyond just common interests of the team or specific interests within a department, they did not know where to start. They suddenly realised how lucky they had been that they never had to take any major decisions with a real cost to their own people and budgets. They also realised how they had perfected the art of 'not offending anyone', working around and accommodating many ingrained interests and 'no go areas' from within the team. Now this was no longer possible for this decision, they were completely blocked, and not just for a meeting: for months on end. The team coach helped the team to understand for the first time 'who' was on the team, how personalities appeared diverse but basic common interests were quite plain to see for all. After exchanging personal histories, values, habits and formative moments in their lives, the feel of the team changed considerably. They were interacting much more freely and started to negotiate for real. Within a week they resolved themselves on the decision, which had been obvious all along (as they could now openly attest). As a consequence, they were much more united as a team. They even managed to go back to the Ministry of Finance for more liquidity in the short term.

11.2   How leadership and derailment are ultimately related

As we have argued in *The Leadership Shadow* (De Haan & Kasozi, 2014), all forms of leadership necessarily involve suppression – not only in trying to win over and suppress opposing or differing proposals – but also suppression *inside the leader*. With every act of leadership, we prioritise certain views and actions, contribute to a narrative or a decision, at the cost of other possibilities and countering views, which arguably we also hold inside. From a systems-psychodynamic view (see Chapter 4) we may hold many different positions inside our conscious and less conscious minds, different positions that are vying for attention and influence. When exercising leadership, we are bound to suppress some of our own viewpoints, positions, skills, or talents, in order to contribute clearly and strongly with our leadership view or position. In the external world, countervailing ideas, perspectives, and bids for leadership usually get represented by different individuals inside and outside the organisation, who are able to give free rein to their opposing ideas. In the internal world however, doubts and countervailing ideas usually fall victim to our coping or defence mechanisms. They 'go underground', dropping outside our conscious awareness, where they may pose less direct interference and opposition. This ubiquitous phenomenon of ongoing internal censorship and suppression to allow the exercise of leadership over a sustained period of time, is what we call the *leadership shadow* (De Haan & Kasozi, 2014).

In other words, if an individual (with a leadership bid) steps forward within a team, particularly a top team, this naturally creates a rift within him- or herself at the same time. This can usually be seen as a conflict between the individual's sunny, active, constructive or assertive side that has the ambition to contribute, create and prove something (as expressed by the bid for leadership); and the same individual's doubting, needy, vulnerable, careful and concerned side, which craves recognition and connection (often in vain).

Leadership therefore comes with suppression that may lead to pathology, in the sense that the mind becomes split, and difficulties are not processed but locked away. It is well documented that more senior leaders have larger distortions in their self-perception than junior leaders (Gentry et al., 2007). Moreover, we now have good documentation and evidence that the influence and personal charisma that one obtains through power does in fact corrupt one's judgement and behaviour over time (Robinson & Garrard, 2016). A well-known mechanism of corruption is through hubris or overreach: the phenomenon that more senior and more tenured leaders can influence decisions beyond their own narrowly defined area of responsibility, or that a top team becomes collectively more risk-seeking, manipulative, and corrupted in their decision making.

There seems to be a natural process in which a new leader who has recently come into power is at his or her most vulnerable and experiences the least control or influence. This leader may also experience the greatest amount of doubt, ambivalence, intimidation. But slowly, over time, as though through some kind of osmosis (growing familiarity, skills, expertise, networks, etc.), power clings to a leader and becomes ever greater. With this accumulation of power, the leader's *discretion* to choose their behaviour or force decisions also increases. It is of course through discretion that leaders can begin to make a difference in their organisation. However, discretion is both the currency with which leaders get things done *and* the bribe that will inevitably corrupt them. Kaiser and Hogan (2007) argue that discretion does not only increase with tenure and understanding of your own leadership role, but that it also increases with hierarchical level. Moreover, one is likely to find more leadership discretion in younger and in smaller organisations, and in those organisations with 'weaker' cultures and limited governance or control mechanisms. Hambrick and Abrahamson (1995) have done an exploration of the amount of discretion per industry that shows:

- Academic experts and security analysts agree with each other and across groups that there are significant differences of levels of discretion between industries.
- These same experts agree on which industries have top teams with more discretion: e.g., the software, engineering, pharma and entertainment industries.
- There are four factors in those industries that predict 49 per cent of the variance in the panellists' rankings of discretion: R&D intensity, advertising intensity, market growth and (inversely) capital intensity.

The above has shown that leadership comes with pathology over time. But pathology also comes with leadership. In other words, there are mutually strengthening processes between pathology and (top) leadership. These processes are highly idiosyncratic as the precise nature of the patterns vary by organisation, industry, and individual leader personality.

In *The Mask of Sanity*, Cleckley (1941) was the first to describe the specific configuration of traits that capture the essence of the psychopathic personality. Psychopaths were described as superficially charming, self-centred, fearless, impulsive, articulate, callous, and guiltless. Out of this thinking, the triarchic model of psychopathy evolved (see Patrick et al., 2009), where the most common psychopathic traits are clustered around boldness (e.g. grandiosity, interpersonal dominance), meanness (e.g. lack of empathy, callousness), and disinhibition (e.g. impulsivity, irresponsibility).

Although boldness may add to positive task performance and charismatic leadership, and disinhibition may add to positive adaptive leadership, an overall negative contribution of meanness and a partially negative contribution of disinhibition to *effective* leadership have been reported (Vergauwe et al., 2021). In the latter research, the effectiveness of leaders was rated by subordinates, which we argue in *The Leadership Shadow* (De Haan and Kasozi, 2014) is a very well-chosen perspective for measuring leadership effectiveness. In fact, honest rankings by direct reports are probably the best measurement of leadership effectiveness that we have available (see Hogan et al., 1994). So Vergauwe et al.'s study provides rather convincing evidence that more serious pathology leads to a lower leadership performance. The same authors argue that if one measures the impact of psychopathy from the perspective of quality of life on our planet or for future generations, these negative, demonstrated correlations between psychopathy and leadership effectiveness are expected to become even stronger and to also include boldness.

The conclusion has to be that (statistically) leadership tenure enhances psychopathy which in turn decreases leadership effectiveness, whilst also causing harm and damage. Leadership appears to be an important example of 'successful psychopathy' (Dutton, 2012): on the one hand it attracts individuals who are interested in power and self-promotion, and on the other hand the pressures and projections on top leadership have a pathology-enhancing effect, especially over time ('acquired hubris syndrome'; Owen, 2008). This means that either through self-selection or through experience on the job, such as inescapable, strong projections onto leaders, the number of triarchic traits is expected to be greater than in the general population (Patrick et al., 2009). We also have some indications that the groups most at risk for this 'successful psychopathy' are the dominant ones in society: male, white, heterosexual, etc.

The factors at play that have the worst impact on the leadership shadow and growing toxicity are the following: neuroticism (Furnham, 2016); highly personal derailment factors such as personality tendencies or disorders (Torregiante, 2005); and projective identification (Petriglieri & Stein, 2012). These are the factors at play that make it worse – and they need to be managed by responsible leadership teams and organisations, with help of their coaches.

From the research as quoted in this section we can safely conclude that leaders who are members of top teams have higher risk factors in terms of their hubristic overreach and their coping strategies under pressure, which may show beginnings of well-known leadership derailment patterns. We just do not know if this is because of a process of 'self-selection' in stepping up to higher levels of leadership, or whether these higher positions and their pressures and expectations influence the leaders towards hubris and derailment. Probably it is both. But what we do know is that there is a higher risk in these teams, and that therefore the mitigating influence of coaching on personality derailment (as found in a number of outcome studies in coaching: Allan et al., 2018, Zanchetta et al., 2020, and De Haan et al., 2019) may be all the more helpful at these senior levels.

Once the patterns are sufficiently noticeable to play a role in the dynamic of a team it is impossible to determine conclusively if they have individual and biographic origins, or whether they are related to the primary process and history of the organisation, or whether they are the product of the intense projections and expectations onto the top of the organisation. Freud's idea of 'overdetermination' or 'multicausality' (Freud, 1900) always applies in these cases: there are more causes than one, and every single cause is sufficient for attribution of the psychological (team) phenomenon. Thanks to multicausality we can be confident as team coaches that we can sense derailment patterns early on as they also seem to arise within us: we will often feel guilty or problematic ourselves as we experience the presence of something hubristic, disturbed or excessive. Here is one recent example.

Case vignette: When a leadership team is suffering from 'shadow patterns' or 'derailers' then this is often quite clear to a team coach at the very beginning of working with the team. I was recently asked by a former client to help the Board of a transportation company with the help of team coaching for only the first day of their twice-yearly three-day retreat. I was invited to meet the CEO in person, in preparation for this event. I arrived after a considerable journey to discover that my meeting was to be one hour in the CEO's diary. I was then given a cup of coffee. After some 20 minutes I asked again at Reception and was asked to wait but I sensed the discomfort of the receptionist. I was thinking many things, sitting there with my second coffee. Because I am at work, I tend to not pick up any extraneous reading nor consult my mobile phone, but just pay attention to my felt sense, emotions, and thoughts. Just to be kept there waiting for the meeting triggered quite strong emotions as I felt essentially kept a prisoner (something which many CEOs fail to realise or to remember when they keep their waiting lounges populated). I was thinking to myself, perhaps something important had happened on the day, which was distracting the CEO a great deal. When I was finally welcomed in, a full 50 minutes had elapsed, and it was made clear to me that we would have just the ten minutes remaining for our meeting. One of the first comments or rhetorical questions from the CEO was, "why would he and me be working together anyway?", which was followed fairly soon by a comment on the HR Director who had advised about this meeting: "I don't trust her, but I can make good use of her. She is very useful". After I inquired why the HR director might want to arrange this meeting and us to collaborate, I was left none the wiser. The only thing I could inject in the remaining two minutes was "I can see what the problem is, just from my experience here with you". This comment did lead to a moment of reflection for the CEO, after which the next visitor was ushered in. Later I understood that in fact the idea of team coaching had not come from the two people I had now spoken with, but from a new member of the team who was rather perplexed by the toxic behaviours she had encountered already in the first weeks. I later heard this person was already seriously considering leaving within two months of having arrived.

11.3   Radical ways to think about decision making in top teams

Given that there are so many ways the decision-making process can be distorted by the pressures of working in top teams, it is of vital importance to think about how we can keep those top teams as healthy and balanced as possible, so that they can continue to make the best decisions for the whole organisation, even when they are under considerable pressure. In *The Leadership Shadow* (De Haan & Kasozi, 2014) we argue that this means that top teams must obtain regular feedback on how they are making decisions including a critical appreciation of their patterns and coping mechanisms under pressure. Similarly, we argue that healthy top teams organise a form of 'upwards feedback' so that they take on board as much information as possible from within the next levels in the organisation, from subject-matter experts but also line managers who will have to implement new decisions. In my view such middle managers are also important experts: experts on the organisational context in which decisions are being made, with a deep knowledge about what goes on at their level and how people are feeling. It is well known that having more experts (i.e., a range of differing autonomous and informed viewpoints) influence a decision, produces qualitatively better decisions (Surowiecki, 2005). Top leadership teams can facilitate high-quality upwards communication including reflection on patterns within their organisation, by setting up quality assurance, feedback and protective systems for their staff; e.g., whistleblowing can help to receive vital upwards feedback information. However, it is important then that firstly whistle-blowers are protected and secondly triangulation (Dunn, 2006) is avoided in dealing with the feedback.

I think it is possible and necessary to go further than just balancing team dynamics through e.g., team coaching, multisource feedback, and upwards communication. I believe that with the growth of our large organisations and the increasing crises on our planet (many of which are arguably caused by leadership failures – De Haan, 2022), we need to radically democratise leadership in organisations (see also Semler, 2001). In our current fast-changing and pressurised world-in-crisis, we need to bring more relevant viewpoints to the table, we need to get better and faster at problem solving, and we need higher levels of commitment once a decision is made, but most of all we need a healthier morale and higher levels of honesty and integrity. All of these can be delivered by a working democracy especially near the top levels of an institution. Democracy will make top leaders more dependent on the people who receive their leadership, by participatory, voting and influencing mechanisms, and that will create better decisions, commitment, transparency, and morale.

Here is a current example that may teach us something about the power of democratic mechanisms in the exercise of leadership.

Case vignette: One prominent feature of the Russo-Ukrainian war which currently is just about contained to Ukraine is the degree to which it appears to be a conflict between 'good' and 'evil', especially on the leadership level. On the one side we see an isolated leader with totalitarian control of his country, not allowing any dissent or even truthful information about the war or leadership bids at the top to percolate through to the masses in 'his' country – a leader who seems to be riddled with fear, needing total control, and lacking a positive vision of the future. On the other side we see a leader who appears open and direct, personable, fiercely democratic and setting an example for many in his own country and around the world with his decisiveness, openness to dialogue, and selfless compassion for the afflicted. Part of this split into 'good' and 'evil' is to do with the partisan projections that leaders naturally attract, but even if we take those into account, I believe the differences in the implementation of leadership are stark in this conflict.

I have been studying leadership over the years, including differences between 'good' and 'bad' leadership. Such differences can always be biased by one's own points of view and political affiliation, so I have learned that it makes more sense to look at the differences between 'good' and 'successful' leadership. Both these country leaders are obviously successful, but their impact and style could not be any different, and the amount of 'goodness' that they bring is often contrasted. We see the same differences playing out in today's large organisations. There are many successful leaders who lead empires with up to a million employees, but the amount of 'goodness' that they bring is often debated. We know from reliable estimates that less than 50% of leaders would get the predicate 'good enough' from within their own team, provided free polls are taken which is not always straightforward (Chénard-Poirier et al., 2022, and Hogan et al., 2021).

Most of the larger institutions in today's world are essentially non-democratic as leaders are not elected. I think this is partly what is causing some of the unpopularity of our organisations' leaders. So, before becoming distracted by circular debates about good versus evil, what is good leadership and what is successful leadership, and how are they different?

Successful leadership is easiest to define and recognise. It is the influence or rank/position that a leader or team has achieved. The higher the position the more leadership they can exert. Leaders in larger institutions generally become more successful as they can convince the layer above them to take them on, i.e., to promote or elect them for a vacancy. The President of Russia is a straightforward example of this kind of success, as he essentially owes his position to one man and one man only: Boris Yeltsin, who promoted him and then made him into the 'succession plan' for his own job. In a democratic country or organisation, one must convince a great many more people to obtain similar success.

Good leadership can be defined by contributions to the process of making an organisation more effective, more competitive, more sustainable, or more strategic (Campbell, 1956). Good leaders help others to become more effective as a team or organisation.

I think just as we instinctively know who has higher morals in the Ukrainian war, and we can back up this intuition by arguments and facts, so we also know how to recognise 'good' leadership in organisations. My own research (as summarised in De Haan & Kasozi, 2014) has led me to think that good leadership consists mostly of organising upwards feedback, i.e., taking on board as many views as possible so that the organisation can make use of the 'wisdom of crowds' (Surowiecki, 2005). Good leaders are able to facilitate a dynamic ebb and flow of such information, feedback and feelings of motivation. They welcome diverse views including dissident and critical voices, which they summarise into a broadly shared sense of direction, which in turn helps to give meaning and purpose to the work of the team. We can see this process work in all implementations of leadership, including during wars and stressful transitions.

To summarise, I believe the science of work and organisations still has a lot to learn from free democracies. We can see that the political world is shaping up increasingly as a rivalry between free democracies and exceedingly controlling autocracies. Yet what is less reflected upon is that we see the same conflict very much playing out in the leadership of large organisations too. Effective leaders manage to take the 'dressing room' with them and they are aware of a multiplicity of views. Authoritarian leaders can afford not to do that, but only to the detriment of their team and decisions.

Here are a few of my more specific learnings from the horrendous ordeal we have seen playing out in Ukraine:

1. As team coaches we should have some awareness of how the exercise of central power can be implemented in society, and within a Western context we should actively support democratic leaders and democratic processes within organisations. It was Pericles who already realised the fragility of a democracy and spoke about it in his famous funeral speech to the war victims. Tolstoy was recently quoted by Alexander Navalny, the Russian freedom fighter: "War is a product of despotism. Those who want to fight war must only fight despotism" (Tolstoy's diary entry on 4 June 1904).
2. We should be in support of fixed terms for leaders, and not just in political appointments. Fixed working terms of four to five years in the role are very healthy at board level, and it is indeed something we are increasingly seeing across the world, at least in the public sector. However, the implementation is

often less rigorous than would be desirable, so that more authoritarian leaders can easily extend their 'formal' terms.

3. We should actively help senior teams to contain their authoritarian traits, such as narcissism, hubris syndrome and other derailment factors, by regularly collecting feedback about their reputation in the workplace and by actively challenging them when reflecting on their reputation and the risks of their leadership offers.

4. When dealing with relatively authoritarian leadership teams, sometimes called 'petty tyrants' or 'dark triads', it is important to encourage free expression and multilateral pressures, to form coalitions and maintain a sense of personal purpose, as it does take a huge, costly and risky effort to refresh and emancipate such leadership.

5. More generally, we should nurture and listen to opposing views by (a) encouraging debate about key (strategic) decisions; (b) strengthening the practice of "listening up" (Reitz & Higgins, 2019) internally; and (c) nurturing whistle-blowers (Miceli & Near, 2002). Whistle-blowers should have the right of anonymity together with identity and job protection. If organisations implement the policies which can already be found in national guidelines, they raise the chances that whistle-blowing stays internal and will not escalate outwards from the organisation into the public domain. Such organisations acquire earlier opportunities to identify and manage risk, which helps to avoid or limit financial and reputational damage.

11.4   What team coaches need to know in working with top teams

Team coaching for top leadership teams can be quite an exposing ordeal, especially in periods of change and renewal, or when vital decisions need to be taken. To help team coaches remain reflective and helpful in these circumstances, I would recommend the following:

1. Stay calm and relational – pressures may be passed on to you. It is important to keep training your awareness for co-created emotions and to keep wondering what the particular tension, fear, doubt or pressure that you experience might be about: what can it tell us about the current challenges for the team?

2. Stay open, curious and spontaneous – in the circumstance this may not feel natural but truly courageous and anxiety-provoking; nevertheless, plain, open speaking offers not only a rich outsider's perspective on what is going on in the team currently, it also models a form of speaking up that would benefit the team and the organisation more generally. In team coaching we sense the emotions that are being felt in the organisation (through 'parallel process' – Searles, 1955), so if it feels extremely difficult to speak up then that is meaningful in itself, and it might be very helpful just to say that: "it seems difficult to speak up".

3. Stay balanced and reflective – following from a general calm and open stance, it is important to remain balanced between feeling the pressures and observing

them, in fleeting moments of noticing (De Haan, 2019a). It may very well be necessary to work with a second coach just to honour both the subjective and the objective, both the team and their organisation, both the decisions and the overall purpose. Moreover, if it does not feel safe for a single coach it is often a lot better to go seconded, so that you can keep the leadership shadow in ongoing observation.

4. Focus on the data and the phenomenal – decisions need to be based on good data (which includes feelings!), reading the room and reading the experts (i.e., both subjective here-and-now data and objective longer-term data), so where you can help as a team coach is in collecting and highlighting data-driven, upwards-feedback decisions.

These contributions of team coaches are also argued in other chapters of this book but for boardroom team coaches they are even more pertinent. Following on from the previous section I think a 'fiercely democratic' stance would behove team coaches. It is important for team coaches to keep in mind the less powerful employees that this team leads, and to remain aware of consequences for others in the organisation of any reputational or policy impacts of the changes in the top team. This is hard to do of course, as the team coaches will not be free from the strong projections around the team or their own authority countertransference patterns (for a definition see Chapter 4), but it is at least worth keeping in mind another 'client' in the team coaching, which is the organisation or subsystem that this top team is responsible for (just like individual coaches do when they are aware of the organisation in the room represented by their coachee). I also believe team coaches need to be fiercely democratic in the sense that they should speak out for what they are observing and noticing, and not be held back by power dynamics. They should remind themselves regularly that they are not inside the hierarchy and that they are independent. Also, they need to keep looking into their own corruptibility as a team coach in the presence of power.

It is important to create the right conditions for top team coaching to work. It is helpful to have a formal contract in place, which specifies the confidentiality and independence of the team coach, the importance of challenge, and other basics. Team coaches often regret it later if they haven't spoken with the CEO or overall commissioner about the need to afford a team coach solid space (freedom, trust, tolerance) to become a trusted, critically involved, supportive outsider. In nearly every assignment there is a moment when the whole team unites in attacking the team coach for having an independent view, and at that very moment it would be nice to be able to say "see, I told you this would happen", or "at least you seem united now, for a change, in your unanimous critique of your powerless supportive outsider" – almost like a court jester.

As top team coaches are in a small minority up against a big, powerful team, they should try to find a deep confidence that the top team needs them as a critically involved, supportive outsider. As I have argued, top teams cannot function very well without outside observations and challenge ('upwards feedback'). It would be best if a multitude of relevant views on the bigger challenges in the organisation would percolate upwards from other layers in the organisation, but in reality (in most large organisations) such views are often in short supply. Modern organisations are not democracies, they are strictly speaking autocracies where ultimate power resides in a small number of autocratically selected individuals (according to an 'opting in' principle which means minorities are nearly always under-represented – see also Chapter 12). This model usually gets replicated in other layers of management as well: it is rare to see whole departments voting for important decisions or for the appointment of their next leader (although according to the evidence reviewed above that would be good practice leading to better decisions). One can see the form of governance in most current organisations as a bounded autocracy: there are clear limits on the power of the rulers, who can only rule on organisation-related and therefore work-related issues and their instruments of power are also limited to non-violent, essentially persuasive ones. The harshest measure that they have in their toolkit is exclusion, depriving someone from the work role, privileges and/ or contract with the organisation, which does stretch to exile or even something approaching a 'death penalty' but only as far as organisational life is concerned.

To come to the best decisions in autocracies – but also in democracies – it is crucial for information to flow to the top where the important decisions are being taken. At the same time, information is power for those that do not enjoy the position power of sitting at the top table. Moreover, information may be unwelcome, as it can contradict existing views in the board. In other words, there are many barriers for information flowing upwards. Open and honest reporting can lead to a loss of felt relevance or repressive counteraction. Team coaches can help both with the information flow upwards (e.g., by summarising the findings from interviews) and with the consideration of fresh information and minority perspectives. For both these reasons it is vital in my view that team coaches are frank and courageous, and that they do not themselves become a filter or censor for potentially crucial information. Similarly, it is important for team coaches not to advise or advocate; to just hold out the information *as* information, as something for the team to consider, to take on board, integrate or discard as leaders see fit. Advising by team coaches, i.e., promoting certain ideas over others, has the same effect as filtering: it constrains rather than expands the potential for decision making at the top of the organisation.

As argued, team coaches for top teams need to be rather direct and challenging, as well as truly deep listeners and observers, without becoming advisors or co-leaders. Our work is entirely non-directive, opening up a possible flaw or elephant in the room, or pointing out what may not be working or does not seem coherent. This is why a combination with expert consulting is not generally so helpful for team coaches. Moreover, certain relatively directive approaches to coaching, such as step methods (GROW, GROUP, CLEAR, etc.) or Solution-Focused Coaching, are less powerful at the board level, because they do not use much challenge or interpretation at all. On the other hand, approaches that encourage emergence of new thinking from within the team, such as relational Gestalt (Chapter 2), or that support the formulation of hypotheses and new insight, such as systems psychodynamics (Chapter 4) and other systemic perspectives (Chapter 3), have much more to offer to top leadership themes. It is therefore important for top coaches to quietly observe, hold hypotheses, and to be able to interpret what is going on, as well as letting go of an interpretation in order to continue to listen freely and compassionately again. Team coaches at this level should be able to tolerate, to a degree, the anxieties in the team and their own pain of not knowing, whilst staying observant. Only then can they tirelessly flirt with their hypotheses without ever marrying them. Many authors have already remarked that coaching can then be a very helpful, tailored intervention at top levels, particularly as it seems to be an effective approach for highly personal tensions and leadership derailment (see, e.g., Nelson & Hogan, 2009; Warrenfeltz & Kellett, 2016; De Haan et al., 2019).

Similar to Greek democratic politicians in the fifth century before Christ, current top leadership teams will need not just an infusion of democracy if they are to stand any chance in the crises of tomorrow, but they will also need something like the institution of Greek tragedy, a place where they can look at the hubris, guilt, shame and revenge patterns which are never far from their decision-making powers.

Case vignette: Here is a recent case example of a university institute's leadership team where researchers are working on one of the global crises that are keeping our minds focused across the world. They asked me to offer a series of team coaching sessions to help the research leaders to overcome boundaries between an archipelago of autonomous research groupings. In these various teams, methodologies and scientific inspirations were different and they were in a sense in competition in trying to understand the current crisis. As a result of working in relative silos for several years they were now not talking with one another much and blaming each other for lack of delivery or wasting the centralised funding of the institute. Before the team coaching, I asked for the opportunity to do interviews and to write a report for the leadership team which was doing its best to keep a neutral stance presiding above the various warring factions. My interviews were emotional and sometimes dramatic, as I felt most of the research leads tried to win me over to their view of the world but also to a very dark estimation of some of the other groups. There were regular hints at unethical practice but despite probing I could not find any evidence of malpractice, except perhaps for some posturing or claiming deeper insight than appeared to be warranted in purely scientific terms. It was straightforward for me to not blame any individuals in my report. In fact, my main hypothesis was that the primary process – research into a highly problematic issue – had spilled over into the dynamics of the group, as has been well documented in organisations that deal with anxiety, loss or crisis (starting with Menzies Lyth, 1960). I interpreted some of the difficult experiences of the teams as possibly being the result of "secondary" defences originated within the research organisation that had been built around the extremely difficult study material. I offered to go ahead with the team coaching where we could process some of this and could look into a better containment for the researchers.

What was interesting about the top leadership was that they had the reputation of being rather 'hands off', that they gave the researchers a lot of freedom, and were often ill-prepared in meetings with them – something that I also felt when I had my meeting with the lead researchers following the writing of the report. In that meeting my report was heavily criticised by the team leads and appeared to become the object of a new scientific debate where the team leaders could unify in their universal disparaging response. I decided to hold on to the report's interpretations as my subjective and preliminary views, offered a date and a frame for team coaching, and refused to give an agenda for that meeting. Then I arrived on time, waiting for what would emerge. To my delight the report and the overall leadership faded away and the negative experiences and rivalry between the teams gained centerground.

Although no formal outcomes were achieved in that first session, everyone felt heard and united in a new way – some reported they had not felt this close for two whole years. A very impactful session as everyone went beyond the toxic dynamics into a shared space where they shared the same humanity. They shared how hurt they had felt in some interactions, but also how warm and generous individuals had been at times. This proved to be a good basis for the next team coaching sessions and the beginning of a slow process 'back' from the fragmentation and crisis they had experienced before.

11.5 Conclusion

I hope I have been able to convey in this chapter how crucial the role of a team coach can be for top leadership teams, and how exciting it can be to play this role and make a difference to major decisions in organisations and to the quality of reflection in top teams. The team coach is often the odd person out, someone who attends to very different aspects than the leaders around the room, and may well look somewhat out of her depth, bedraggled, or clumsy. But, as Shakespeare wrote, "jesters do oft prove prophets" and from the background or the shadows of the team's dynamics a team coach can make a very profound difference to the sustainability and validity of decisions of top teams. The secret of the successful fool is that he is no fool at all. And a jester unemployed is nobody's fool. Just to quote a few well-known sayings that apply very well to boardroom team coaches.

Chapter 12

Working with equity, diversity, and inclusion in teams

Tammy Tawadros and David Birch

Not everything that is faced can be changed. But nothing can be changed until it is faced.
(James Baldwin, 1962, p. 12)

12.1 Introduction

Team coaching is always concerned, to some extent, with change. As Baldwin remarked, "Not everything that is faced can be changed; but nothing can be changed until it is faced", therefore the team has to really face and confront the issues and conflicts they hold before they can begin to change them. Facing the issues means that team members look at how they collaborate and learn, across differences and systemic boundaries. The meaning and significance of questions of 'Equity, Diversity and Inclusion' (EDI) within a team will depend on a myriad of factors, including the lived experience of team members, and the ways in which social differences are understood (and responded to within the organisation and in the wider systemic context). Our universal social need for psychological safety (Edmondson & Lei, 2014) and relational security (Baumeister & Leary, 1995) is, in part, mediated through our experiences of equity and fairness, of diversity and difference and of inclusion and belonging (see for e.g., Nembhard & Edmondson, 2006; Workman-Stark, 2021)

The EDI themes and patterns that present themselves in team coaching, may emanate from within the team itself, impacting the team as a whole and then the organisation beyond. Or the converse may be the case, in that what happens within the team, may be manifestations or 're-presentations' of wider organisational or societal dynamics. This inside-out, outside-in dynamic can be disorientating for teams, who may find themselves dealing with powerful ideas, behaviours and feelings that seemingly 'belong' in several places at once. What might seem to be about an individual team member may simultaneously be about the norms, values and the

DOI: 10.4324/9781003325789-16

climate of the team, or for that matter the wider organisation's culture and practices, or the many social oppressions and injustices currently 'out there' in the 'past-present' of unheeded and unhealed wounds of history (see for e.g.,Olusoga, 2016).

Our experience of coaching diverse teams is that they often face episodes of becoming 'stormy' or getting 'stuck'. Team coaching can support them as they reflect, surface their differing experiences, and explore how this impacts their collaborative endeavours. It can also help create the conditions for building the habits of deep dialogue and perspective-taking.

The scope of this chapter

Providing a comprehensive or complete understanding of EDI is beyond the scope of this chapter. Instead, we want to share the understandings and approaches that have helped us as we have grappled with the issues. We find that we are, in any case, continuously re-examining and evolving our approaches and practices. We know that we are simultaneously part of the rich picture that we are seeking to describe, understand and change. This is inevitably part and parcel of relational team coaching work: we are 'in relationship with' and embedded in the personal, interpersonal, and wider systems within which we live and work.

Our use and choice of terms

The current terminology is derived from the egalitarian language of human rights and social justice. Most organisations and institutions will refer to one or more of the following terms:

- D&I: diversity and inclusion
- EDI: equity, diversity, and inclusion
- DEIB: diversity, equity, inclusion and belonging
- EDIJ equity, diversity, inclusion, and justice

Our preference is to use the phrase 'equity, diversity and inclusion' (EDI) because it serves as both an expedient shorthand for talking about difference, but also as an indication of the normative values which inform our practice as team coaches. In our view, equity encompasses justice and inclusion and implies a felt sense of belonging. We take diversity (and difference) as constant features in all of our lives. For us, it is the social value which we might attach to these dimensions, and what this implies for the participation and representation of different groups that matters most. That said, we also have some reservations about the use of EDI terminology, which has arguably become something of a ubiquitous corporate acronym. As a result, it may invite a rather 'mindless' engagement with checklists or with sloganeering and a rallying call for groupthink or token gestures. In such cases, the possibility of reflection and dialogue is stifled, as is the potential for relational connection and shared understanding. Nonetheless, we believe that it is expedient and pragmatic to adopt the most-used terms by way of shorthand, and an entry point into this area. We will elaborate below on how we understand and interpret these terms, together with some brief examples based on our practice.

Why the topic matters to us

Equity, diversity, and inclusion are themes which have received renewed attention over recent years. We are living through an era of profound upheaval and uncertainty, causing many of us to re-evaluate our fundamental relationships and contracts with ourselves, with each other and with our planet. Any fantasies we might have entertained of a benign, secure, stable existence have been violently shaken by the widespread abuse, exploitation, and corruption on the part of powerful individuals and institutions. Now, more than ever, we are confronted by widespread ableism, classism, misogyny, and racism, as well as the oppression of other marginalised and minoritized groups, such as LBTQ+, neurodiverse and many other groups.[1] The growing awareness and concern for rights and justice has also underlined the need to consider 'intersectionality', or how identities and oppressions overlap and operate together.[2] As a result, there has been a good deal more public debate and understanding about equity and social justice, which has in turn led to greater efforts by organisations and institutions to respond positively and responsibly.

Tammy writes: These are themes that touch my own personal history growing up as a member of a religious minority in a newly independent nation, its culture hollowed out and its prospects for economic and political autonomy eroded by decades of colonial occupation. The legacy of empire shaped my experience of migration and of living in Britain, settling a 'racialised' identity for me-as an exile, as a stranger in someone else's green and pleasant land, and a lesser citizen, for all the privileges that modest material comfort, class and education conferred on me. This relationship with race overlapped and intersected with my experiences of gender and of disability. I was politically active as a student, a young professional and an educationalist, but grew disillusioned with the apparently slow rate of meaningful structural change. The intense emotional and social trauma of Covidian times and the killing of George Floyd, served as uncomfortable reminders. Uncomfortable reminders not only of my own vulnerabilities, but also of the power and potential of transracial and intersectional solidarity[3] and other areas of humanity, of society and inevitably of group and team life. This prompted me to re-engage more consciously, with the professional values and practices of anti-discriminatory and anti-oppressive work in the helping professions that had felt so much more present and vital during the earlier part of my career. Knowing that hard-won progress continues to come from the struggle of marginalised and minoritized groups has inspired me to renew my own contract with the world, and with the core values of social justice. What endures for me in my own practice is the commitment to continue to find ways of bringing these values to life in the work with individuals, teams, and organisations.

David writes: Growing up in the 1960s in white suburban Britain I was educated at a selective boys' school where we were often reminded of our social and academic privilege. I didn't feel particularly special and felt confused by the injustice and inequity in my situation. Leaving home, I was attracted by the radicalism and inclusiveness of the peace movement and the Anti-Nazi League of the early 1980s. I joined a men's group and learned about assertiveness, facilitation, and non-violent direct action. By my late 20s I was living at an ashram in India, seeking inner peace and enlightenment through the teachings of a guru. My transformation into a suit-wearing, mortgage-paying corporate citizen came later, when I was recruited by one of the 'big 4' accountancy firms as an internal OD consultant. Here I found ways of expressing my erstwhile radicalism in my process work with individuals and teams. My subsequent training as a psychotherapist included inner-city placements where I was once again confronted by my whiteness and male privilege. Since then I have been co-inquiring into my lifelong biases and prejudices, noticing and regulating their impact on my relationships and professional practice.

Why EDI matters to team coaching

The experiences and changes described above have influenced and impacted team coaches, as well as the coaching profession itself.[4] These values are of course controversial to those holding more individualistic and conservative world views. This can sometimes lead to a troubling discourse of denialism[5] and denigration. In the UK and elsewhere, this often masquerades as the moderating of unbridled 'political correctness' or as active resistance in the 'war on woke'. From a psychodynamic perspective we understand these regressive forces as individual, group and societal defences against shame, fear and the dread of dislocation and dissolution. At the same time, we have seen the emergence of 'cancel culture', a vehement intolerance of ambiguity and nuance, that leaves little room for open debate and dialogue. Our experience is that critique, debate, and strong emotions are a necessary and inevitable part of any conversation that reaches into the heart of who we are and how we relate to each other.

During an era of radical disruption and societal dysregulation, we are confronted with fundamental questions about our human relations and social condition, that bring us face-to-face with contested ideas, passionate disagreements, and the bewildering complexity of our human experience. This requires us to 'tune in', to understand ourselves and our relationships at a deeper level. This means grappling with past and present traumas of social power and privilege, becoming more conscious of our emotional and social shadow and, in time, coming together more fully and authentically.

As team coaches, we take into account multiple perspectives, layers of experience and a multiplicity of interconnected relationships. We find ourselves flooded with information and faced with an array of possibilities and hypotheses to consider. This is particularly the case when we are dealing with the complexity that EDI encompasses and the way these dimensions simultaneously interact.

We have found that the three 'relational lenses' we describe below, can provide a useful starting point, and means of focusing the attention of the team coach on some key aspects of the team and its relationship with EDI:

(a) By considering how the team may 're-present' experiences of *equity* and fairness as a fractal[6] of the wider systemic context. This often takes the form of a recapitulation or 'replay' of existing inequities in the team's wider social context.

(b) By noticing how the expression and suppression of *diversity* and difference influences the climate of psychological safety within a team. As team coaches, we can help teams to notice and make sense of the emotional tensions they may be holding and enacting, for example by suppressing difference. Or we may help the team track the ways in which openness and acceptance of diversity enhance psychological safety (Edmondson, 1999).

(c) By looking at how the team can offer opportunities for *inclusion* and belonging by providing a secure base for its members. The notion of a secure attachment and the idea of the team as a secure base (Schofield & Beek, 2014) derive from Bowlby's theories of attachment (Bowlby, 1969). According to Biggart et al. (2017), the team can operate as both a safe haven and a secure base that helps its members cope with the demands of their roles. Key to the functioning of the team as a secure base, is team belonging.

We will return to these through case vignettes described below as we demonstrate how the work of a team coach can be naturally and robustly underpinned by EDI and our understanding of the dynamics of difference.

12.2   Relational equity: honouring the E of EDI

For us, 'equity' comes first. It is both a value *and* an outcome of fair and just practices. Also, the pursuit of equity, in contrast to equality, takes account of the differential privileges that individuals and groups possess, and which confer certain advantages to them. Equitable practices acknowledge the existence and consequences of oppression and recognise that we are so embedded within a psychic and social context of power and privilege that objectivity is impossible, and 'neutrality' is essentially a myth.

As coaches, we need to recognise that whilst we cannot be 'neutral', 'objective' or 'impartial', we can at least be transparent about this. In team coaching, we arguably hold an ethical and professional responsibility to actively challenge oppression. This may mean witnessing and validating team members' lived experience of ableism, homophobia, patriarchy, misogyny, racism or transphobia, among the many oppressions that exist. Our task in coaching teams is to form supportive alliances with our clients, at the same as holding up a mirror to the unhealthy patterns of relationship that we witness. We also explicitly hold ourselves open to looking at the power and privilege we carry and express. In doing so, we keep in mind the awareness that some social groups are exalted, while others are devalued, and that we ourselves are complicit in this.

We should also remain alert to the simultaneous layering and interplay of the EDI issues. Team dynamics may reflect both issues of social power and privilege, *and* themes of envy, rivalry, attachment, and dependency. We strive to adopt an approach that takes into account the multiple relationships between our co-created emotional worlds, our organisational systems, and our social and political power relations. We see social justice as integral to our ethical practice, and we are unapologetic in our emphasis on equity as a paramount, guiding principle in our work.

Implications for practice: contracting

What and how we contract with a team is always a matter of judgement, rather than a hard and fast rule. In many instances, we find that it is not only what we share about our approach, but more importantly how we make contracts in the moment that enables these perspectives to be voiced and heard. Much depends on our felt sense of readiness and the safety climate that we have encouraged and co-created with them.

Whatever the presenting issues or goals we set for the team coaching work, we usually include something about our values when contracting more generally for *how* we work. We might begin by asking about the team and their organisation's approach to equity. Then we might say something like:

> We believe it's important to talk about what happens in this organisation and in this team and how you feel about the things that may be fair or unfair, just, or unjust. We see it as part of our job to notice the themes and feelings to do with equity, fairness, and justice during the sessions and to ask you about them. It's probably something we'll come to take responsibility for together, to pay attention and notice when it comes up, and to look into its significance for the team.

We find this makes it easier to inquire robustly into any themes connected to oppression that present themselves as the work unfolds. Teams tend not to talk about these issues directly because they may feel inhibited or because the thoughts and feelings are outside conscious awareness. Our work as team coaches is often to listen for and inquire into seemingly inconsequential complaints and tensions, such as being 'irritated', 'hacked off', 'pissed off' and so on, and into apparently 'ordinary' everyday skirmishes.

Where the felt climate of psychological safety feels 'robust enough', we might also contract a 'general permission' for how we work with the team to exploring the dynamics of social power. We might open with something like:

> It's not unusual for us to make space to address questions about power and privilege that come up in teams, and to come to an understanding about what actually happens to us individually and collectively.

And follow up with a statement along the lines of:

It's important for us to let you know that as part of our commitment to help-ing you grow as a team will be to encourage you to look into questions like what you stand for, who you stand with, and how you empower and value each other. When we find ourselves exploring these questions, we stand in support of those individuals whose identity, presence, and contribution may be unwittingly devalued.

Implications for practice: developing sensitivity

As team coaches we can develop our sensitivity to the experience of difference by learning how systems of discrimination, subordination, and privilege exist in our wider culture. Oppressive processes such as sexism, racism, classism, ableism and heterosexism give rise to unconscious biases, stereotypes, and assumptions that implicitly discourage or silence those who feel different to the prevailing or dom-inant societal norms.

These processes play out in organisations all the time. For example, in an organ-isation where the leader is an archetypal assertive white man, Black women may be criticised for being loud and aggressive, thus finding themselves in a double bind: they either can conform to the organisation's norms and risk being marginal-ised by their group, or they can do the opposite. Either way they risk opprobrium and ostracism.

Team coaches can create the connection and psychological safety needed to share these experiences, *moving towards difference* instead of staying silent. This means facilitating conversations where people from different backgrounds find the confidence to voice their lived experiences, perspectives, and world views.

These kinds of conversation can be difficult and uncomfortable because they name and confront oppressions that will have been out of peoples' conscious awareness. Team members – and indeed team coaches – may fear the reactions or reprisals from those in more privileged or powerful positions, so it's important that people's feelings are respected and that different perspectives are welcomed. By adopting a non-judgemental stance of compassionate curiosity, we can avoid pre-mature meaning-making and support reflection on the discomfort and eventually the learning that lies on the other side.

As team coaches, we may struggle to maintain our curiosity when we encounter difference. We may feel caught between attachment and separation, and in such moments we can notice and share our defensiveness, exercise humility and use 'I statements' to describe our thoughts, feelings, and interpretations. There will always be different perspectives which cannot be reduced to a single truth.

We find it important to remember that conversations about equity, diversity and inclusion take time and emotional energy, so we often pause for reflection and then return to the conversation with a fresh perspective.

Case vignette 1: Using the lens of Team as a Fractal: 're-presenting' experiences of equity

One of us worked with a project team that reported to the Executive Leadership Team (ELT) responsible of the construction of a multi-billion-pound transport hub. Within the team there were subgroups looking after passenger modelling and infrastructure design, with one person (Sean) responsible for the construction of the hub. The team was all-male, with a woman leader (Kate) who was also a member of the ELT. Sean was Irish, Kate was Australian (as were most of the ELT), the rest of the team were British.

The team coaching intervention was timed shortly before a reporting deadline. The team was under stress and a split was emerging between Sean, Kate, and the rest of the team. Sean, a civil engineer was results-oriented and had a reputation as 'a talented fixer'. The planners and modellers, mostly former civil servants, were more laid back and absorbed in the design of computer models predicting passenger flows according to alternative designs and scenarios.

With the reporting deadline drawing close, Sean told the team that he felt let down and unsupported by them. He was worried that he had 'nothing substantial to say about progress' in his report to the project board. He blamed his planning colleagues for the delay, accusing them of being 'public school toffs' of 'not living in the real world' and of 'playing around with modelling software'. Kate stepped in and tried to mediate, pointing out the importance of getting the modelling right and suggesting that she use her influence 'to smooth things over with the board'. Kate's display of concern for Sean seems to infuriate him further. He rejected her offer of help, telling her that she and her Australian colleagues were secretly referred to as 'the colonials with the keys to the executive toilet.'

As the team coach, I was taken aback by Sean's outburst and his apparent contempt for his team members, not to mention his views about Kate and the ELT. I felt caught between wanting to validate Sean's deep sense of hurt and drawing attention to the social divisions between Sean and the planners and his ideas about 'commonwealth colonialism' with respect to Kate and her ELT colleagues. After reflecting for a few moments, I said: "it sounds like it may be hard for people and their contribution to be valued in this organisation?". This seemed to resonate with the team, who went on to talk about the impact of pressure and stress on them. As the tense atmosphere began to ease, I gently returned to Sean's provocative statements and the polarisation I had witnessed.

Role of the team coach

This was an intense and demanding process for me. My thinking was drawn to the social and ethnographic dimensions of the discussion, but I had a visceral experience of how it felt to work in this team and organisation. I knew from being in a difficult or high-stakes situation in my family or in the teams I had been part of, that I often went into my head, and the realm of ideas, especially when I had intense feelings of distress and discomfort in my body, particularly, my stomach. It occurred to me that Sean's denigration of his colleagues was in some way a fractal of society's relationship with public transport; the way we take it for granted, complaining about it and devaluing it, whilst still needing it throughout our lives. I wanted to share my insight, without blame or criticism, and without dismissing Sean's experience. I wanted to show my compassion for Sean. His comments had clearly invoked the social inequities of class and perceived cultural superiority and dominion of Britain over Australia. It seemed that a powerful experience from his own background had been evoked for him, perhaps in re-presentation and replay of his class position and his country's history of colonial entanglement with England. This had lent his words a particular force and meaning, which resonated with me, and got me reflecting on what past hurts were perhaps remaining unheeded and unhealed for him personally, and in what way he was an unwitting conduit, 'channelling' and voicing the team's discomforts and divisions.

In this case we can discern some of the processes and mechanisms underpinning 'othering', 'splitting', and social power that operate in the intrapsychic layers of individual and team experience (inside out), and the layers of external, historical, political, and social influence that shape our experience (outside in). It was Freud who originally posited that the ego, or "I", protects itself against the threats to identity presented by otherness through unconscious defence mechanisms, which may include denial, disavowal, and projection (Freud, 1946). The notion that differences needs to be 'defended against' has long been central to our understanding of 'othering' (Klein, 1964). This can be explained as the way we defend against the anxiety by reducing those who are different from "us" to the status of "things". For Sean, these defences may have come to the fore in response to the hidden and internalised oppressions he experienced in relation to class and the historic power relations between Ireland and England, though disavowal, denial, and projection may well have been at play for him and indeed his teammates and for Kate, the leader of the team. At the level of the group, othering enables groups and group members with more power and privilege to define the boundaries of who is 'in' and who is in the 'out' group. And although we don't know what the interactions and dynamics that preceded the team coaching sessions were like, it is possible that Kate and the sub-group of modellers held more social power and privilege than Sean.

12.3   Valued diversity: expanding the D of EDI

The term 'diversity' has evolved in its usage over the years. It is currently used to refer to a wide range of human attributes that differentiate groups and people from one another. Difference tends to be defined in relation to the socially dominant culture or group, which explicitly or implicitly signifies a 'lesser than' status and departure from a given norm or 'standard'. Working with difference is invariably a feature of life in a team, as it is in the wider systems within which the team exists. Appreciating and actively harnessing diversity has long been recognised as being advantageous for teams (see for example, Rock & Grant, 2016; West, 2012). There is growing evidence of the benefit that women and LGBTQ+ people (to name but two examples of what has become known as 'diversity dividend'), bring to leadership teams and boards. However, as we have already noted, difference throws up many psychological and relational dilemmas for teams, notwithstanding the potential advantages. These are sometimes the unspoken challenges that cause an executive team or board to seek team coaching, or they may simply show up spontaneously during a session.

Case vignette 2: Using the lens of Team Climate: noticing how the team suppresses or expresses difference and the impact on psychological safety
The executive team of this property and entertainment business was struggling to maintain a constructive dialogue between the different generations and cultures represented within the team. The founder and owner of the business was a 66-year-old man from a south Asian background with the rest of the team comprised of six younger men and women of white European or Asian British heritage.

The founder had stated his intention to retire from his CEO role but had not identified a successor and was struggling to relinquish control of the business. This was causing frustration amongst the team, which sometimes erupted into full-blown arguments, usually when the founder was challenged by younger women executives. Small disagreements would rapidly escalate into loud arguments, with shouting, swearing, and people leaving the meeting in tears.

Team members reacted to these incidents in different ways. Some would avoid any kind of conflict with the founder, adopting a compliant and passive attitude towards him. Others would continue to confront him, arguing that his "command and control" leadership style was unacceptable and that he needed to work more collaboratively as he prepared for his retirement.

There were many issues at play in this team, not the least of which was the founder's ambivalence about retiring, but more immediately the need to address the recurring pattern of arguments and conflict.

Over a period of several months, as part of a team coaching engagement, one of us worked with this team. I worked primarily to facilitate a process of storytelling in the group, where each team member shared their life-story, including their hopes and dreams for the future. This revealed, among other things, that the founder had grown up in the 1950s in a socially conservative Punjabi family, where boys were idolised as 'little princes' and where gender roles were strictly delineated. He felt that he was being "disrespected" when he was challenged, which triggered strong, visceral feelings of anger and an irresistible desire to control. This in turn had a retraumatising effect on those in the team who had grown up in families where the men were similarly domineering.

This opened a rich dialogue into changing gender roles (particularly in south Asian communities) and eventually some agreement about what appropriate social behaviour looked like in the team. The founder acknowledged his power and the effect that his aggressive style had been having on his colleagues. He and the team agreed ground rules for offering alternative or opposing points of view to reduce the risk of them being taken personally as they had been before. They also learned and consciously practised active listening skills that they deployed when things became heated.

Role of the team coach

I saw my role in this case as being to negotiate and facilitate a process that acknowledged the effect of different experiences, assumptions, and biases that team members brought to their meetings. Over time, this helped the team respect and honour their differences, whilst creating a sense of separation between what was tolerable "back then" and what was appropriate "right now". An important part of this differentiation between past and present was linguistic: I encouraged team members to say "I used to think" or "I used to feel" when describing archaic reactions that they were letting go of. This was a symbolically important change of mindset that helped reduce the reactive potential in the team.

I focused first of all on maintaining a calm and accepting presence when conflict was expressed. This carried the message that high emotion and disagreement was something that could be bearable and contained. Next, I concentrated on observing how the team interacted, noticing what differences needed to be expressed. Encouraging the team to give voice to their experience, indirectly through the medium of story, helped them to surface the tensions engendered by differing expectations about gender roles across generations. Perhaps in part because the founder had placed a good deal of trust in me, and perhaps because like him, I was a man (albeit one who was providing him with a challenge to his gender role expectations), I was able to set an expectation about the value of open acknowledgement with team members.

Doing this in a purposefully gentle manner, and 'staying with' the team over time, as they worked through their differing needs and perspectives, helped them to acquire the habit of patience, openness, and skilled listening. By attending closely to the patterns and themes in the team's conversations and rounds of interaction, and fostering a climate of openness and curiosity, they were eventually able to cultivate the requisite team climate.

In this scenario, I operated to some extent as an 'agent provocateur' and an agent of social valorisation, in giving and directing attention to gendered and generational differences that threatened the team's capacity to collaborate. This involved me confronting and 'normalising' the conflict, ambivalence, dependency, rivalry that emerged, whilst acknowledging the operation of social difference and structural power and supporting the voices of those who would be marginalised to be heard.

This case shows us that it is as a result of attuning to and working through the discomforts of different expectations, frames of reference, differentials of social power, privilege, and status that the teams realise the so-called 'diversity advantage'. In this case, team coaching enables the team to arrive at a point where, having witnessed each other's narratives, they are better able examine their experience from multiple perspectives, to deliberate more thoroughly and carefully before reacting emotionally or rejecting different viewpoints, as well as tolerate ambiguity and disagreement. Team coaching can help teams to confront discomfort and to build habits and practices that engender a relational climate of greater psychological safety.

12.4   Secure inclusion: taking responsibility for the I of EDI

'Inclusion' refers to the ways in which differences are welcomed, enjoyed, and respected in a team. Attending to inclusion inevitably invokes issues about belonging, which in turn can be bound up with identity, difference, status, and power within the team. These are themes which structure and pattern social relationships not only in teams, but the wider context of the organisation and the external world. Questions of diversity, difference and inclusion can stir up powerful emotions in the team which have hitherto been repressed or unacknowledged. They may remain under the surface, or they may be expressed in overt or covert conflict and contention.

There is a myriad of subtle and unconscious ways in which team members may be excluded and 'othered' by their colleagues. What gives these exchanges their very particular emotional charge and social meaning is the combination of current and historic power relationships, and how these intersect and combine to contextualise the meanings of words, gestures, interactions, and relationships.

For example, to exhort a team member to 'get back in the kitchen!' may be a playful injunction to a male teammate in the context of them preparing the team's Christmas lunch, but it may suggest a completely asymmetric interaction if it is spoken by the male team leader to the only woman member of the team. The idiom, to 'crack the whip', apparently goes back to and originates from practices connected to horse-drawn vehicles (Ames, 2020), but takes on the connotations of slavery, when used by a white leader with a majority Black nursing team already carrying an excessive workload, whatever the intentions and circumstances of the situation.

Although the number of studies remains small, the available evidence supports the value of inclusive behaviours in facilitating positive outcomes in diverse teams. Focused on investigating inclusive leadership, the work of Ashikali et al. (2021) offers some important pointers that are consistent with the literature on bias and belonging at work (for example, Waller, 2022; Wilcox, 2011), and with our own experiences of team coaching. Namely, that to feel included in a team, individuals need to feel that they belong in the group. At the same time, each team member needs to be treated as an insider ('one of us') whilst having the opportunity to be different, unique, and distinctive. There is also growing evidence that leader and team member behaviours that promote inclusion also foster psychological safety (Edmondson, 2018; Shore et al., 2018).

As team coaches it behoves us to model and signal inclusive leadership. This is not only in service of being congruent with our values, but also because our work is concerned with coaching teams of leaders whose own inclusive behaviours matter hugely. Inclusive leadership behaviours have been shown to be a critical factor in cultivating a welcome climate for organisational employees with a diversity of social identities. Ashikali et al. (2021), identify the key behaviours of inclusive leaders as being:

1. Valuing and welcoming difference.
2. Setting the expectation that multiple, unique, and dynamic social identities are the 'norm'.
3. Encouraging people to maintain curiosity, openness, and authenticity.
4. Actively seeking out and using difference in decision-making.

Case vignette 3: The Team as a Secure Base: offering opportunities for inclusion and belonging

This senior clinical team at an NHS Trust was responsible for the care and treatment of vulnerable women with a history of childhood trauma, self-harm, domestic violence, sex work and substance abuse.

Structural changes at the Trust required the clinical leader to spend more time with the trust executive and less time with the team. This resulted in the rest of the team feeling excluded from strategic decisions affecting their work with other departments at the trust. There was a strong sense of 'them and us' with the 'us' being the all-women team, united in their anger and frustration with what they felt was a needless introduction of hierarchy and stratification.

At the time that one of us had begun coaching the team, there had been some recent changes in team composition with some staff reducing their hours or working part time. Not only were team members competing for the attention of their leader, but they were competing with one another, meeting less frequently and withdrawing into their disciplinary 'tribes' of social work, psychology, psychiatry, and nursing. Envy, rivalry, and mistrust now characterised what had hitherto been a collaborative multidisciplinary team. Psychologically, their sense of loss mirrored the distress felt by their patients, many of whom also felt commodified and abused.

The intervention was designed to recreate the sense of the team as a 'secure base' – much as they sought to do with their patients. The team coach used a psychologically informed 'team-narrative' approach, where each team member contracted to alternate sharing their narrative accounts of the team with listening and noticing the quality of the individual story, including its emotional tone and salient themes. This enabled a shared appreciation of the team's narrative, including nostalgia for a bygone 'golden age' where there were men on the team and manageable levels of demand. Since then, the demands on the team had grown, with ever more patients with multiple and complex needs and an erosion of in-person time together and with the clinical lead. Talking about how things were then and how they are now, including their distinctive and shared concerns, helped the team contain huge anxieties and begin discussing what they needed from the clinical leader and each other.

Role of the team coach

I saw that my role was primarily to facilitate a process that allowed the team to witness, acknowledge, and accept the experiences that had not been previously shared in the team. By creating a safe container – a 'secure base' – where team members felt listened to and taken seriously, team coaching helped the team reframe their narrative of subordination and co-construct one better suited to their role in the Trust and the community. This 'secure base for exploration' worked to reduce anxiety and enabled them to engage with their internal world of feelings, and the external reality, as well as to consider the internal world of their colleagues without regressing or falling prey to defensive behaviours and 'routines'.

Looking at a more granular level, I also worked to provide a here-and-now opportunity for team members to state their needs, and accept their vulnerability, to make themselves available to each other. This process enabled them to recognise their feelings, to re-kindle a sense of belonging, and to collaborate on a non-work task, away from the huge pressures of daily demands. In turn, this gave them the chance both to re-create what they had once had in terms a safe haven and secure base, back then, whilst demarcating the experience from their past and locating it in the present.

This case shows us how multiple simultaneous changes and uncertainties influence and often distort the experience of team life, shrinking the psychic space and reducing the amount of time we have to make ourselves available to our colleagues, to offer them a safe haven when they most need it to cope with growing demands. As it is, our internal psychic world is made up of different parts jostling to be recognised. When we feel calm and untroubled, we largely manage to accommodate the ambivalence and multiplicity within. Under pressure, we may lose our ability to process, and instead project the qualities we cannot bear in ourselves onto others invested with our 'badness' or other unwanted characteristics (Bollas, 2013). In this way, we can continue to be 'good', better even, than the designated 'other' (Turner, 2021). These splits and projections manifest in the external world of our relationships, as an expression of the individual and the collective, team level psyche, when we are under pressure. We may 'regress' and find ourselves unable to hold a picture of all the parts or indeed a shared sense of responsibility for including each other and co-creating or maintaining the sense of a team. This unconscious 'reneging' on our view of ourselves as team players, may be disavowed in the context of power imbalance or social difference. The other becomes 'bad', whether they are bosses, men, women, people of colour, members of another profession or different in some other way. The qualities and attributes that are disowned in this way not only militate against safety, inclusion, and security in the team, but they also multiply and further exclude those who are vulnerable to being othered in the collective cultural psyche, or the wider organisational and societal system. When we interrupt and draw attention to these processes it becomes possible for the team to re-experience the sense of being and belonging together. The role of the team coach is to help the team to co-regulate and to re-create the secure base. This can then become the foundation for more dialogue and reflection in future sessions. Over time, these may bring a greater awareness of the 'shadow sides' of our experience, and the capacity to understand and own our unconscious defences, examine our social positioning, and appreciate the oppressions and privilege that difference confers. It may also help us to recognise our entanglement in the turmoil and trauma of our past.

12.5   Conclusion: resourcing ourselves to work with EDI in team coaching

As team coaches, we need to resource ourselves for EDI work. First, by raising our awareness of how privilege and social power permeate teams and organisations. Second, by facing and working through the anxiety and pain that we feel when we address these issues. At a personal level this means reflecting on our identity and experience of social difference, becoming more conscious of how we project onto others with less privilege and social power than ourselves. Group supervision is one possible source of support, ideally one that is diverse not only demographically, but also in terms of experience and perspective. Another option is to join a local 'consciousness awakening' or 'equity circle' group. These groups are usually self-facilitated and convened in and around universities or centres of professional education.

In this chapter we have highlighted why the topic of EDI matters for us personally and why we believe it matters for team coaching. We believe that surfacing issues of equity, diversity, and inclusion is important because they have such a profound effect on the ability of the team to function and collaborate. We also know that these kinds of conversations can be difficult to broach. Contracting with teams at the outset can help 'normalise' conversations about EDI, as can contracting 'in the moment' to address any implicit or explicit tensions.

As team coaches, we need to trust our intuitive judgement and sensitivity to EDI. In teams, the simultaneous layering of other dynamics such as envy or competition can combine and interact with EDI, resulting in a bewildering complexity. Our three relational lenses can help focus our attention and inquiry. The lens of 'team as a fractal' draws attention to how the team may be a 're-presentation' of the wider societal or organisational context. The lens of 'team climate' helps us notice how the team suppresses or expresses difference and the impact that this has on psychological safety. When we use the lens of the team as a 'secure base', the focus is on whether and how the team offers opportunities for inclusion and belonging.

Addressing issues of equity, diversity, and inclusion, is demanding work. We need support to improve our understanding of how privilege and social power permeates our lives and relationships. But while facing and working through these issues will undoubtedly challenge us, it also represents a unique opportunity for us to learn and grow.

Notes

1 We appreciate that we may not be naming and addressing many human rights and social justice concerns or indeed naming the myriad of oppressed groups. This may reflect a bias and a lack in our practice. Nonetheless, our intent is to speak about the questions and issues that we have sufficient experience of in our lives and our practice to date. We recognise that there are limits to our understanding and we are open to critique, to learning, and to enhancing and evolving our approach and our practice.
2 The notion of intersectionality recognises that identity and experience is not unitary, and that our identity and experience of multiple simultaneous oppressions intersect in a complex and nuanced manner. For example, being a person of colour, gay, and a woman produces a mosaic of different identities, that produce a very particular social experience.
3 That is, a feeling of unity and mutual sympathy and support across different groups.
4 See for example, the EMCC Diversity and Inclusion Declaration, 2018, updated 2020 and the ICF's July 2020 declaration of commitment to the core values of diversity, equity, inclusion, and justice and to placing these at the forefront of all its activities.
5 We are using the term denialism to mean the denial of current reality or historical event(s), as a way to avoid a psychologically or socially uncomfortable truth. The US journalist, Michael Specter, has defined societal denialism as happening "when an entire segment of society, often struggling with the trauma of change, turns away from reality in favor of a more comfortable lie" (2009).
6 For a full explanation of the dynamic systems concept of fractals and a description of teams as dynamic systems, see for example Gorman et al. (2017).

Chapter 13

Ending well as a team coach

Rachael Hanley-Browne

> Nothing in the world is permanent, and we're foolish when we ask anything to last, but surely, we're still more foolish not to take delight in it while we have it. If change is of the essence of existence, one would have thought it only sensible to make it the premise of our philosophy.
>
> (W. Somerset Maughan, 1944, p. 223)

My interest in endings is due to my own experiences throughout my career, what I would describe as the process of drawing a close to a business relationship, as an employee, colleague, supplier, consultant, and coach.[1]

My experiences with organisations ranged from being celebrated to ignored. With the resulting mixed emotions as I left of sadness, validation, and sometimes pure relief! Exploring and reflecting on our experiences in this liminal or transitional space offers us fertile ground as team coaches. Because endings matter.

Paradoxically in a team coach-client relationship, in comparison to our personal life, we work hard over time to build trust and a depth of understanding between us, in the full knowledge that we intend to exit and no longer work with the team. This is not part of our usual relationship modus operandi; as we already know at the beginning that there will be an intentional separation and loss. And in team coaching there are multiple relationships to end. Yet, during my coaching career I have found minimal literature or studies into how, and when, to end a team coaching relationship. Mostly, the research emphasis was on client outcomes and objectives (Graßmann et al., 2020; Peters & Carr, 2013, 2019), how to begin team coaching (Maseko et al., 2019) or the coaching process (Hauser, 2014), but not the ending of the relationships themselves. To date, research in one-to-one coaching has implied that whatever the approach or methodology used, it is the relationship between coach and client that is at the heart of positive outcomes (De Haan & Gannon, 2017). In team coaching there was fertile ground to explore, so I decided to research relationships at this key juncture and in 2021 published a paper, 'What Do Team Coaches Experience at the End of a Client Relationship?' in the International Journal of Evidence

DOI: 10.4324/9781003325789-17

Based Coaching and Mentoring. My study (Hanley-Browne, 2021) took an interpretive phenomenological analysis (IPA) approach (Bryman, 2016), in that it was about exploring, understanding, and making sense of team coach experiences in the field. There is a close parallel between coaching and phenomenology in that it centres on experience (Bachkirova et al., 2020; Rajasinghe, 2020). In this chapter I draw upon my study, my own experiences as a team coach and apply this learning so as to bring endings to life for you. This is not a definitive account.

13.1   Introduction: why do endings matter?

What do we mean by 'ending well' and what does this mean in practice? The ending of a team coaching assignment can be bittersweet. At its best, it is where we as coaches gain both the satisfaction of co-creating change, and experience a rich learning process, alongside the loss of a meaningful relationship. At its worst it may offer the unforgettable combination of a transactional relationship which fails to develop, a sense of disappointment about what might have been, and a raw learning experience which may result in a sense of failure or inadequacy.

An ending is the last part of a process, it is where we bring a story to a conclusion and permanently change the nature of our relationship. Therefore, it is a significant relational crossroads for both team coach and team. So, what can we learn from relationship endings? First, let us suspend the constraints of trying to formally evaluate team coaching. Why? Because it is often complex and messy work, where the composition of the team is unlikely to be the same at the beginning and end of our assignment. Also, if you support the premise that coaching is grounded in andragogy or adult learning (Knowles et al., 2014), outcomes become the joint responsibility of both the coach and the team. Success is reliant on the team applying their knowledge and using their systemic awareness when no longer in your presence. Also, I believe that both the individual and team's learning continues to develop and embed itself way beyond the confines of our work together. So, let us instead shift our focus to the relational aspects of our work, as this is where we access a deeper understanding of self and how we made contact with our clients. Because at its heart, team coaching is relational work.

This chapter will explore the complex nature of endings, the experiences of practitioners in the field and the correlation between relationship beginnings and ending well. In the following three sections I will offer you a frame of reference to make sense of endings in team coaching. Based on my research, the frame divides coaching relationships into three dimensions:

1. Your relationship to the coaching context;
2. Your relationship to the learning process; and
3. Your relationship with your client.

Each section includes vignettes and a set of reflective questions or exercises. You may approach this chapter purely from a cognitive perspective and as a source of further reading. Or you may decide to go deeper and use this opportunity for self-guided development, or as a prompt for a discussion with your co-coach. Alternatively, for peer-to-peer dialogue or in group supervision.

So first, let us pull into your awareness your own experiences of endings, both in your career and then latterly in your role as coach. This will help you to connect with the subject of endings from a less cerebral, and more phenomenological, perspective.

Reflective exercise and questions

Create a timeline for your career and working life highlighting significant relationship endings. Illustrate your experiences using drawings, images, metaphors, words, or music, and try to capture as many feelings, emotions, and senses as you can. You may want to do this with the support of a co-coach or supervisor.

* What do the endings evoke in you?
* Are any particularly memorable or symbolic? If so, why?
* Which relationships do you consider 'ended well'; why?
* What did you learn about yourself or others from those endings?
* Do you notice any patterns emerging?

Now do the same exercise specifically for your coaching assignments, this may include both individual and team coaching clients. Then compare your responses to endings in your career and working life with your coaching assignments:

1. What are the similarities or differences between how you end relationships with your clients and your own workplace experiences? What do you notice?
2. Taking your own experience of ending relationships well, how can you replicate that for your clients? How might your practice change as the result of your reflections?

13.2   What matters at the end?

Endings in team coaching can be a troublesome topic, because when they end without a sense of accomplishment, herein may lie shame, emotional triggers about loss, or abandonment, and negative feelings about our sense of worth and identity as a coach. For example, if our work ends prematurely or with unexpected challenges, we may feel a sense of failure or regret. Alternatively, if we consider that we ended well, what does that really mean? Did we believe that we delivered the outcomes agreed at the beginning of our work, did we establish strong relational connections with the team, and/or did we make a constructive impact on their social systems? How do we know? What matters at the end of your work will be unique to you, your client, and their context. It will depend on your purpose, your values, approach and intended outcomes. I subscribe to Somerset Maughan's observation, "Nothing in the world is permanent, and we're foolish when we ask anything to last, but surely, we're still more foolish not to take delight in it while we have it. If change is of the essence of existence, one would have thought it only sensible to make it the premise of our philosophy" (Somerset Maughan, 1944, p. 223). So, before you start coaching a team find the space to reflect on why you are doing this work. Can you clearly articulate what matters to you when ending and why? If you co-coach, are you aligned on endings?

Endings involve the sponsor and coach, the leader and the team, their colleagues, and stakeholders with whom you have had contact; what we may describe as their systems (Meadows, 2011). Team coaching typically follows a circuitous route and all assignments end, but how they end is impacted by your relationships. Endings are where we consciously move away from our client team, and intentionally bring our work to a close. This process of bringing work to an end is symbolic. By symbolic, I mean that it is a manifestation of the client and coach relationship. Research by Halinen and Tähtinen (2002) and Havila and Tähtinen (2012) offers descriptors of endings, which capture the nature of commercial relationships. For example, if it ends abruptly or without acknowledgment it may be deemed transactional, if it is a planned and gradual process then it has been a partnership. In coaching, if it leads to observable and significant change within the team and their broader systems, it may be transformational. And I would add that, if you sit with the feelings of joy in the changes you made, and simultaneously the loss of the human connections, it has been relational.

Why might a relationship be stuck at transactional? Relationships tend to be transactional when there is a material misalignment or misunderstanding between the coach and client. Where might this misalignment show up? My research, and experience, highlighted three scenarios which may significantly impact endings. They included:

1. Your values, purpose and approach are misaligned with the client. There is an unresolvable tension between yourself, the team, and their systems
2. There is a resistance, or the external conditions do not support a learning environment within the team. This may be because they are a pseudo team, or the team has not yet defined their common goals or purpose. Or individuals are ready to check out and move on from the team or organisation; this may be unspoken or avoided by the leader or their colleagues
3. You fail to build trust and psychological safety, this may be a defence mechanism by the team or team members, e.g., splitting. The relationship is not given enough time and attention or is undervalued. Alternatively, an event shatters the connection.

In the above scenarios, supervision helps, exploring transactional endings mitigates the possibility that we try to fix ourselves or introject systemic issues beyond our control. We may internalise shame (Wheeler, 1997) or other organisational forces at play (Armstrong, 2018), and this can impact our confidence and future practice.

13.3   How might we approach the end?

The skill of a team coach is to recognise and negotiate the appropriate time to end a coaching relationship and do it effectively. This may be informed by budgets or contractual agreements, but here we are focusing on relationships. In my view, the ability to plan, acknowledge and celebrate the end of your relationship with a team is a privilege. It is a transient moment; every team is unique. You have a singular opportunity to look back and consider what you have achieved together, to appreciate where you are now, and then to turn to the future and say a fond farewell. Now let us look in more detail at the process:

Your own relationship to the coaching and context

In team coaching we are active political agents in a social context (Louis and Dichon, 2018). We are there to facilitate change and our very presence intentionally interrupts the team dynamics and a team's relationship with their environment or field (Lewin, 1951). Furthermore, our role is to actively assist the team to work more effectively in relation with their broader systems, and we do this through raising their awareness and ability to read and respond to their context. We may facilitate relational agility with their colleagues, their sponsor e.g., HRD, the executive, or board, and stakeholders (shareholders, investors, the local community, suppliers, and/or customers). As coaches we have influence about what we choose to surface, the relationships we prioritise and the way in which we facilitate. This inherent power requires us to understand and be clear about our own motivations and intentions. We are not in a neutral position. Because our well-developed organisational antenna allow us to notice and observe systemic issues which may or may not be in service of the team, leader, or sponsor. Where do we draw the line in our coaching intervention, decide to step aside and to end our work?

Reflective questions

- How do you maintain boundaries and relationship parameters for you and your client?
- Where do you see the boundary between your own needs and your clients?
- How would you handle 'ethical dilemmas,' and what might they be?
- What would trigger you to prematurely end a coaching relationship?
- How closely is your professional identity aligned with the outcomes of your team coaching work?
- How do you retain perspective on your contribution to the ending?

In your role as an interpreter of contextual relationships, a knowledge of organisational development theories and practices (Cheung-Judge and Holbeche, 2011) are essential. As is social intelligence, in particular diversity, inclusion and working with difference in organisational life. Otherwise, we could inadvertently be reinforcing racism, exclusion, or inequity (Fanshawe, 2022; Shah, 2022). Our knowledge allows us to make sense of, and to effectively navigate our relationship with the business, organisational and social context in which we are working. It also provides us with a language and way of interpreting relationships in organisational life in a meaningful way for our clients. In my work I draw on a relational organisational Gestalt approach (Chidac, 2018), holism (Stevenson, 2018) and whole intelligence (Parlett, 2018).

My study suggested that culture, power, and influence will play a key role in how your work with the team progresses and ends. The culture, or environment in which you are working may or may not align with your value system; you may have to speak up or actively challenge power and authority (Reitz and Higgins, 2019). Consider how the culture of the organisation reveals itself to you and may impact the end of your work. For example, how do people leave the organisation or how are commercial contracts brought to a close? How relational or otherwise are they? Are endings with colleagues avoided? This information will allow you to prepare for the way your work is likely to conclude or to raise awareness with the team, and to challenge the status quo.

In my research, power dynamics were frequently mentioned as contributing to a coach withdrawing from an assignment. This may be inside the team, where a significant imbalance of power led to the inability of the coach to create an atmosphere of trust. Or between the coach and team; the coach feeling powerless and unable to get any traction or movement with the team, possibly due to the forces of transference upon their own feelings, leading to countertransference feelings of ineffectiveness or lack of agency (for definitions of counter/transference see Chapter 4). Or, between the coach, team, and their broader systems, where the team and coach are aligned, but their desired changes are contextually misaligned. Here the coach needs to make a value judgment whether to push through this resistance or consider bringing their work to an end. As a team coach knowing your appetite for personal risk is essential self-knowledge. This risk is vastly different as an internal coach or when representing a consultancy, rather than the relative freedom you enjoy with your own business. A significant influence on your decision will be the quality of your relationship, and ability to explore this dynamic, with the sponsor or the team leader. As is the wisdom and perspective of a co-coach or supervisor. Below is an example of where I made a choice to bring a team coaching assignment to a close, because of the team's lack of power, influence, and authority within their organisational context. Whilst I had a trusting relationship with the sponsor, they did not have the positional power to influence key stakeholders e.g., the executive, and this meant that the initial objectives of our work were unachievable. However, by taking personal risk and sharing my sense of powerlessness and vulnerability, the team opened up about their feelings and our ending became relational.

Case vignette: Drawing on your lived experience

An international manufacturing company undergoing a business transformation. The team coaching assignment was with a programme management team and instigated by the learning and development (L&D) manager. The team was cross-functional, and the members either reported directly into an executive or were seconded as subject matter experts. The team of 12 people were leading an enterprise-wide IT change programme; there were 11 men and 1 woman. An external contractor appointed by the overseas head office was acting as programme director. The team had hit challenges and it was deemed that a coaching intervention would be helpful. My role was to bring the team together, to co-create a working agreement and facilitate an improvement in their relationship with their external stakeholders, including a supplier.

If we look at this coaching assignment through the lens of power and politics, what might we anticipate about how it would end?

As my work progressed numerous challenges emerged: the team's nominal leader had little social capital within the business; the IT director was on long-term sick; the business was underperforming; there was a new CEO and decisions about big numbers were pending. The team had been created months before the coaching started and was based in a different country from their executive.

As the business was underperforming the commercial leaders on the team did not have the capacity to fully commit to what they perceived as an 'IT initiative'. It required yet more effort on top of their overstretched schedule. There was an absence of structural power within the team e.g., no executive presence and this resulted in a sense of disempowerment for the team. In fact, they were a team in name only, they were a group of interested parties who were lacking direction, and common objectives or budgetary authority. Each had their own agendas as to how the new IT system would impact their directorate. Whilst the programme director was highly skilled (he had expert power), he struggled to influence the executive decision makers or key stakeholders. He lacked proximity to them; distance, culture, and authority separated him.

Here there was a parallel process. The coaching assignment unravelled just as the programme had, and at every turn a new obstacle revealed itself. The team could not find alignment, they would not, or could not, find time in their diaries to work together and their energy levels were rapidly declining. They were in conflict with their supplier and had developed factions within the team. The only woman in the team quietly left the business. Despite requests, I was not given access to the CEO or Exec., there was an understandable concern that this might further expose the programme or put the team members at risk. Therefore, I felt powerless to support the overarching aims of their work, but there was a contribution I could make.

Taking a systemic and OD perspective, I was able to offer the team a way of making sense of their predicament by looking at power, authority, and influence. The team appreciated the clear re-framing of their challenges, and I was able to share my feelings, and sense of what it was like for me to work with them and their organisation; my lived experience. How I was losing my voice; literally and metaphorically. It seemed that these disclosures mirrored how they felt. Which led to an open and frank conversation amongst the team about their own situation. They volunteered that it would have been helpful for the coaching to have commenced at the beginning of the programme and questioned why this investment had not happened for what was considered to be a 'business-critical' implementation? Their frustrations with the programme director were also explored and his lack of agency was now better understood. They concluded that their lack of clarity or direction, disunity, and fear of taking action reflected that of the executives as they navigated the uncertainties of a new CEO and a business in crisis.

However, previous experience taught me that I had influence in my way of being and how I responded to the challenges we faced; by showing vulnerability, admitting being stuck and not knowing where to take this work. Also, in giving the team a sense of how they actually showed-up from an external perspective. We reviewed what we had already done together, and the team considered how they might set up future change initiatives. They were able to re-focus on positive learning outcomes from their experiences. At a fundamental level, psychological safety, trust, and awareness had started to emerge within the team. Also, a newly acquired ability to start to read the context in which they were working and its' impact on them, rather than jumping in to immediately judge colleagues or blame themselves. I agreed with the L&D manager that my coaching should end at this point. Without the executive taking ownership of the overall change programme, giving the team authority, and taking key budget decisions, it could not progress. We concluded our final workshop by speaking up, being heard, and sharing our learning. We did this through individual reflections, by appreciating the connections we had made and offering generative feedback. After I left, and in short time, the team was disbanded, and latterly many left the organisation.

Reflective question

- What might you have done differently at the beginning now you know the ending?

13.4 What is your role as a team coach in relation to the learning process?

Knowing how to guide a team through a learning process so that they achieve their stated objectives is a key skill of a team coach. You act as coach, mentor, facilitator, and consultant; it is a multi-faceted role, and this is why it is vastly different from one-to-one coaching (Hartog, 2019). Through the process, you will be an "advisor, educator, catalyzer, and assimilator" (Hauser, 2014) by thoughtfully finessing your interventions to move towards a formative ending. Therefore, an understanding of adult learning theory, group process, systems theory, psychology, and leadership development theories and techniques will offer you a solid foundation for team coaching. This includes having thought in advance about activities or ways of ending your working relationship with the team that are appropriate and congruent with their context. For example, being mindful of both the prevailing internal and macro culture. My research suggested that national context may impact the need for evidence-based outcomes (Schein and Schein, 2017; Hofstede, 2017). As a consequence, it is helpful to begin the coaching process with the end in mind. Care at the outset will enable you to contract more effectively with your clients, e.g., to uncover a preference for working with survey data or ROI measures, versus valuing the learning experience itself. You may need to compromise and include a qualitative pre and post 360° survey. As with all surveys, you should know their pitfalls and limitations, how to evaluate the results and to effectively manage the feedback process.

Your role is to work in partnership with the team, but it is the team who takes accountability and responsibility for their own contribution and the application of their learning. This includes giving you iterative feedback and a commitment to ask you for what they need during the coaching process. To achieve this level of accountability, openness and trust requires the coach to demonstrate that your work is in service of the team, not to individual agendas and to be clear about your expectations from the outset. Also, to be clear about your role, ways of working and to actively encourage feedback and challenge. What we may call contracting and setting boundaries for behaviour; both for the team and yourself. When working on-line it may take a greater investment of time, or focused attention, to achieve the same outcome as face-to-face interaction (Blanchard, 2021). This partnership builds over time, and your role as coach is to navigate the team through the systemic and social forces of structure, culture, and context. Your purpose is to enable them to achieve their shared objectives, being mindful that you may need to frequently course correct. Indeed, this course correction may come about because of a teams' progress; their newly acquired systemic awareness leading to a shift in their focus or direction. Contracting with the team continues throughout the coaching process.

Getting out of the way

Once you see continuous signs and signals of the transfer of learning happening within the team or outcomes, such as ripples of positive change happening internally or externally, it may be time to consider ending your work together. This could be evidenced in their use of language, behaviours, integration of activities or ways of working. Or, through decisions or actions by colleagues, positive feedback from stakeholders or evidence of new relationships being established. Your role is to reveal these new capabilities and shifts so that the team is conscious of the changes they have made and what they have achieved together. It is helpful to leave the team with outstanding actions so that they are motivated to take ownership and apply their learning independently of you. At this stage you become a custodian, by capturing and curating their learning outcomes and enabling the team to express and verbalise what is different.

In order to begin the ending process, you may take a phenomenological approach whereby you heighten the team's awareness of their changed feelings, senses, and experiences of being within the team from the beginning to their current state. Also, to surface and notice what is different about their relationships with each other, as well as those outside of the team. You bring their embodied learning (Stolz, 2015) to consciousness. To support this, you may hold up a mirror to the team and reveal what you see, your experience of working with them and what you have noticed is different. You may wish to reciprocate and ask them for feedback on their perceptions of you both at the beginning and at this stage of your partnership. This will accelerate your own learning and self-awareness.

The team, with their newly heightened awareness, may themselves come to the realisation that they have achieved what they wanted or need from team coaching. They may tell you that they feel ready to end the work. That they can be this direct and clear in communicating what they need is a testimony to the relationship itself and the level of trust you have established. If this does not happen it may be because your embodied work has surfaced unmet needs and there is more work to do. Or it reinforces deeper vulnerabilities, and you may see signs of dependency developing for a team member or leader. Individuals may require personalised support, e.g., one-to-one coaching, or skills and leadership development. Alternatively, their systemic awareness may highlight a larger issue, e.g., the need for an organisational restructure or change in the leadership team composition. Here support from an organisational design or HR specialist may be required.

Case vignette: 'We're foolish when we ask anything to last'

The CEO of a small charity based in the UK approached me to work with her team in order to support them to change the culture of their organisation. It was partly as a result of a poor staff engagement survey, multiple changes in their team, and pressure from the board of trustees to address the issues raised. The current CEO had a desire to create more dialogue and engagement with the staff, and to build a shared vision for the future of the organization, as they faced major disruption in their sector.

We initially had robust and tough sessions together; there was a lot of stress, mistrust, and underlying tension in the team. But after several months of hard graft by us, it became clear that their initial objectives were nearing completion. They had undertaken an extensive staff engagement project and had co-designed new values and ways of working in partnership with them. The team had notice-ably become more actively engaged with other staff, their behaviours had shifted to being more open with each other and in sharing their challenges or doubts. The dialogue amongst the team was more balanced and dominant leaders lis-tened more effectively to those who had previously not spoken up. The lead-ership team still had a lot to do, including commencing a relocation, so I could have easily continued with them. But I sensed they needed to take ownership of their learning and work through the next phase of building their culture by embedding their working practices and evidencing congruence between their actions and verbal commitments. So, I decided it was time for me to exit as I had completed the piece of work we had contracted to do. Had I stayed and extended our work, I would have been stepping into different territory, by being drawn into the role of a management consultant giving advice. It would confuse our purpose and blur accountability for the changes that needed to happen. I found supervision helpful in holding up the mirror to me and my actions. I reflected on how important it was to hand over the baton to the CEO and in doing so to create the space for her and the team to coach each other.

We brought the learning process to an end in a landmark way. The CEO asked me to support the co-design of a day where she brought everyone together; a great example of how things had changed! The team wanted to celebrate their progress with all the staff at an off-site. The CEO launched the day, with each of the team sharing their own stories and leadership lessons; we all saw them in a new light.

The staff then led the majority of the day with activities that culminated in a celebration. I left partway through the day, which was a symbolic act for me, with mixed emotions; feeling the loss of my bond with the team, but with satis-faction in the deeper connections the team had with their colleagues. What a gift to end an assignment in such an uplifting way.

Reflective questions

How do you know when learning has become embodied or transferred and change has commenced? Think of client examples and using a phenomenological approach, e.g., drawing on your feelings, all senses, memories, and experiences:

- What are the signs and signals that move you towards an ending? What do you experience, notice, and act upon? What is different?
- In what circumstances might you stay with a client, extend an assignment, or change role? What relational or ethical dilemmas might this cause?
- What would you do if you sensed a delegation of responsibility to you for the outcomes of the coaching?

If you are co-coaching, then discuss your answers afterwards to look for align-ment or dissonance. You could also use this exercise for group supervision.

Your relationship with the client

A much-neglected topic in team coaching literature is the interpersonal relationship between coach and client, here we explore and acknowledge its importance. As described above, there is an essential paradox to team coaching; to build trust and a rich learning environment you need to develop close relationships with the team, but the closer and more influential you become, the nearer you are to moving away and planning your exit. You work continuously with the polarities of proximity and distance. As a consequence, at the end of a team coaching assignment you may have poignant emotions. The metaphors frequently used by team coaches in my study were those of a parent saying goodbye to their adolescents as they leave. As I am not a parent, I would say that it is like having a talented member of your own team who you have mentored and developed, leaving to take a promotion elsewhere, but multiplied! In both cases, pride that you have fulfilled your role in developing them, but a keen sense of their absence. However, if a relationship has been transactional, turbulent, or brief, there may be a sense of relief on both sides!

Not all relationships end

Take a moment to consider the range of relationships you may have; with the leader, the individual team members (past and present), the sponsor/s, your co-coach (who may be internal), and other stakeholders you have met or interviewed. What is the most appropriate approach to ending your relationship in each case? Will a follow-up activity be required? How do you differentiate between them, and how do you end well? Saying goodbye might not be with everyone, for example you may intend to stay connected with the leader or sponsor. However, you will not stay connected with the whole team as an entity, as this is the formal end of your work together. So, this requires preparation, and considerations about ethics (Iordanou et al., 2016), attachment, and dependency (Holmes, 2014); for both you and the team. You may want to continue to coach them for reasons driven by ego or identity. Alternatively, sentiments may be imbalanced, with you ready to exit and move on, whilst the team does not feel ready or willing to let you go. Drawing on the work of Thornton (2016) regarding team relationships, I like these questions: what will your absence mean to the team and what will their absence mean to you? By considering the answers, you get to the essence of what you represent to the team and what you bring to the coaching relationship.

Ending is a process that requires reflection, signposting, preparation, and sensitivity. My experience, and that of the coaches I interviewed, suggests that a figurative way of saying goodbye allows all parties an opportunity to transition into a different phase of your relationship, from present to past. This acknowledges the importance of your relationships, the trust you established and honours what you have achieved together. How you say goodbye with the team depends on budgets, context, culture, and the personalities involved, it could range from a whole day event through to a meal, an activity or a shared conversation to symbolic pictures, images, or words. It may happen virtually or in person; my preference would always be in person. They can mirror your signature style, or you could co-design each ending together with the team; how you approach this could be a learning opportunity in itself. Reflecting on relationship endings can raise powerful emotions in us and sitting with these can be helpful to build self-awareness and therefore, improve our practice.

Reflective questions

Consider the different types of relationships we defined earlier in the chapter; transactional, partnership, transformational, and relational. Use these to frame your answers.

- Why or when might you avoid discussing or planning endings with your client?
- How could you end client relationships in a way that fits with your values and approach?
- How do you address the emotions and feelings left behind by unsatisfactory or avoided endings?

It could be helpful to discuss your experiences with a co-coach or supervisor. Especially if you notice patterns in how you, or your clients, end relationships.

Below is an example of how I brought a coaching assignment to an end in an unusual way, but which truly represented the special nature of our connection.

Case vignette: 'Change is of the essence of existence'

A division of an international corporate. I commenced a lengthy team coaching assignment which involved working with a small team of four relatively new leaders whose remit was to transform their business operation into profitability. Their division had been through a challenging time having been treated as non-core business; they were under-funded and essentially isolated from the parent business. On achieving profitability, the future of the business was unclear, it may have been integrated into a prospective acquisition or divested. So, success meant more change.

We had worked through some incredibly tough conversations within the team, we had handled challenging feedback from stakeholders, as well as navigating an initially hostile staff environment. But in navigating these risky conditions, we created what could be described as a high performing team; where there was congruence between the quality of relationships, business outcomes, and key stakeholder engagement. It became clear once we had navigated the initial challenges they were on the right track, and I observed that they probably no longer needed me; they were effectively coaching each other. I noticed them saying, 'what would Rachael ask?' Evidence that we had built deep trust, but that perhaps my influence was becoming problematic, or I was becoming de facto team leader. I did some deep reflective work; was I staying with this team in order to validate myself or was I becoming attached and in doing so creating co-dependency. Was my anxiety about their uncertain future delaying my exit. I concluded that, reluctantly, it was time for me to leave and to acknowledge that they were more than ready to face any future changes.

From my perspective the ending with the sponsor and key stakeholders was staged and formal, as is typical in a corporate environment. It included review meetings and a concluding report about our work, which they described as transformational. But in this instance the ending with the team was not just about the work, it required something special. We decided to share an evening meal together. This meal figuratively marked the conclusion of our assignment, but the nature of the event symbolised that our relationship was such that we wanted to spend social time together. We have not met each other since. When I reflect back, I feel appreciation for the opportunity and a sense of joy about the time we spent together; we had ended well.

13.5   Conclusion: endings matter, so 'take delight in it while we have it'

The intention of this chapter is to acknowledge the importance and complexity of relationship endings in team coaching. In sharing my experiences, research, and client vignettes my aim is to bring to life the highs and lows of team coaching practice. What matters to us at the end gives us a window into our professional selves as coaches (Bachkirova, 2020). Because it is in these transitory moments, when saying goodbye, that we make contact with our core purpose and fully appreciate the depth of our relational connection.

Note

1   This chapter is dedicated to my Dad, Bill Scott (1937–2022).

The future of team coaching

An epilogue by all contributors

(Erik)

Here are some professional trends in the world of team coaching as I see them:

As far as I can establish the emergence of coaching as an important developmental practice for leadership in large organisations (over the last 25 or so years) can be ascribed to profound societal changes, such as globalization, individual search for meaning with a lessening influence from religious or traditional narratives, technological change, and a growing awareness of the many crises caused by our own consciousness. All these large-scale and in-depth changes have prompted a deep sensitivity and yearning to use our 'mind' better at work, including our ability to retain good decision-making and communication under high pressure (see also Chapter 11). Improving software applications are causing on the one hand that the operational tasks of managers and leaders can now be largely taken over by machines, and on the other hand a powerful transparency for decision makers in a globally connected and accountable world. These conspire to bring phenomena such as doubt, confidence, emotion, motivation and theory of mind (ability and nature of thinking and deciding) very much to the fore for leaders. Executive (team) coaching is one of the very few practices that can help nurture, process, develop and sustain these very phenomena for leaders, especially because coaching is so tailored to the client's existing challenges, goals, thinking style – or at least should be.

My prediction for the future will be that this trend strengthens and deepens and that the human mind and human minds interacting ('teamwork') will become even more strategically important and problematic at the same time. Drucker's famous twenty-first-century knowledge worker will become a whole mind-in-body worker. There will be many more scientific breakthroughs, so that we begin to really understand emotions, personality and neurodiversity. Team coaches and their clients will benefit because they will be able to apply the new knowledge, to tailor their interventions even better and to get still better results. This may mean new psychometrics, live opinion polling, or other technology, but I am not so sure. Thinking under stress, containing leadership derailment, arriving at better decisions in top teams, will remain competences that cannot just be taken over by new technology nor can

DOI: 10.4324/9781003325789-18

they be enhanced by IT systems. Currently, I notice that laptops and mobile phones in the room, or teleconferencing tools for virtual team coaching, are not improving team coaching at all. In most cases they actually dilute our interventions.

Although there will be lots of software upgrades and measurement/communication technology, I do not believe team coaching will change in its core. Just that team coaches will become better informed. Being physically together with few distractions will still be preferable. For this reason, there is a good chance we might move in the opposite direction: meeting without any electronics, more observations of teams ('accompaniment') inside organisations providing full immersion for the team coach, and thinking sessions with an emphasis on movement, mindfulness meditation and exercise.

In sum, I expect the following challenges to become more important: (1) what does good mean for this team versus what will good mean for clients, other teams and for humankind; (2) how can we offer the quality of team coaching for the many teams that will need it, in other words: how can we team coach for the many; and (3) how can we keep offering quality despite increasing electronic interference and virtual working.

(Tammy)

As climate change, global pressures, and technology rapidly advance, the future of team coaching will be uneven: diversifying, segmenting, and fracturing the 'marketplace' in a variety of ways. As disruption and upheaval take hold, we may see a convergence of team coaching and team mediation. Schools of thought on team coaching will tend to polarise with instructive, mechanistic, linear approaches firmly at one end, and the dialogic, relational, and systemic at the other. We may see DIY team coaching: team leader or team led, following protocols and manuals. In-person team coaching where it remains affordable, desirable, or indeed possible, will increasingly rely on the use of technology and AI. Virtual or not, it will incorporate the use of various technologies, including AI. Software will offer different and imaginative ways to work with team constellations and stimulate perspective taking. Wearable technologies will deliver real-time data and immediate feedback on the relational 'health' and performance of teams as they work together. Virtual reality will offer the opportunity for teams to have immersive experiences of real and possible scenarios that provide for different levels of psychological safety, collaboration, and various team dynamics. Technology will augment and enhance team development in some instances. In others it won't. In many cases the objective of team coaching will be to restore the relational dimensions of team life, and in many others, it will be used to enhance and augment the technology itself.

(Andrew)

Team coaching is a new and emerging field of practice that has developed out of the coaching profession. As with other emerging professions we can expect to see a similar trajectory of growth. First, we have a period of considerable energy, optimism and excitement. The risk in this stage is that team coaching is seen as a panacea for all kinds of organisational problems. At some point there is a reckoning when a more realistic appraisal of the practice can develop. With further growth, we can expect questions and debates around rigour, theories and methods, evidence-based practice, ethics, training and professional standards and professionalisation to surface. We can also expect to see sub-groupings and fragmentation around philosophical and professional differences. Team coaching will also need to find an identity in relation to the overlapping fields of facilitation, team development, T-group training and organisation development. Is it a case of old wine in new bottles or is it genuinely a new field of practice?

For me, the edges and challenges to my practice lie in how to help teams to access the deeper emotional influences on their behaviour, particularly those that hold them back from confronting the bigger existential questions facing their organisations. I am increasingly working with leadership teams that are concerned about the impact of their organisations on society and the environment. To act differently and make a difference requires courage and the willingness to challenge and take politically contentious, yet necessary decisions. As a coach, what is our role in challenging leadership teams and when might we be guilty of colluding or turning a blind eye?

(Simon)

Team coaching has established itself as a significant practice for developing individuals, leaders and their ability to work effectively together in often challenging and unpredictable contexts. In this book we have attempted to show how team coaching can be informed by focusing on the relational processes at work within teams. Attending to these fundamental human processes requires team coaches to hold the tension between structured approaches and the space in which possibilities can arise for team members to participate in making sense of their experience moment by moment in relation to one another, their tasks and ways of achieving these. This way of working develops in individuals their capacities for self-reflection, self-other observation, relating, sense-making and collaborating. It allows for questions to be raised in relation to the current status quo and enables experimentation with new forms of being, relating and acting. My hope is that relational team coaching influences patterns of relating beyond team boundaries to shape organisational cultures, where dialogue and human connection are at the heart of the enterprise. It is only by connecting with this shared humanity that we might be able to navigate the existential crises we face on our planet and as a species.

(Rachael)

What are the boundaries between team coaching and OD? Team coaching has primarily been an extension of one-to-one coaching. In that its focus has been on making an impact at both the group and individual membership level. Most coaches come to team coaching having mastered one-to-one coaching. Indeed, training and accreditations in team coaching often requires this route (EMCC Global). However, I believe that there is a stronger confluence of team coaching practice towards organisational development. Especially as people typically have multiple team memberships and that there is an increased fluidity to teams in a post-pandemic world; are we ever really working with, or in, a single team? If we believe we are not, and that our work makes ripples across the client organisation, would we not consider this as being at the boundaries of OD practice? Especially when working with the leadership team who have organisational power and influence.

More importantly, when we shift our perspective of team coaching beyond a single team, and then deploy it at an enterprise level it offers us an impactful way of accessing and leveraging hidden social capital for effective organisational change. If we shift our lens to coaching 'teams of teams', we facilitate the following: the development of a coaching culture that fosters active listening and improves communication skills; a shift of focus from 'the hero leader' to a recognition that sustained performance requires both teaming and cooperation between teams; that by surfacing and working with these interdependencies we create opportunities for creativity and innovation. In summary, it is our relationships across and between teams that ultimately drives outcomes.

Beyond the enterprise, team coaches may move even further into the community or societal realm by working at the boundaries of organisations, e.g., by bringing together internal and external teams. Here there are exciting opportunities to make an impact beyond the organisation, and to increase connectivity and reciprocity with its key stakeholders. For example, with a contract supplier team and a customer team, to foster a partnership role that incorporates all the benefits outlined above. Furthermore, technology enables us to do this work at scale and provides additional channels of communication and influence; the rapid adoption of Zoom during the pandemic being an excellent example. The ability to bring local teams together in real life whilst simultaneously connecting national or international teams together on-line, in a hybrid setting, creates huge possibilities for large-scale team-coaching work. We can work on both local and collective development simultaneously.

The implications of this shift are pertinent to team-coach training and supervision. In that there is a need for both individual-coaching skills and organisational-development capability. But I'd go beyond that and say that more attention needs to be paid to developing co-coaching skills, which may include how to work as a team of coaches. These large-scale interventions go beyond a single coach or co-coaching capability. Supervision practices will also need to develop in tandem. So, there is an opportunity to revise our curriculum and to be far more ambitious about the collective power of team coaching to bring about relational change at scale.

(Alexandra)

As the 2010s were drawing to a close we witnessed, perhaps participated in, a marked increase in attention to the unfolding crises in climate and nature. With Greta Thunberg leading school strikes, record-breaking heatwaves making headlines and

David Attenborough bringing vivid images of climate impacts into sitting rooms, leaders in business and government were stirred to action. Finally, for a coach whose practice is grounded in nature and climate response, it felt wholly legitimate to *ethically and sensitively* bring the natural world as stakeholder into coaching conversations.

In the early 2020s pandemic, war and economic crises diverted attention, but for many a heightened nature awareness and the impulse to action sustained. If anything, maybe a by-product of increased hybrid working, the urge to be in nature became greater than ever. Opportunities to coach teams in natural spaces became more frequent.

Practically, team coaching in a natural context offers a number of possibilities, not least the pleasure of being away from the desk. A natural context can be as ordinary as the local park, or quite extraordinary – a nature reserve, mountainside or fjord. What matters is holding space for encounter, the deepening of connection with self, others, and powerfully, with non-human other, becoming present to, exquisitely alive to our sentient world (Mathews, 2003).

At first encounter, nature can a source of rich metaphor. Webs of relationship in ecosystems, from the abundant microbial action in a handful of soil, to the vast invisible networks of subterranean mycelium, offer inspiration for new insight into complex human relationships (Capra, 2004; Simard, 2021). Our corporate world is already rich with natural metaphor – (work)streams, hedging, product lifecycles, viruses! – so drawing on the environment directly isn't much of a stretch. It's a safe conventional space, ontologically, for a team to inhabit.

Coaching in nature however can afford deeper inquiry, reflection on personal and collective purpose. Exploration of values, pushing ontological edges through experiential encounter, acknowledging one's part in the anthropogenic forces driving climate breakdown, can compel deep questioning and reframing of purpose (Esbjörn-Hargens & Zimmerman, 2009).

For teams prepared to go further (and a thoughtful coach can help here), such inquiry becomes a route to connecting more fundamentally to themselves as embodied beings, a part of and wholly inter-reliant with our world. For some this may be a spiritual connecting, an exploration of soul and source (Roszak et al., 1995).

In keeping with core principles in coaching, this work requires that we come alongside our coachees as active co-inquirers rather than knowledgeable guides. It is an active practice, opportunity to learn and deepen awareness ourselves. Indigenous wisdoms can be a source of powerful insight, but scrupulous cultural sensitivity is required, starting with attending to our own stories and inherited belief systems (Kimmerer, 2020). What this form of work is not, is using nature as a zip-wired playground or a test of mettle in competitive team-building.

Executive coaching has drawn upon a number of evocative metaphoric source domains over the years – sports, psychotherapy, complexity science (Gallwey, 1974; De Haan, 2008; Stacey, 2003). What has too often been missing in the coaching relationship, however, just as in the corporate world more broadly, is the non-human. So where is team coaching going? Outside to the natural world and inward, to purpose and soul.

(Charlotte)

What is the direction of team coaching:

As we go to publication, the world is consciously or unconsciously reverberating with its reaction to the likely end of our species. Is humanity going to die out – in a slow and extremely painful way – or will it transform itself in some other way?

The COP 28 talks in Egypt ended with most people feeling disappointment and despair at so little being agreed. Many had already despaired and decided not to attend (e.g. Greta Thunberg) because they saw how few of last year's agreements have been carried out.

Cynics/realists point to the trend in global 'disaster capitalism' where businesses are getting massive subsidies for various schemes that justify delaying change.

Team coaches need first to do their own work in coming to terms with the significance of what is happening. Then team coaching can be an important factor in working within organisations to make huge adjustments to their ways of measuring success and their expectations of life – perhaps using the process of 'Deep Adaptation' described by Bendell and Read (2021), which offers a framework of resilience, relinquishment, restoration and reconciliation. As Professor Will Steffen says: "Collapse followed by transformation is a common way that complex systems evolve. Perhaps collapse of our high consumption, climate-destabilising society can lead to transformation towards a brighter human future. The Deep Adaptation framework outlined in this book is a helpful way to seek that transformation".

(David)

How many of the teams that we work with come close to having a shared purpose, collaborate in service of common goals, are psychologically safe, or share trust and accountability? Not many in my experience, although I have worked with plenty who aspire to doing so. Useful as these concepts may be, they are by themselves insufficient if we are serious about addressing the challenges faced by our organisations and communities, now and in the future.

Vested interests and established power structures have reinforced corrupt, oppressive and profoundly damaging practices that are a source of so much of the harm being perpetrated across our planet. Team coaching has the potential for providing a radical alternative to the collusion that so many teams exhibit when faced with such huge discrepancies in power and influence.

In practice, this means supporting teams in recognising, owning and facing their complicity in these processes, learning to support each other in finding alternatives to top-down, self-serving models of leadership and organisation. This doesn't mean opposing in an adversarial way, in fact some of the most progressive and impactful teams that I have worked with bring a sense of fun and radical creativity to their work, combined with an impatience and frustration with the established ways of doing things. Subversive team coaching means helping teams tap into this latent creative potential, enabling dissent, improvisation and innovation as part and parcel of everyday life. Team coaches need the awareness and personal skills to question and confront themselves and their teams as they do so, recognising and owning their erstwhile complicity, whilst taking up radical, and where necessary militant roles, instead.

(Ann)

"Please stay", helping teams to stay at the contact boundary and in so doing to maintain their sense of agency in the face of existential challenges.

The essence of leadership team coaching is usually working with some form of the question, "how can we be the most effective leadership team that we can be for our organisation in our current context?"

The thing is that in the last few years, whilst they may still come with that good old question, the inquiry is no longer straightforward, if it ever was. Whether they acknowledge it or not, teams, organisations, social groups – even societies – are experiencing echoes of what is referred to in some religious texts as the 'end times'. I'm not saying, 'the end is nigh!' exactly, but every team I've worked with in the last three years has been faced with some fundamental realisation that what they had previously taken as a given, whether about their identity, their 'goodness' or even their right to existence – no longer holds.

This is not the same old crap about a VUCA world. We are in a time of existential crisis at a systemic level. We in the rich countries of the West are being brought back to Earth (capital intended) with a bump. Our world is burning, flooding, freezing, dying and we are learning that we are, however well intended, prejudiced and 'schuldig'. We are having to live with the pain of being the problem – and the absolute requirement to be part of the solution.

Our work for a long time now has been supporting teams as they engage with 'adaptive challenges' (Heifetz et al., 2009) where values, loyalties and losses are activated and challenged. We have been working to help teams to resist the temptation towards polarisation, where for one perspective to be right, the other must be wrong and instead to acknowledge the potential for multiple realities to coexist.

In one recent team coaching session, the team leader found himself no longer able to tolerate the very difficult messages he was receiving from his colleagues about the impact of his leadership on the organisation, its customers and his colleagues. He got up to leave, and my co-coach gently said, "please don't do that… stay". This is the work, to support (and challenge) the client teams to stay in contact, in relationship, even though the work, the messages, the projections, the reality is difficult to bear. Because we have all seen the consequences of isolation and retreat from contact.

Peter Block asks teams to consider, "What is my part in the problem I am concerned with?" (Block, 2003). It is a question rich with purpose, forgiveness and possibility. It is a 'contactful' question. It puts the team in contact, in relationship with its own experience, its relationship with others involved and with the multiple realities of the situation (Denham-Vaughan & Chidiac, 2013). As Michael Vincent Miller writes, "the exchange that goes on unceasingly between the human organism and its surrounding environment in all areas of life ties person and world inextricably to one another" (Perls et al., 1951; introduction to the 1996 edition). Our role is more than ever to re-integrate even in the face of primary conflicts (Yalom, 1980), or more accurately, to bring the team back into contact with their own experience in the service of meaningful collective stewardship of their part of our world.

(Judith)

Humankind is confronting an existential crisis. The climate emergency, war, habitat destruction and infection are impacting us exponentially and bring loss and trauma in their wake. As the poet Rumi (13th century) wrote: "Be silent and sit down, for you are drunk and we are on the edge of the roof". In such circumstances it is imperative that we keep trying to listen, communicate, think and relate. The super-wicked problems that we encounter require an openness to the other as never before. These issues arouse strong, painful emotions that are defended against by equally strong social and personal defences. Only by opening a space for the relational in how we work together can we effectively enable people to hear what is being said, to feel heard by others and to make sense of what is going on around them. Through self-awareness and reflection on what is being observed team coaching can contribute to greater capacity for cooperation, collaboration, dialogue and mutual understanding within teams, whole organisations and beyond. My aspiration for team coaching is that through this focus it will promote understanding meaning making beyond the workplace to society and humanity.

(Dorothee)

As global health issues, climate change with its implications for the environment and societies, ongoing wars are becoming increasingly our reality on this earth, death is ever present not only for us individually, but on the level of community and whole society. We are all on some level grappling with our own mortality, the potential for our living spaces to perish and the knowledge that massive societal change is inevitable. This includes the potential 'death' of work practices, individual organisations or even whole sectors (e.g. certain parts of the energy industry). Climate anxiety and climate depression are now beginning to be recognised as common conditions, particularly in younger generations.

In many Western societies we are notoriously bad in talking openly about death and increasingly work is done at community level to enable conversations about death, e.g. death cafes or death talks. This enables many of us to see death much more as part of life. The introduction of the role of a 'death doula', described as a community-led response to support and come emotionally, practically and spiritually alongside those at the end of life, and those close to them is increasing in popularity. When one dives into the world of death and bereavement, one can't help but be struck by the similarities to the reality of organisational life.

Team coaches are already supporting teams through all sorts of losses – loss of team members, loss of leaders, loss of identity, loss of meaning in regards to work tasks, etc. In future there is the potential for team coaches to have to go even further. Helping teams to think about their 'organisational mortality', whether this is in relation to a potential perishing (dismantling) of the team, the end of particular work practices or even the potential of the death of their organisation or sector. The role of the team coach might become more geared towards becoming their doula, coming alongside the team for a period of time, helping them to have much more existential conversations and getting in touch with something much more fundamental and final.

References

Allan, J., Leeson, P., De Fruyt, F. & Martin, S. (2018). Application of a 10-week coaching program designed to facilitate volitional personality change: Overall effects on personality and the impact of targeting. *International Journal of Evidence Based Coaching and Mentoring*, *16*(1), 80–94.

Ames, J. (2020). Cracking the whip racism claim fails. *The Times Online, May.* www.thetimes.co.uk/article/cracking-the-whip-racism-claim-fails-qg9b6md8d. Consulted November 2022.

Armstrong, D. (2018). *Organisation in the mind: Psychoanalysis, group relations and organisational consultancy.* London/New York: Routledge.

Armstrong, D. (2005). Emotions in organisations: Disturbance or intelligence? In: D. Armstrong & R. French (Eds), *Organization in the Mind: Psychoanalysis, Group Relations, and Organizational Consultancy* (pp. 90–110). London: Karnac.

Ashikali, T., Groeneveld, S. & Kuipers, B. (2021). The role of inclusive leadership in supporting an inclusive climate in diverse public sector teams. *Review of Public Personnel Administration*, *41*(3), 497–519.

Bachkirova, T. (2020). Understanding yourself as a coach. In *The Coaches' Handbook* (pp. 39–47). London/New York: Routledge.

Baldwin, J. (1962). As much truth as one can bear. *New York Times Book Review*, *14*(2).

Bandiera, O., Guiso, L., Prat, A. & Sadun, R. (2011). *What do CEOs do?* Available at SSRN 1758445.

Barber, P. (2006). *Becoming a practitioner researcher: A Gestalt approach to holistic inquiry.* London: Middlesex University Press.

Bateson, G. (1978). *Steps to an ecology of mind.* New York: Ballantine.

Baumeister, R.F. & Leary, M.R. (1995). The need to belong: Desire for interpersonal attachments as a fundamental human motivation. *Psychological Bulletin*, *117*(3), 497.

Bell, J. (2021). Individual, group and organisational dynamics. In: E. Jackson & A. Berkeley (Eds), *Sustaining depth and meaning in school leadership* (pp. 73–93). London/New York: Routledge.

Bendell, J. & Read, R. (Eds) (2021). *Deep adaptation: Navigating the realities of climate chaos.* Hoboken (NJ): John Wiley & Sons.

Berne, E. (1961). *Transactional analysis in psychotherapy.* New York: Grove Press.

Berne, E. (1963). *The structure and dynamics of organisations and groups.* New York: Grove Press.

Berne, E. (1964). *Games people play.* New York: Grove Press.

Berne, E. (1966). *Principles of group treatment.* New York: Oxford University Press.

Berne, E. (1972). *What do you say after you say hello?* New York: Grove Press.

Biggart, L., Ward, E., Cook, L. & Schofield, G. (2017). The team as a secure base: Promoting resilience and competence in child and family social work. *Children and Youth Services Review, 83*, 119–130.

Bion, W.R. (1961). *Experiences in groups.* London: Tavistock.

Bion, W.R. (1962). *Learning from experience.* London: Heinemann.

Blanchard, A. (2021). The effects of COVID-19 on virtual working within online groups. *Group Processes & Intergroup Relations, 24*(2), 290–296.

Block, P. (2003). *The answer to how is yes: Acting on what matters.* Oakland, CA: Berrett-Koehler Publishers.

Bogdanoff, M. & Elbaum, P. L. (1978). Role lock: Dealing with monopolizers, mistrusters, isolates, helpful Hannahs, and other assorted characters in group psychotherapy. *International Journal of Group Psychotherapy, 28*(2), 247–262.

Boin, A., Kofman-Bos, C. & Overdijk, W. (2004). Crisis simulations: Exploring tomorrow's vulnerabilities and threats. *Simulation & Gaming, 35*(3), 378–393.

Bollas, C. (2013). *Being a character: Psychoanalysis and self experience.* London/New York: Routledge.

Boston Change Process Study Group & Nahum, J. P. (2008). Forms of relational meaning: Issues in the relations between the implicit and reflective-verbal domains. *Psychoanalytic Dialogues, 18*(2), 125–148.

Boston Change Process Study Group (2010). *Change in psychotherapy – A unifying paradigm.* New York: Norton.

Bowlby, J. (1969). *Attachment and loss: Attachment (Vol. 1).* London: Random House.

Brown, J. (1997). Circular questioning: An introductory guide. *Australian and New Zealand Journal of Family Therapy, 18*(2), 109–114.

Bridger, H. (1976). The changing role of pets in society. *Journal of Small Animal Practice, 17*(1), 1–8.

Bridger, H. (1990). Courses and working conferences as transitional learning institutions. *The Social Engagement of Social Science, 1*, 221–245.

Bryman, A. (2016; 5th edition) *Social research methods.* Oxford: Oxford University Press.

Buber, M. (1965). *Das dialogische Prinzip.* Heidelberg: Schneider.

Buber, M. (1970). *I and Thou* (translated by W.A. Kaufmann from original published 1923). New York: Scribner.

Buber, M. (1999). *Martin Buber on psychology and psychotherapy: Essays, letters, and dialogue* (J. Buber Agassi, Ed.). New York: Syracuse University Press.

Bunge, M. (2017; 4th edition) *Causality and modern science.* London/New York: Routledge.

Burr, V. (2015; 3rd edition) *Social constructionism.* London/New York: Routledge.

Bushe, G.R. & Marshak, R.J. (2015). *Dialogic organisation development: The theory and practice of transformational change.* Oakland, CA: Berrett-Koehler.

Campbell, D.T. (1956). *Leadership and its effects upon the group.* Columbus, OH: Ohio State University.

Campbell, D., Draper, R. & Huffington, C. (1991). *A systemic approach to consultation.* London/New York: Routledge.

Campbell, D. & Huffington, C. (2008). *Organisations connected.* London: Karnac.

Capra, F. (2004). *The hidden connections: A science for sustainable living.* Palatine, IL: Anchor.

Cardona, F. (2020). *Work matters: Consulting to leaders and organisations in the Tavistock tradition.* London/New York: Routledge.

Carr, A. (2008). *Family therapy: Concepts, processes and practice*. Hoboken, NJ: John Wiley & Sons.

Carroll, M. (2015). Psychological contracts: Hidden agreements in life and work. In: R. Tribe & J. Morrissey (Eds), *Handbook of professional and ethical practice for psychologists, counsellors and psychotherapists* (2nd edition, pp. 19–31). London/New York: Routledge.

Casey, D., Roberts, P. & Salaman, G. (1992). Facilitating learning in groups. *Leadership & Organisation Development Journal, 13*(4), 8–13.

Cavanagh, M. (2006). Coaching from a systemic perspective – A complex adaptive conversation, in D.R. Stober & A. M. Grant (Eds), *Evidence Based Coaching Handbook*. Hoboken, NJ: John Wiley & Sons.

Cavicchia, S. & Gilbert, M. (2018). *The theory and practice of relational coaching – Complexity, paradox and integration*. London/New York: Routledge.

Cecchin, G. (1987). Hypothesizing, circularity, and neutrality revisited: An invitation to curiosity. *Family Process, 26*(4), 405–413.

Chénard-Poirier, L.A., Morin, A.J., Boudrias, J.S. & Gillet, N. (2022). The combined effects of destructive and constructive leadership on thriving at work and behavioral empowerment. *Journal of Business and Psychology, 37*(1), 173–189.

Cheung-Judge, M.Y. & Holbeche, L. (2011). *Organisation development: A practitioner's guide for OD and HR*. London: Kogan Page.

Chidiac, M.A. (2018). *Relational organisational gestalt: An emergent approach to organisational development*. London/New York: Routledge.

Chidiac, M. & Denham-Vaughan, S. (2007). The process of presence: Energetic availability and fluid responsiveness. *British Gestalt Journal, 16*(1), 9.

Cleckley, H.M. (1941). *The Mask of Sanity: An attempt to clarify some issues about the so-called psychopathic personality*. St Louis, MO: Mosby.

Clemmens, M.C. (2012). The interactive field: Gestalt therapy as an embodied relational dialogue. In *Gestalt Therapy* (pp. 39–48). London/New York: Routledge.

Clemmens, M.C. & Bursztyn, A. (2003). Culture and body: A phenomenological and dialogic inquiry. *British Gestalt Journal, 12*(1), 15–21.

Compernolle, T. (2007). Developmental coaching from a systems point of view. In: M. Kets de Vries, K. Korotov & E. Florent-Treacy (Eds), *Coach and couch – The psychology of making better leaders* (pp. 41–63). London: Palgrave Macmillan.

Cornish, E. (2004). *Futuring: The exploration of the future*. Chicago, IL: World Future Society.

Cozolino, L. (2006). *The neuroscience of human relationships: Attachment and the developing social brain*. New York: W.W. Norton and Company.

Cozolino, L. (2013). *The social neuroscience of education: Optimising attachment and learning in the classroom*. New York: W.W. Norton and Company.

Dalal, F. (1998). *Taking the group seriously: Towards a post-Foulkesian group analytic theory*. London: Jessica Kingsley.

Dallos, R. & Draper, R. (2002). *An introduction to family therapy: Systemic theory and practice*. Maidenhead: Open University Press

Damasio, A. (2000). The feeling of what happens: Body. *Emotion and the making of consciousness*. London: Vintage.

Darwin, C. (1859). *On the Origin of Species by Means of Natural Selection*. London: John Murray.

Day, A. (2020). *Disruption, change and transformation in organisations: A human relations perspective*. London/New York: Routledge.

De Haan, E. (2008). *Relational coaching: Journeys towards mastering one-to-one learning.* Hoboken (NJ): John Wiley & Sons.

De Haan, E. (2017). *The Team Coaching Pocket Book.* Alresford: Management Pocketbooks.

De Haan, E. (2019a). Team coaching: A fleeting moment of noticing? *Coaching Today,* January, 12–19.

De Haan, E. (2019b). Coaching begins at hello. *The Training Journal* (October), *5*, 29–31.

De Haan, E. (2021). *What works in executive coaching – Understanding outcomes through quantitative research and practice-based evidence.* London/New York: Routledge.

De Haan, E. (2022). Love for the planet: Our contract with the world and the crisis of leadership. *Coaching Today,* January, 8–11.

De Haan, E. & Gannon, J. (2017). The coaching relationship. In: *The SAGE handbook of coaching* (pp. 195–217). London: Sage.

De Haan, E. & Kasozi, A. (2014). *The leadership shadow: How to recognise and avoid derailment, hubris and overdrive.* London: Kogan Page.

De Haan, E. & Metselaar, C. (2015). A critique of the use of diagnostic instruments in executive coaching. *Coaching Today,* July, 16–17.

De Haan, E., Gray, D.E. & Bonneywell, S. (2019). Executive coaching outcome research in a field setting: A near-randomized controlled trial study in a global healthcare corporation. *Academy of Management Learning and Education, 18*(4), 1–25.

Denham, J. (2006). The presence of the trainer. *British Gestalt Journal, 15*(1), 16–22.

Denham-Vaughan, S. (2005). Will and Grace: An integrative dialectic central to gestalt psychotherapy. *British Gestalt Journal, 14*(1), 5–14.

Denham-Vaughan, S. & Chidiac, M.A. (2013). SOS: A relational orientation towards social inclusion. *Mental Health and Social Inclusion 17*(2), 100–107.

Dunn, T. (2006). Triangulation and the misuse of power. *Human Development, 27*, 18–26.

Dutton, K. (2012). *The wisdom of psychopaths.* London: Random House.

Edmondson, A.C. (1999). Psychological safety and learning behavior in work teams. *Administrative Science Quarterly, 44*(2), 350–383.

Edmondson, A.C. (2018). *The fearless organisation: Creating psychological safety in the workplace for learning, innovation, and growth.* Hoboken, NJ: John Wiley & Sons.

Edmondson, A.C. & Lei, Z. (2014). Psychological safety: The history, renaissance, and future of an interpersonal construct. *Annual Review of Organisational Psychology and Organisational Behavior, 1*(1), 23–43.

English, F. (1975). The three-cornered contract. *Transactional Analysis Journal, 5*, 383–384.

Eoyang, G. & Holladay, R. (2013). *Adaptive action – Leveraging uncertainty in your organisation.* Stanford, CA: Stanford University Press.

Esbjörn-Hargens, S. & Zimmerman, M. (2009). *Integral ecology: Frequently asked questions.* Boston, MA and London: Integral Books.

Fanshawe, S. (Ed.) (2022). *The power of difference: Where the complexities of diversity and inclusion meet practical solutions.* New York: Kogan Page.

Fogel, A. (2009). *Body sense: The science and practice of embodied self-awareness.* New York: W.W Norton and Company.

Freud, A. (1946). *The ego and the mechanisms of defense.* New York: International Universities Press.

Freud, S. (1900). *The Interpretation of Dreams.* Translation: Standard Edition, 4–5. London: Hogarth Press, 1953.

Freud, S. (1905). Fragment of an analysis of a case of hysteria. In: James Strachey (Ed.), *The standard edition of the complete psychological works of Sigmund Freud* (Vol. 7, pp. 1–122). London: Hogarth Press, 1953–1974.

Freud, S. (1912). Recommendations to physicians practicing psycho-analysis. In: James Strachey (Ed.), *The standard edition of the complete psychological works of Sigmund Freud* (Vol. 12, pp. 111–120). London: Hogarth Press, 1953–1974.

Freud, S. (1921). Group psychology and the analysis of the ego: The future of an illusion. In: James Strachey (Ed.), *The standard edition of the complete psychological works of Sigmund Freud* (Vol. 18, pp. 65–144). London: Hogarth Press, 1953–1974.

Furnham, A. (2016). *The elephant in the boardroom: The causes of leadership derailment.* London: Springer.

Gaffney, S., Gaffney, S. & Chidiac, M.-A. (2013). *Groups, teams and groupwork revisited.* Scotts Valley, CA: CreateSpace.

Gallwey, T. (1974). *The inner game of tennis* . London: Random House.

Gaudart, M. (2021). The first moments. *The Coaching Psychologist, 17*(2), 52–62.

Gendlin, E.T. (1997). *Experiencing and the creation of meaning: A philosophical and psychological approach to the subjective.* Evanston, IL: Northwestern University Press.

Gentry, W.A., Hannum, K.M., Ekelund, B.Z. & de Jong, A. (2007). A study of the discrepancy between self- and observer-ratings on managerial derailment characteristics of European managers. *European Journal of Work and Organisational Psychology, 16,* 295–325

Gibb, J.R. (1978). *Trust: a new view of personal and organisational development.* Los Angeles, CA: Guild Tutors Press.

Gilbreth, F.B. (1911). *Motion study.* New York: Van Norstrand.

Gorman, J.C., Dunbar, T.A., Grimm, D. & Gipson, C.L. (2017). Understanding and modeling teams as dynamical systems. *Frontiers in Psychology, 8,* 1053.

Gould, S.J. (2007). *Punctuated equilibrium.* Cambridge, MA: Harvard University Press.

Grant, A. M. (2020). An integrated model of goal-focused coaching: An evidence-based framework for teaching and practice. *Coaching Researched: A Coaching Psychology Reader,* 115–139.

Graßmann, C., Schölmerich, F. & Schermuly, C.C. (2020). The relationship between working alliance and client outcomes in coaching: A meta-analysis. *Human relations, 73*(1), 35–58.

Halinen, A. & Tähtinen, J. (2002). A process theory of relationship ending. *International Journal of service industry management, 13*(2), 163–180.

Hambrick, D.C. & Abrahamson, E. (1995). Assessing managerial discretion across industries: A multimethod approach. *Academy of Management Journal, 38*(5), 1427–1441.

Hankinson, J. R. (1998). *Cause and Explanation in Ancient Greek Thought.* Oxford: Oxford University Press.

Hanley-Browne, R. (2021). What do team coaches experience at the end of a client relationship? *International Journal of Evidence Based Coaching & Mentoring, 15,* 20–36.

Harris, J.B. (2001). *A Gestalt perspective on working with group process.* Available from www.mgc.org.uk

Hartog, M. (2019). Becoming a team coach. In *The practitioner's handbook of team coaching* (pp. 365–378). London/New York: Routledge.

Hauser, L.L. (2014). Shape-shifting: A behavioral team coaching model for coach education, research, and practice. *Journal of Psychological Issues in Organisational Culture, 5*(2), 48–71.

Havila, V. & Tähtinen, J. (2012). Definitions of business relationship ending-A literature review. In *7th Nordic Workshop on Relationship Dynamics (NoRD 2012), Umeå, 10–12 October.*

Hawkins, P. (2021). *Leadership team coaching: Developing collective transformational leadership.* London: Kogan Page Publishers.

Heifetz, R.A., Grashow, A. & Linsky, M. (2009). *The practice of adaptive leadership: Tools and tactics for changing your organisation and the world.* Cambridge, MA: Harvard Business Press.

Heron, J. (2001; 5th edition) *Helping the client.* London: Sage.

Hirschhorn, L. (1998). *Reworking authority – Leading and following in the post-modern organisation.* Boston, MA: MIT Press.

Hirschhorn, L. & Barnett, C. (Eds) (1993). *The psychodynamics of organisations.* Philadelphia, PA: Temple University Press.

Hobart, B. & Sendek, H. (2014; 2nd Edition). *Gen Y now – Millenials and the evolution of leadership.* Hoboken (NJ): John Wiley & Sons.

Hofstede, G.J. (2017). Culture. In: Buchanan, D.A. and Huczynski, A. (Eds), *Organisational behaviour* (9th edition; pp. 108–144). Harlow, UK: Pearson.

Hogan, R., Curphy, G. J. & Hogan, J. (1994). What we know about leadership: Effectiveness and personality. *American Psychologist, 49*(6), 493.

Hogan, R., Kaiser, R.B., Sherman, R.A. & Harms, P.D. (2021). Twenty years on the dark side: Six lessons about bad leadership. *Consulting Psychology Journal: Practice and Research, 73*(3), 199–213.

Holmes, J. (2014). *John Bowlby and attachment theory.* London/New York: Routledge.

Husserl, E. (1912–1929). Ideen zu einer reinen Phänomenologie und phänomenologischen Philosophie. Allgemeine Einführung in die reine Phänomenologie. Translated as *Ideas: General Introduction to Pure Phenomenology.* (Translated by W.R. Boyce Gibson). New York: Collier, 1972.

Husserl, E. (1935). *Die Krisis der europäischen Wissenschaften und die transzendentale Phänomenologie: Eine Einleitung in die phänomenologische Philosophie.* Translated as *The Crisis of the European Sciences and Transcendental Phenomenology: An Introduction to Phenomenological Philosophy.* Evanston, IL: Northwestern University Press, 1970.

Iordanou, I., Hawley, R. & Iordanou, C. (2016). *Values and ethics in coaching.* London: Sage.

Jacobs, M. (2012; 4th edition). *The presenting past.* Maidenhead: McGraw-Hill.

Jacobs, M. & Rowan, J. (2002). *The therapist's use of self.* Maidenhead: Open University Press.

Janis, I. (1972). *Victims of groupthink: A psychological study of foreign policy decisions and fiascos.* Boston, MA: Houghton, Mifflin.

Kaiser, R.B. & Hogan, R. (2007). The dark side of discretion: Leader personality and organisational decline. In *Being there even when you are not* (pp. 173–193). Bingley: Emerald Group Publishing.

Kant, I. (1965). *Critique of pure reason* (Translated by N.K. Smith from original published 1781). New York: St Martin's Press.

Karpman, S. (1968). Fairy tales and script drama analysis. *TA Bulletin, 7*(26), 39–43.

Kegan, R. (1998). *In over our heads: The mental demands of modern life.* Cambridge, MA: Harvard University Press.

Kepner, J. (2003). The embodied field. *British Gestalt Journal, 12*(1), 6–14.

Keyes, M.F. (1983). *Inward journey: Art as therapy.* La Salle, IL: Open Court.

Kimmerer, R.W. (2020). *Braiding sweetgrass.* Minneapolis, MN: Milkweed Editions.

King, K., Higgins, J. & Schroeder, H. (2018). Resilience is a team sport. *Dialogue, Q2,* 66–67.

Klein, M. (1964). Love, guilt and reparation. In: M. Klein & J. Riviere (Eds), *Love, hate and reparation* (pp. 57–94). New York: W.W. Norton & Company (Original work published 1937).

Kline, N. (1999). *Time to think: Listening to ignite the human mind.* London: Cassell.

Knowles, M.S., Holton III, E.F. & Swanson, R.A. (2014; 8th edition). *The adult learner: The definitive classic in adult education and human resource development.* London/New York: Routledge.

Koffka, K. (1935). *Principles of Gestalt psychology.* Harcourt, Brace & World.

Krantz, J. (1998). Anxiety and the new order. In: E. Klein & F. Gabelnick (Eds), *Leadership in the 21st century* (pp. 77–107). New Haven, CT: Yale University Press.

Lapworth, P. & Sills, C. (2011). *An introduction to transactional analysis.* London: Sage.

Laszlo, C. & Zhexembayeva, N. (2011). *Embedded sustainability – The next big competitive advantage.* Stanford, CA: Stanford Business Books.

Lawrence, W.G., Bain, A. & Gould, L. (1996). The fifth basic assumption. *Free Associations, 6*(1), 28–55.

Lawrence, G. & Robinson, P. (1975). *An innovation and its implementation: Being a study of the development of syndicate methods in six colleges of education.* London: Tavistock Institute of Human Relations.

Leary-Joyce, J. & Lines, H. (2018). *Systemic team coaching.* London: AoEC Press.

Lencioni, P. (2002). *The five dysfunctions of a team.* San Francisco, CA: Jossey-Bass.

Levinas, E. (1989). *The Levinas reader* (S. Hand, Ed.). Oxford: Blackwell.

Lewin, K. (1947). Frontiers in group dynamics I. Concept, method and reality in social science; social equilibria and social change. *Human Relations, 1,* 5–41.

Lewin, K. (1951). *Field theory in social science: Selected theoretical papers* (Edited by Dorwin Cartwright). London: Tavistock.

Lines, H. & Scholes-Rhodes, J. (2013). *Touchpoint Leadership – Creating collaborative leadership across teams and organisations.* London: Kogan Page.

Louis, D. & Fatien Diochon, P. (2018). The coaching space: A production of power relationships in organisational settings. *Organisation, 25*(6), 710–731.

Lyons-Ruth, K. (1999). The two-person unconscious: Intersubjective dialogue, enactive relational representation, and the emergence of new forms of relational organisation. *Psychoanalytic Inquiry, 19*(4), 576–617.

Marris, P. (1993). *Loss and change.* London/New York: Routledge.

Mathews, F. (2003). *For love of matter: A contemporary panpsychism.* Albany, NY: Suny Press.

Maughan, W.S. (1944). *The razor's edge.* New York: Doubleday Doran.

McLean, A. (2013). *Leadership and cultural webs in organisations: Weavers' tales.* Bingley: Emerald Group.

Mead, G.H. (1967). *Mind, self and society* . Chicago, IL: University of Chicago Press.

Meadows, D.H. (2011; 3rd edition) *Thinking in systems: A primer.* London: Earthscan.

Menzies Lyth, I.E.P. (1960). A case study in the functioning of social systems as a defence against anxiety: A report on a study of the nursing service of a general hospital. *Human Relations, 13*(2), 95–121.

Merleau-Ponty, M. (1969). *The essential writings of Merleau-Ponty* (A. Fisher, Ed.). New York: Harcourt.

Miceli, M.P. & Near, J.P. (2002). What makes whistle-blowers effective? Three field studies. *Human Relations, 55*(4), 455–479.

Micholt, N. (1992). Psychological distance and group interventions. *Transactional Analysis Journal, 22*(4), 228–233.

Miller, E.J. (1979). Autonomy, dependency and organisational change. In: D. Towell and C. Harries (Eds), *Innovation in patient care: An action research study of change in a psychiatric hospital* (pp. 172–190). London: Croon Helm.

Miller, E.J. (1995). Dialogue with the client system: Use of the "working note" in organizational consultancy. *Journal of Managerial Psychology, 10*(6), 27–30.

Miller, E.J. & Rice, A.K. (1967). *Systems of organisation: Task and sentient systems and their boundary control*. London: Tavistock Publications.

Mills, J. (2005). A critique of relational psychoanalysis. *Psychoanlaytic Psychology, 22*(2), 155–188.

Naranjo, C. (1993). *Gestalt therapy: The attitude and practice of an atheoretical experientialism*. Nevada City, CA: Gateways.

Nelson, E. & Hogan, R. (2009). Coaching on the dark side. *International Coaching Psychology Review, 4*(1), 7–19.

Nembhard, I.M. & Edmondson, A.C. (2006). Making it safe: The effects of leader inclusiveness and professional status on psychological safety and improvement efforts in health care teams. *Journal of Organisational Behavior: The International Journal of Industrial, Occupational and Organisational Psychology and Behavior, 27*(7), 941–966.

Nevis, E.C. (1987). *A Gestalt approach to organisational consulting*. New York: Gestalt Institute of Cleveland/Gardner.

Newton, T. (*2006*). Scripts, psychological life plans and the learning cycle. *Transactional Analysis Journal, 36*(3), 186–195.

Nietzsche, F. (1966). *Beyond good and evil* (translated by W. Kaufmann from original published 1886). New York: Random House.

Obholzer, A. & Zagier Roberts, V. (Eds; 1994). *The unconscious at work – Individual and organisational stress in the human services*. London/New York: Routledge.

Olusoga, D. (2016). *Black and British: A forgotten history*. London: Pan Macmillan.

Orange, D. (2010). *Thinking for clinicians – Philosophical resources for contemporary psychoanalysis and the humanistic psychotherapies*. London/New York: Routledge.

Oshry, B. (2007). *Seeing Systems – Unlocking the mysteries of organisational life*. San Francisco, CA: Berrett Koehler.

Owen, D. (2008). Hubris syndrome. *Clinical Medicine, 8*(4), 428–432.

Parlett, M. (1991). Reflections on field theory. *British Gestalt Journal, 1*(2), 69–81.

Parlett, M. (2018). *Future sense: Five explorations of whole intelligence for a world that's waking up*. Market Harborough: Troubador.

Patrick, C., Fowles, D. & Krueger, R. (2009). Triarchic conceptualization of psychopathy: Developmental origins of disinhibition, boldness, and meanness. *Development and Psychopathology, 21*(3), 913–938.

Perls, F., Hefferline, R.E. & Goodman, P. (1951). *Gestalt therapy excitement and growth in the human and personality*. London/New York: Bantam.

Perls, F., Hefferline, R.F. & Goodman, P. (1969). *Ego, hunger and aggression: The Gestalt therapy of sensory awakening through spontaneous personal encounter, fantasy, and contemplation*. Big Sur, CA: Esalen.

Peters, J., & Carr, C. (2013). Team effectiveness and team coaching literature review. *Coaching: An International Journal of Theory, Research and Practice, 6*(2), 116–136. https://doi.org/10.1080/17521882.2013.798669

Petriglieri, G. & Stein, M. (2012). The unwanted self: Projective identification in leaders' identity work. *Organisation Studies, 33*(9), 1217–1235.

Pfeiffer, J.W. (Ed.) (1990). *The encyclopedia of team-development activities* (Vol. 1). San Francisco, CA: Jossey Bass.

Philippson, P. (2001). *Self in relation. Gouldsboro*: Gestalt Journal Press.

Phillips, A. (1997; Reprint Edition). *Terrors and experts*. Cambridge, MA: Harvard University Press.

Pöhlker, C., Wiedemann, K.T., Sinha, B., Shiraiwa, M., Gunthe, S.S., Smith, M., Su, H., Artaxo, P., Chen, Q., Cheng, Y. & Elbert, W. (2012). Biogenic potassium salt particles as seeds for secondary organic aerosol in the Amazon. *Science 337*(6098), 1075–1078.

Polster, E. & Polster, M. (1974). *Gestalt therapy integrated: Contours of theory and practice.* New York: Vintage.

Proctor, B. (2008). *Group supervision: A guide to creative practice.* London: Sage

Rainey Torbert, M.A.R. & Hanafin, J. (2006). Use of self in OD consulting – What matters is presence, in B. Jones and M. Brazzel (Eds), *The NTL Handbook of Organisation Development and Change* (pp. 69–82). San Francisco, CA: Jossey-Bass.

Rajasinghe, D. (2020). Interpretative phenomenological analysis (IPA) as a coaching research methodology. *Coaching: An International Journal of Theory, Research and Practice, 13*(2), 176–190.

Raven, B.H. & French Jr., J.R.P. (1958). Legitimate power, coercive power, and observability in social influence. *Sociometry, 21*(2), 83–97.

Reitz, M. & Higgins, J. (2019). *Speak up: Say what needs to be said and hear what needs to be heard.* London: Pearson.

Rice, A.K. (1969). Individual, group and intergroup processes. *Human Relations, 22*(6), 565–584.

Robinson, G. & Garrard, P. (Eds; 2016). *The intoxication of power: Interdisciplinary insights.* London: Springer.

Rock, D. & Grant, H. (2016). Why diverse teams are smarter. *Harvard Business Review, 4*(4), 2–5.

Rogers, C. (1971). My way of facilitating encounter groups. *The American Journal of Nursing, 71*(2) (February 1971), 275–279.

Roszak, T.E., Gomes, M.E. & Kanner, A.D. (1995). *Ecopsychology: Restoring the earth, healing the mind.* San Francisco, CA: Sierra Club Books.

Rumi, J.A.D. (13th Century). *Mystical poems of Rumi* (Translated by Arberry, A. J. and Javadi, H). Chicago, IL: University of Chicago Press, 2010.

Schein, E.H. (1999). *Process consultation revisited: Building the helping relationship.* Reading, MA: Addison-Wesley.

Schein, E.H. & Schein, P.A. (2017; 5th edition). *Organisational culture and leadership.* Hoboken, NJ: John Wiley & Sons.

Schoemaker, P.J. (1995). Scenario planning: A tool for strategic thinking. *Sloan Management Review, 36*(2), 25–50.

Schofield, G. & Beek, M. (2014). *Promoting attachment and resilience: A guide for foster carers and adopters on using the Secure Base model.* London: BAAF.

Schön, D.A. (2017). *The reflective practitioner: How professionals think in action.* London/New York: Routledge.

Schutz, W.C. (1958). *FIRO: A three dimensional theory of interpersonal behavior.* New York: Holt, Rinehart & Winston.

Schwartz, H. (1990). *Narcissistic process and corporate decay – The theory of the organisation ideal.* New York: New York University Press.

Schwartz, R.C. (1989). The internal family systems model: An expansion of systems thinking into the level of internal process. *Family Therapy Case Studies, 3*, 61–66.

Searles, H.F. (1955). The informational value of the supervisor's emotional experience. *Psychiatry, 18*(2), 135–146.

Selvini, M. P., Boscolo, L., Cecchin, G. & Prata, G. (1980). Hypothesizing–circularity–neutrality: Three guidelines for the conductor of the session. *Family Process, 19*(1), 3–12.

Semler, R. (2001). *Maverick! The success story behind the world's most unusual workplace.* New York: Random House.

Shah, S. (2022). *Diversity, inclusion and belonging in coaching: A practical guide.* London: Kogan Page.

Shaw, P. (2002). *Changing conversations in organisations – A complexity approach to change.* London/New York: Routledge.

Shohet, R. (Ed.) (2018). *Love in the NHS: Stories of caring, kindness, and compassion.* New York: Productivity Press.

Shore, L.M., Cleveland, J.N. & Sanchez, D. (2018). Inclusive workplaces: A review and model. *Human Resource Management Review, 28*(2), 176–189.

Siegal, D.J. (1999). *The developing mind: How relationships and the brain interact to shape who we are.* New York: The Guildford Press.

Silsbee, D. (2008). *Presence-based Coaching: Cultivating self-generative leaders through mind, body and heart.* San Francisco, CA: Jossey-Bass.

Sills, C. (Ed.) (2006). *Contracts in counselling and psychotherapy.* London: Sage.

Sills, C. (2012). The coaching contract: A mutual commitment. In: E. de Haan & C. Sills (Eds), *Coaching relationships: The relational coaching field book* (pp. 93–109). London: Libri.

Sills, C. (2015). Role Lock – When the team gets stuck. *Training Journal,* July, 26–29.

Sills, C. & Mazzetti, M. (2009). The comparative script system: A tool for developing supervisors. *Transactional Analysis Journal, 39*(4), 305–314.

Sills, C. & Salters, D. (1991). The Comparative Script System. *ITA News, 31*, 11–15.

Sills, C., Lapworth, P. & Desmond, B. (2012). *An introduction to Gestalt.* London: Sage.

Simard, S. (2021). *Finding the mother tree: Uncovering the wisdom and intelligence of the forest.* London: Penguin.

Slotnick, S.D. (2017). *Cognitive neuroscience of memory.* Cambridge: Cambridge University Press.

Somerset Maugham, W. (1944). *The razor's edge.* London: Heinemann. Quote from London: Vintage Books, 2008, Part Six, p. 223.

Specter, M. (2009). *Denialism: How irrational thinking harms the planet and threatens our lives.* London: Penguin.

Spretnak, C. (1997). *The resurgence of the real: Body, nature and place in a hypermodern world.* Harlow: Addison-Wesley.

Stacey, R. (2001). *Complex responsive processes in organisations.* London/New York: Routledge.

Stacey, R. (2003). *Complexity and group processes: A radical social understanding of individuals.* London/New York: Routledge.

Stevenson, H. (2018). Holism, Field Theory, Systems Thinking, and Gestalt Consulting: How each informs the other – Part 1, Theoretical Integration. *Gestalt Review, 22*(2), 161–188.

Stiehm, J.H. & Townsend, N.W. (2002). *The US Army War College – Military education in a democracy.* Philadelphia, PA: Temple University Press.

Stolz, S.A. (2015). Embodied learning. *Educational Philosophy and Theory, 47*(5), 474–487.

Stubbings, A. & Ceasar, N. (2012). *Sustainability as usual.* Berkhamsted: Ashridge Publications.

Surowiecki, J. (2005). *The wisdom of crowds.* New York: Anchor.

Taylor, F.W. (1911). *Principles of scientific management.* New York: Harper and Row.

Thornton, C. (2016; 2nd edition) *Group and team coaching: The secret life of groups.* London/New York: Routledge.

Tolman, C.W. (Ed.) (1996). *Problems of theoretical psychology*. Concord, ON: Captus Press.

Tomm, K. (1988). Interventive interviewing: Part III. Intending to ask lineal, circular, strategic, or reflexive questions? *Family Process, 27*(1), 1–15.

Torregiante J. (2005). Destructive personality traits and leadership performance: A pattern-oriented approach. Unpublished master's thesis, North Carolina State University, Raleigh, NC.

Tuckman, B.W. (1965). Developmental sequence in small groups. *Psychological Bulletin, 63*, 384–399

Turner, D. (2021). *Intersections of privilege and otherness in counselling and psychotherapy: Mockingbird*. London/New York: Routledge.

Turquet, P. (1975). Threats to identity in the large group. In L. Kreeger (Ed.), *The large group: Dynamics and therapy* (pp. 87–144). London: Maresfield reprints.

Van Wyk, R., Odendaal, A. & Maseko, B.M. (2019). Team coaching in the workplace: Critical success factors for implementation. *SA Journal of Human Resource Management, 17*(1), 1–11.

Vergauwe, J., Hofmans, J., Wille, B., Decuyper, M. & De Fruyt, F. (2021). Psychopathy and leadership effectiveness: Conceptualizing and testing three models of successful psychopathy. *Leadership Quarterly, 32*(6), 101536.

Warrenfeltz, R. & Kellett, T. (Eds; 2016). *Coaching the dark side of personality*. Hogan Press.

Watzlawick, P., Weakland, J.H., Fisch, R. (1974). *Change; Principles of problem formation and problem resolution*. New York: W.W Norton and Company.

Wertheimer, M. (1944). Gestalt theory. *Social Research, 11*(1), 78–99.

West, M.A. (2012). *Effective teamwork: Practical lessons from organisational research*. Hoboken, NJ: John Wiley & Sons.

Western, S. (2012). *Coaching and mentoring – A critical text*. London: Sage.

Western, S. (2013). *Leadership – A critical text* (2nd Edition). London: Sage.

Wheeler, G. (1997). Self and shame: A Gestalt approach. *Gestalt Review, 1*(3), 221–244.

Whittaker, D. & Lieberman, M. (1964/2008). *Psychotherapy through the group process*. New York: Basic.

Wilke, G. (2014). *The art of group analysis in organisations: The use of intuitive and experiential knowledge*. London: Karnak Books.

Willard, B. (2012). *The new sustainability advantage*. Gabriola (BC): New Society.

Workman-Stark, A.L. (2021). Fair treatment for all: Testing the predictors of workplace inclusion in a Canadian police organisation. *Management and Labour Studies, 46*(1), 94–110.

Wosket, V. (1999). *The therapeutic use of self: Counselling practice, research and supervision*. London/New York: Routledge.

Yalom, I.D. (1980). *Existential psychotherapy*. New York: Basic.

Yontef, G. (2007). The power of the immediate moment in Gestalt therapy. *Journal of Contemporary Psychotherapy, 37*(1), 17–23.

Zanchetta, M., Junker, S., Wolf, A.M. & Traut-Mattausch, E. (2020). "Overcoming the fear that haunts your success" – The effectiveness of interventions for reducing the impostor phenomenon. *Frontiers in Psychology, 11*, 405.

Zinker, J. (1977). *Creative process in Gestalt therapy*. New York: Brunner/Mazel.

Index

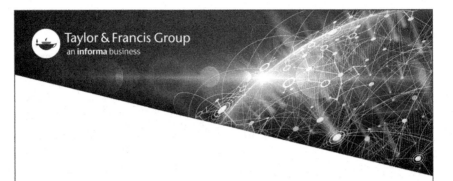

Taylor & Francis eBooks

www.taylorfrancis.com

A single destination for eBooks from Taylor & Francis
with increased functionality and an improved user
experience to meet the needs of our customers.

90,000+ eBooks of award-winning academic content in
Humanities, Social Science, Science, Technology, Engineering,
and Medical written by a global network of editors and authors.

TAYLOR & FRANCIS EBOOKS OFFERS:

A streamlined
experience for
our library
customers

A single point
of discovery
for all of our
eBook content

Improved
search and
discovery of
content at both
book and
chapter level

REQUEST A FREE TRIAL
support@taylorfrancis.com

Printed in the United States
by Baker & Taylor Publisher Services